T0328891

International Strategic Management

SERIES ON INTERNATIONAL BUSINESS AND TRADE

SERIES EDITOR-IN-CHIEF
Khosrow Fatemi

International Strategic Management
Challenges and Opportunities

Edited by

Franklin R. Root
University of Pennsylvania

Kanoknart Visudtibhan
The George Washington University

Routledge
Taylor & Francis Group

LONDON AND NEW YORK

First published 1992 by
FRANK CASS AND COMPANY LIMITED
2 Park Square, Milton Park, Abingdon, Oxon OX14 4RN
711 third Avenue, New York, NY 10017

Published 2013 by Routledge

Routledge is an imprint of the Taylor & Francis Group, an informa business

This book was set in Times Roman by Hemisphere Publishing Corporation. The production supervisor was Peggy M. Rote; the editors were Miriam Gonzalez and Lisa Speckhardt; and the typesetter was Phoebe Carter. Cover design by Michelle Fleitz.

A CIP catalog record for this book is available from the British Library.

⊗ The paper in this publication meets the requirements of the ANSI standard Z39.48–1984 (Permanence of Paper)

Library of Congress Cataloging-in-Publication Data

International strategic management: challenges and opportunities /
[edited by] Franklin R. Root, Kanoknart Visudtibhan.
    p.   cm.

    Includes bibliographical references and index.
    1. International business enterprises—Management.   2. Strategic management.   I. Root, Franklin R.   II. Visudtibhan, Kanoknart.
HD62.4.I566   1992
658.4′.012—dc20   92-6356
                                                           CIP

ISBN 978-0-844-81666-1 (pbk)

Contents

Preface

No single definition of international or global strategic management can hope to capture its many dimensions, and we are not so foolhardy as to offer one here. Instead, we have used four criteria in selecting articles for this book. The first criterion is a focus on the multinational (transnational) enterprise; the second, a top-management perspective encompassing the entire multinational enterprise system; the third, a normative, decision-making emphasis that is useful to international managers; and the fourth, recency of publication, specifically no earlier than 1985. In making our final selections, it was unfortunately necessary to exclude some excellent articles because of limitations of space.

We found that the selected articles fell naturally into six categories, representing several (albeit interdependent) dimensions of international strategic management. In reaching decisions that affect the entire multinational enterprise system, managers use concepts and theories (if only implicitly) to formulate strategies that are intended to create competitive advantages in regional and global markets. Today, the dominant source of international competitive advantages is continuing technological innovation. Again, managers must design organizations that can implement their international strategies. To do so, they may "extend" the multinational enterprise beyond its conventional boundaries through the formation of international strategic alliances with other multinational firms. And once again, international managers must formulate and carry out strategies that are responsive to political environments.

We are confident that readers will agree that our final selection of articles represents a high order of excellence in research on international strategic management.

Part One: Concepts and theories of international strategic management. In chapter 1, Sumantra Ghoshal delineates his conceptual framework with a map of the global strategic management field. In chapter 2, Bruce Kogut takes issue with Ghoshal and also proposes a concept of the multinational corporation as a network that transfers acquired capabilities across borders. Balaji Chakravarthy and Howard Perlmutter in chapter 3 review four generic planning systems that are available to multinational corporations. Franklin Root and Kanoknart Visudtibhan close out Part One with chapter 4, an exploratory effort to measure empirically the concept of international strategic focus.

Part Two: Creating strategies for international competitive advantage. In chapter 5, Michael Porter investigates the meaning of international competition, as contrasted with domestic competition, for planning competitive strategy. His model is based on the configuration and coordination of the activities of a value chain in global markets. Allen Morrison, David Ricks, and Kendall Roth in chapter 6 contend that multinationals need to pay more attention to regional competitiveness in North America, Europe, and the Pacific rim instead of rushing to adopt full-fledged global strategies. In chapter 7, George Yip, Pierre Loewe, and Michael Yoshino propose a systematic approach to developing and implementing a global strategy that stresses "internal drivers" of industry potential for globalization and factors internal to the firm that facilitate a global strategy.

Part Three: Designing organizations to carry out international strategies. Part Three kicks off with an article in chapter 8 by William Egelhoff that, first, tests the Stopford and Wells model of strategy and structure in multinational corporations and then introduces the relative size of foreign manufacturing as an additional predictor of structure. In chapter 9, Philip Rosenzweig and Jitendra Singh examine the concepts of organization-environment relations of multinational enterprises, develop several hypotheses about those relations, and then offer refining concepts of the organization environment.

Part Four: Managing technological innovation on a global scale. Chapter 10, by Farok Contractor and V. K. Narayanan, provides a technology planning framework for the multinational firm, covering technology scanning, strategy development at the product level, and implementation at the country level. Arnoud de Meyer and Atsuo Mizushima, in chapter 11, study European and Japanese firms and conclude that globalization of research and development (R&D) has become a necessity for multinationals, requiring a new framework for the management of decentralized R&D laboratories located throughout the world.

Part Five: Forming international strategic alliances. In chapter 12, Farok Contractor and Peter Lorange create a framework to assist international managers in choosing between fully-owned operations and cooperative arrangements with another international firm. C. Christopher Baughn and Richard Osborn, in chapter 13, investigate the role of technology in the formation of new cooperative arrangements between U.S. and Japanese industrial firms.

Part Six: Managing the political environment. In chapter 14, Peter Ring, Stephanie Lenway, and Michael Govekar offer a model for analyzing the political imperative that faces international managers. The authors postulate that a geocentric predisposition is likely to enhance the competitive position of a multinational firm because of the firm's ability to respond to the political imperative regardless of industry structure.

The book ends with a Postscript on the current state of research in international strategic management.

We believe that this book will appeal to faculty who want to add depth to courses in international business and management or want to internationalize courses in strategic management and business policy. Also, we anticipate that it will appeal to managers who are facing the challenges and opportunities of international strategic management.

Franklin R. Root
Kanoknart Visudtibhan

Part One
Concepts and Theories of International Strategic Management

Chapter 1

Global Strategy: An Organizing Framework

Sumantra Ghoshal
INSEAD

Abstract *Global strategy has recently emerged as a popular concept among managers of multinational corporations as well as among researchers and students in the field of international management. This paper presents a conceptual framework encompassing a range of different issues relevant to global strategies. The framework provides a basis for organizing existing literature on the topic and for creating a map of the field. Such a map can be useful for teaching and also for guiding future research in this area. The article, however, is primarily directed at manager so multinational corporations, and is aimed at providing them with a basis for relating and synthesizing the different perspectives and prescriptions that are currently available for global strategic management.*

Over the past few years the concept of global strategy has taken the world of multinational corporations (MNCs) by storm. Scores of articles in the *Harvard Business Review, Fortune, The Economist* and other popular journals have urged multinationals to 'go global' in their strategies. The topic has clearly captured the attention of MNC managers. Conferences on global strategy, whether organized by the Conference Board in New York, *The Financial Times* in London, or Nomura Securities in Tokyo, have invariably attracted enthusiastic corporate support and sizable audiences. Even in the relatively slow-moving world of academe the issue of globalization of industries and companies has emerged as a new bandwagon, as manifest in the large number of papers on the topic presented at recent meetings of the Academy of Management, the Academy of International Business and the Strategic Management Society. 'Manage globally' appears to be the latest battlecry in the world of international business.

MULTIPLE PERSPECTIVES, MANY PRESCRIPTIONS

This enthusiasm notwithstanding, there is a great deal of conceptual ambiguity about what a 'global' strategy really means. As pointed out by Hamel and Prahalad (1985), the distinction among a global industry, a global firm, and a global strategy is somewhat blurred in the literature. According to Hout, Porter and Rudden (1982), a global strategy is appropriate for global industries which are defined as those in which a firm's competitive position in one national market is significantly affected by its competitive position in other national markets. Such interactions

Reproduced by permission of John Wiley and Sons Limited from *Strategic Management Journal*, Vol. 8, pp. 425–440, 1987.

between a firm's positions in different markets may arise from scale benefits or from the potential of synergies or sharing of costs and resources across markets. However, as argued by Bartlett (1985), Kogut (1984) and many others, those scale and synergy benefits may often be created by strategic actions of individual firms and may not be 'given' in any *a priori* sense. For some industries, such as aeroframes or aeroengines, the economies of scale may be large enough to make the need for global integration of activities obvious. However, in a large number of cases industries may not be born global but may have globalness thrust upon them by the entrepreneurship of a company such as Yoshida Kagyo KK (YKK) or Procter and Gamble. In such cases the global industry—global strategy link may be more useful for ex-post explanation of outcomes than for ex-ante predictions or strategizing.

Further, the concept of a global strategy is not as new as some of the recent authors on the topic have assumed it to be. It was stated quite explicitly about 20 years ago by Perlmutter (1969) when he distinguished between the geocentric, polycentric, and ethnocentric approaches to multinational management. The starting point for Perlmutter's categorization scheme was the world-view of a firm, which was seen as the driving force behind its management processes and the way it structured its world-wide activities (see Robinson, 1978 and Rutenberg, 1982 for detailed reviews and expositions). In mush of the current literature, in contrast, the focus has been narrowed and the concept of global strategy has been linked almost exclusively with how the firm structures the flow of tasks within its world-wide value-adding system. The more integrated and rationalized the flow of tasks appears to be, the more global the firm's strategy is assumed to be (e.g., Leontiades, 1984). On the one hand, this focus has led to improved understanding of the fact that different tasks offer different degrees of advantages from global integration and national differentiation and that, optimally, a firm must configure its value chain to obtain the best possible advantages from both (Porter, 1984). But, on the other hand, it has also led to certain dysfunctional simplifications. The complexities of managing large, world-wide organizations have been obscured by creating polar alternatives between centralization and decentralization, or between global and multidomestic strategies (e.g., Hout et al., 1982). Complex management tasks have been seen as composites of simple global and local components. By emphasizing the importance of rationalizing the flow of components and final products within a multinational system, the importance of internal flows of people, technology, information, and values has been de-emphasized.

Differences among authors writing on the topic of global strategy are not limited to concepts and perspectives. Their prescriptions on how to manage globally have also been very different, and often contradictory.

1. Levitt (1983) has argued that effective global strategy is not a bag of many tricks but the successful practice of just one: product standardization. According to him, the core of a global strategy lies in developing a standardized product to be produced and sold the same way throughout the world.
2. According to Hout, et al. (1982), on the other hand, effective global strategy requires the approach not of a hedgehog, who knows only one trick, but that of a fox, who knows many. Exploiting economies of scale through global volume, taking pre-emptive positions through quick and large investments, and managing interdependently to achieve synergies across different activities are, according to these authors, some of the more important moves that a winning global strategist must muster.
3. Hamel and Prahalad's (1985) prescription for a global strategy contradicts that of Levitt (1983) even more sharply. Instead of a single standardized product, they recommend a broad product portfolio, with many product varieties, so that investments on technologies

and distribution channels can be shared. Cross-subsidization across products and markets, and the development of a strong world-wide distribution system, are the two moves that find the pride of place in these authors' views on how to succeed in the game of global chess.

4. If Hout, et al.'s (1982) global strategist is the heavyweight champion who knocks out opponents with scale and pre-emptive investments, Kogut's (1985b) global strategist is the nimble-footed athlete who wins through flexibility and arbitrage. He creates options so as to turn the uncertainties of an increasingly volatile global economy to his own advantage. Multiple sourcing, production shifting to benefit from changing factor costs and exchange rates, and arbitrage to exploit imperfections in financial and information markets are, according to Kogut, some of the hallmarks of a superior global strategy.

These are only a few of the many prescriptions available to MNC managers about how to build a global strategy for their firms. All these suggestions have been derived from rich and insightful analyses of real-life situations. They are all reasonable and intuitively appealing, but their managerial implications are not easy to reconcile.

THE NEED FOR AN ORGANIZING FRAMEWORK

The difficulty for both practitioners and researchers in dealing with the small but rich literature on global strategies is that there is no organizing framework within which the different perspectives and prescriptions can be assimilated. An unfortunate fact of corporate life is that any particular strategic action is rarely an unmixed blessing. Corporate objectives are multidimensional, and often mutually contradictory. Contrary to received wisdom, it is also usually difficult to prioritize them. Actions to achieve a particular objective often impede another equally important objective. Each of these prescriptions is aimed at achieving certain objectives of a global strategy. An overall framework can be particularly useful in identifying the trade-offs between those objectives and therefore in understanding not only the benefits but also the potential costs associated with the different strategic alternatives.

The objective of this paper is to suggest such an organizing framework which may help managers and academics in formulating the various issues that arise in global strategic management. The underlying premise is that simple categorization schemes such as the distinction between global and multidomestic strategies are not very helpful in understanding the complexities of corporate-level strategy in large multinational corporations. Instead, what may be more useful is to understand what the key strategic objectives of an MNC are, and the tools that it possesses for achieving them. An integrated analysis of the different means and the different ends can help both managers and researchers in formulating, describing, classifying and analyzing the content of global strategies. Besides, such a framework can relate academic research, that is often partial, to the totality of real life that managers must deal with.

THE FRAMEWORK: MAPPING MEANS AND ENDS

The proposed framework is shown in Table 1. While the specific construct may be new, the conceptual foundation on which it is built is derived from a synthesis of existing literature.

The basic argument is simple. The goals of a multinational—as indeed of any organization—can be classified into three broad categories. The firm must achieve efficiency in its current activities; it must manage the risks that it assumes in carrying out those activities; and it must develop internal learning capabilities so as to be able to innovate and adapt to future changes.

Table 1
Global Strategy: An Organizing Framework

Strategic objectives	Sources of competitive advantage		
	National differences	Scale economies	Scope economies
Achieving efficiency in current operations	Benefiting from differences in factor costs—wages and cost of capital	Expanding and exploiting potential scale economies in each activity	Sharing of investments and costs across products, markets and businesses
Managing risks	Managing different kinds of risks arising from market or policy-induced changes in comparative advantages of different countries	Balancing scale with strategic and operational flexibility	Portfolio diversification of risks and creation of options and side-bets
Innovation learning and adaptation	Learning from societal differences in organizational and managerial processes and systems	Benefiting from experience—cost reduction and innovation	Shared learning across organizational components in different products, markets or businesses

Competitive advantage is developed by taking strategic actions that optimize the firm's achievement of these different and, at times, conflicting goals.

A multinational has three sets of tools for developing such competitive advantage. It can exploit the differences in input and output markets among the many countries in which it operates. It can benefit from scale economies in its different activities. It can also exploit synergies or economies of scope that may be available because of the diversity of its activities and organization.

The strategic task of managing globally is to use all three sources of competitive advantage to optimize efficiency, risk and learning simultaneously in a world-wide business. The key to a successful global strategy is to manage the interactions between these different goals and means. That, in essence, is the organizing framework. Viewing the tasks of global strategy this way can be helpful to both managers and academics in a number of ways. For example, it can help managers in generating a comprehensive checklist of factors and issues that must be considered in reviewing different strategic alternatives. Such a checklist can serve as a basis for mapping the overall strategies of their own companies and those of their competitors so as to understand the comparative strengths and vulnerabilities of both. Table 1 shows some illustrative examples of factors that must be considered while carrying out such comprehensive strategic audits. Another practical utility of the framework is that it can highlight the contradictions between the different goals and between the different means, and thereby make salient the strategic dilemmas that may otherwise get resolved through omission.

In the next two sections the framework is explained more fully by describing the two dimensions of its construct, viz. the strategic objectives of the firm and the sources of competitive advantage available to a multinational corporation. Subsequent sections show how selected articles contribute to the literature and fit within the overall framework. The paper concludes with a brief discussion of the trade-offs that are implicit in some of the more recent prescriptions on global strategic management.

THE GOALS: STRATEGIC OBJECTIVES

Achieving Efficiency

A general premise in the literature on strategic management is that the concept of strategy is relevant only when the actions of one firm can affect the actions or performance of another. Firms competing in imperfect markets earn different 'efficiency rents' from the use of their resources (Caves, 1980). The objective of strategy, given this perspective, is to enhance such efficiency rents.

Viewing a firm broadly as an input-output system, the overall efficiency of the firm can be defined as the ratio of the value of its outputs to the costs of all its inputs. It is by maximizing this ratio that the firm obtains the surplus resources required to secure its own future. Thus it differentiates its products to enhance the exchange value of its outputs, and seeks low costs factors to minimize the costs of its inputs. It also tries to enhance the efficiency of its throughput processes by achieving higher scale economies or by finding more efficient production processes.

The field of strategic management is currently dominated by this efficiency perspective. The generic strategies of Porter (1980), different versions of the portfolio model, as well as overall strategic management frameworks such as those proposed by Hofer and Schendel (1978) and Hax and Majluf (1984) are all based on the underlying notion of maximizing efficiency rents of the different resources available to the firm.

In the field of global strategy this efficiency perspective has been reflected in the widespread use of the integration-responsiveness framework originally proposed by Prahalad (1975) and subsequently developed and applied by a number of authors including Doz, Bartlett and Prahalad (1981) and Porter (1984). In essence, the framework is a conceptual lens for visualizing the cost advantages of global integration of certain tasks vis-à-vis the differentiation benefits of responding to national differences in tastes, industry structures, distribution systems, and government regulations. As suggested by Bartlett (1985), the same framework can be used to understand differences in the benefits of integration and responsiveness at the aggregate level of industries, at the level of individual companies within an industry, or even at the level of different functions within a company (see Figure 1, reproduced from Bartlett, 1985). Thus the consumer electronics industry may be characterized by low differentiation benefits and high integration advantages, while the position of the packaged foods industry may be quite the opposite. In the telecommunications switching industry, in contrast, both local and global forces may be strong, while in the automobile industry both may be of moderate and comparable importance.

Within an industry (say, automobile), the strategy of one firm (such as Toyota) may be based on exploiting the advantages of global integration through centralized production and decision-making, while that of another (such as Fiat) may aim at exploiting the benefits of national differentiation by creating integrated and autonomous subsidiaries which can exploit strong links with local stakeholders to defend themselves against more efficient global competitors. Within a firm, research may offer greater efficiency benefits of integration, while sales and service may provide greater differentiation advantages. One can, as illustrated in Figure 1, apply the framework to even lower levels of analysis, right down to the level of individual tasks. Based on such analysis, a multinational firm can determine the optimum way to configure its value chain so as to achieve the highest overall efficiency in the use of its resources (Porter, 1984).

However, while efficiency is clearly an important strategic objective, it is not the only one. As argued recently by a number of authors, the broader objective of strategic management is to create·value which is determined not only by the returns that specific assets are expected to

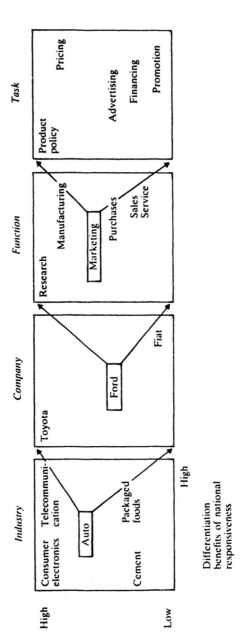

Figure 1 The integration–responsiveness framework (reproduced from Bartlett, 1985).

generate, but also by the risks that are assumed in the process (see Woo and Cool (1985) for a review). This leads to the second strategic objective of firms—that of managing risks.[1]

Managing Risks

A multinational corporation faces many different kinds of risks, some of which are endemic to all firms and some others are unique to organizations operating across national boundaries. For analytical simplicity these different kinds of risks may be collapsed into four broad categories.

First, an MNC faces certain *macroeconomic risks* which are completely outside its control. These include cataclysmic events such as wars and natural calamities, and also equilibrium-seeking or even random movements in wage rates, interest rates, exchange rates, commodity prices, and so on.

Second, the MNC faces what is usually referred to in the literature as political risks but may be more appropriately called *policy risks* to emphasize that they arise from policy actions of national governments and not from either long-term equilibrium-seeking forces of global markets, nor from short-term random fluctuations in economic variables arising out of stickiness or unpredictability of market mechanisms. The net effect of such policy actions may often be indistinguishable from the effect of macroeconomic forces; for example, both may lead to changes in the exchange rate of a particular currency. But from a management perspective the two must be distinguished, since the former is uncontrollable but the latter is at least partially controllable.

Third, a firm also faces certain *competitive risks* arising from the uncertainties of competitors' responses to its own strategies (including the strategy of doing nothing and trying to maintain the status quo). While all companies face such risks to varying extents (since both monopolies and perfect competition are rare), their implications are particularly complex in the context of global strategies since the responses of competitors may take place in many different forms and in many different markets. Further, technological risk can also be considered as a part of competitive risk since a new technology can adversely affect a firm only when it is adopted by a competitor, and not otherwise.[2]

Finally, a firm also faces what may be called *resource risks*. This is the risk that the adopted strategy will require resources that the firm does not have, cannot acquire, or cannot spare. A key scarce resource for most firms is managerial talent. But resource risks can also arise from lack of appropriate technology, or even capital (if managers, for reasons of control, do not want to use capital markets, or if the market is less efficient than finance theorists would have use believe).

One important issue with regard to risks is that they change over time. Vernon (1977) has highlighted this issue in the context of policy risks, but the same is true of others. Consider resource risks as an example. Often the strategy of a multinational will assume that appropriate resources will be acquired as the strategy unfolds. Yet the initial conditions on which the plans for on-going resource acquisition and development have been based may change over time. Nissan, for instance, based its aggressive internationalization strategy on the expectation of developing technological, financial, and managerial resources out of it home base. Changing competitive positions among local car manufacturers in Japan have affected these resource development plans of the company, and its internationalizing strategy has been threatened significantly. A more careful analysis of alternative competitive scenarios, and of their effects on the resource allocation plans of the com-

---

[1]In the interest of simplicity the distinction between risk and uncertainty is ignored, as is the distinction between systematic and unsystematic risks.

[2]This assumes that the firm has defined its business correctly and has identified as competitors all the firms whose offerings are aimed at meeting the same set of market needs that the firm meets.

pany, may have led Nissan to either a slower pace of internationalization, or to a more aggressive process of resource acquisition at an earlier stage of implementing its strategy.

The strategic task, with regard to management of risks, is to consider these different kinds of risks *jointly* in the context of particular strategic decisions. However, not all forms of risk are strategic since some risks can be easily diversified, shifted, or shared through routine market transactions. It is only those risks which cannot be diversified through a readily available external market that are of concern at the strategic level.

As an example, consider the case of currency risks. These can be classified as contractual, semi-contractual and operating risks (Lessard and Lightstone, 1983). Contractual risks arise when a firm enters into a contract for which costs and revenues are expected to be generated in different currencies: for example a Japanese firm entering into a contract for supplying an item to be made in Japan to an American customer at a price fixed in dollars. Semi-contractual risks are assumed when a firm offers an option denominated in foreign currencies, such as a British company quoting a firm rate in guilders. Operating risks, on the other hand, refer to exchange rate-related changes in the firm's competitiveness arising out of long-term commitments of revenues or costs in different currencies. For example, to compete with a Korean firm, an American firm may set up production facilities in Singapore for supplying its customers in the United States and Europe. A gradual strengthening of the Singapore dollar, in comparison with the Korean won, can erode the overall competitiveness of the Singapore plant.

Both contractual and semi-contractual currency risks can be easily shifted or diversified, at relatively low costs, through various hedging mechanisms. If a firm does not so hedge these risks, it is essentially operating as a currency speculator and the risks must be associated with the speculation business and not to its product-market operations. Operating risks, on the other hand, cannot be hedged so easily,[3] and must be considered at the strategic rather than the operational level.

Analysis of strategic risks will have significant implications for a firm's decisions regarding the structures and locations of its cost and revenue streams. It will lead to more explicit analysis of the effects of environmental uncertainties on the configuration of its value chain. There may be a shift from ownership to rental of resources; from fixed to variable costs. Output and activity distributions may be broadened to achieve the benefits of diversification. Incrementalism and opportunism may be given greater emphasis in its strategy in comparison to pre-emptive resource commitments and long-term planning. Overall strategies may be formulated in more general and flexible terms, so as to be robust to different environmental scenarios. In addition, side-bets may be laid to cover contingencies and to create strategic options which may or may not be exercised in the future (see Kogut, 1985b; Aaker and Mascarenhas, 1984; and Mascarenhas, 1982).

Innovation, Learning and Adaptation

Most existing theories of the multinational corporation view it as an instrument to extract additional rents from capabilities internalized by the firm (see Calvet, 1981, for a review). A firm goes abroad to make more profits by exploiting its technology, or brand name, or management capabilities in different countries around the world. It is assumed that the key competencies of the multinational always reside at the center.

While the search for additional profits or the desire to protect existing revenues may explain why multinationals come to exist, they may not provide an equally complete explanation of why

---

[3]Some market mechanisms such as long-term currency swaps are now available which can allow at least partial hedging of operating risks.

some of them continue to grow and flourish. An alternative view may well be that a key asset of the multinational is the diversity of environments in which it operates. This diversity exposes it to multiple stimuli, allows it to develop diverse capabilities, and provides it with a broader learning opportunity than is available to a purely domestic firm. The enhanced organizational learning that results from the diversity internalized by the multinational may be a key explanator of its ongoing success, while its initial stock of knowledge may well be the strength that allows it to create such organizational diversity in the first place (Bartlett and Ghoshal, 1985).

Internal diversity may lead to strategic advantages for a firm in many different ways. In an unpredictable environment it may not be possible, ex ante, to predict the competencies that will be required in the future. Diversity of internal capabilities, following the logic of population ecologists (e.g., Hannan and Freeman, 1977; Aldrich, 1979), will enhance the probability of the firm's survival by enhancing the chances that it will be in possession of the capabilities required to cope with an uncertain future state. Similarly, diversity of resources and competencies may also enhance the firm's ability to create joint innovations, and to exploit them in multiple locations. One example of such benefits of diversity was recently described in the *Wall Street Journal* (April 29, 1985):

> P&G [Procter and Gamble Co.] recently introduced it new Liquid Tide, but the product has a distinctly international heritage. A new ingredient that helps suspend dirt in wash water came from the company's research center near P&G's Cincinnati headquarters. But the formula for Liquid Tide's surfactants, or cleaning agents, was developed by P&G technicians in Japan. The ingredients that fight mineral salts present in hard water came from P&G's scientists in Brussels.

As discussed in the same *WSJ* article, P&G's research center in Brussels has developed a special capability in water softening technology due, in part, to the fact that water in Europe contains more than twice the level of mineral content compared to wash water available in the United States. Similarly, surfactant technology is particularly advanced in Japan because Japanese consumers wash their clothes in colder waters compared to consumers in the US or Europe, and this makes greater demands on the cleaning ability of the surfactants. The advantage of P&G as a multinational is that it is exposed to these different operating environments and has learned, in each environment, the skills and knowledge that coping with that environment specially requires. Liquid Tide is an example of the strategic advantages that accrue from such diverse learning.

The mere existence of diversity, however, does not enhance learning. It only creates the potential for learning. To exploit this potential, the organization must consider learning as an explicit objective, and must create mechanisms and systems for such learning to take place. In the absence of explicit intention and appropriate mechanisms, the learning potential may be lost. In some companies, where all organizational resources are centralized and where the national subsidiaries are seen as mere delivery pipelines to supply the organization's value-added to different countries, diverse learning may not take place either because the subsidiaries may not possess appropriate sensing, analyzing, and responding capabilities to learn from their local environments, or because the centralized decision processes may be insensitive to knowledge accumulated outside the corporate headquarters. Other companies, in which the subsidiaries may enjoy very high levels of local resources and autonomy may similarly fail to exploit global learning benefits because of their inability to transfer and synthesize knowledge and expertise developed in different organizational components. Local loyalties, turf protection, and the 'not invented here' (NIH) syndrome—the three handmaidens of decentralization—may restrict internal flow of information across national boundaries which is essential for global learning to occur. In other words, both centralization and decentralization may impede learning.

THE MEANS: SOURCES OF COMPETITIVE ADVANTAGE

Most recent articles on global strategy have been aimed at identifying generic strategies (such as global cost leadership, focus or niche) and advocating particular strategic moves (such as cross-subsidy or pre-emptive investments). Underlying these concepts, however, are three fundamental tools for building global competitive advantage: exploiting differences in input and output markets in different countries, exploiting economies of scale, and exploiting economies of scope (Porter, 1985).

National Differences

The comparative advantage of locations in terms of differences in factor costs is perhaps the most discussed, and also the best understood, source of competitive advantage in international business.

Different nations have different factor endowments, and in the absence of efficient markets this leads to inter-country differences in factor costs. Different activities of the firm, such as R&D, production, marketing, etc., have different factor intensities. A firm can therefore gain cost advantages by configuring its value-chain so that each activity is located in the country which has the least cost for the factor that the activity uses most intensely. This is the core concept of comparative advantage-based competitive advantage—a concept for which highly developed analytical tools are available from the discipline of international economics. Kogut (1985a) provides an excellent managerial overview of this concept.

National differences may also exist in output markets. Customer tastes and preferences may be different in different countries, as may be distribution systems, government regulations applicable to the concerned product-markets, or the effectiveness of different promotion strategies and other marketing techniques. A firm can augment the exchange value of its output by tailoring its offerings to fit the unique requirements in each national market. This, in essence, is the strategy of national differentiation, and it lies at the core of what has come to be referred to as the multidomestic approach in multinational management (Hout et al., 1982).

From a strategic perspective, however, this static and purely economic view of national differences may not be adequate. What may be more useful is to take a dynamic view of comparative advantage and to broaden the concept to include both societal and economic factors.

In the traditional economics view, comparative advantages of countries are determined by their relative factor endowments and they do not change. However, in reality one lesson of the past four decades is that comparative advantages change and a prime objective of the industrial policies of many nations is to effect such changes. Thus, for any nation, the availability and cost of capital change, as do the availability of technical manpower and the wages of skilled and unskilled labor. Such changes take place, in the long run, to accommodate different levels of economic and social performance of nations, and in the short run they occur in response to specific policies and regulations of governments.

This dynamic aspect of comparative advantages adds considerable complexity to the strategic considerations of the firm. There is a first-order effect of such changes—such as possible increases in wage rates, interest rates or currency exchange rates for particular countries that can affect future viability of a strategy that has been based on the current levels of these economic variables. There can also be a more intriguing second-order effect. If an activity is located in an economically inefficient environment, and if the firm is able to achieve a higher level of efficiency in its own operations compared to the rest of the local economy, its competitive advantage may actually increase as the local economy slips lower and lower. This is because the macroeconomic variables such as wage or exchange rates may change to reflect the overall performance of the economy relative to the rest of the world and, to the extent that the firm's performance is better than this national aggregate, it may benefit from these macro-level changes (Kiechel, 1981).

Consistent with the discipline that gave birth to the concept, the usual view of comparative advantage is limited to factors that an economist admits into the production function, such as the costs of labor and capital. However, from a managerial perspective it may be more appropriate to take a broader view of societal comparative advantages to include 'all the relative advantages conferred on a society by the quality, quantity and configuration of its material, human and institutional resources, including "soft" resources such as inter-organizational linkages, the nature of its educational system, and organizational and managerial know-how' (Westney, 1985: 4). As argued by Westney, these 'soft' societal factors, if absorbed in the overall organizational system, can provide benefits as real to a multinational as those provided by such economic factors as cheap labor or low-cost capital.

While the concept of comparative advantage is quite clear, available evidence on its actual effect on the overall competitiveness of firms is weak and conflicting. For example, it has often been claimed that one source of competitive advantage for Japanese firms is the lower cost of capital in Japan (Hatsopoulos, 1983). However, more systematic studies have shown that there is practically no difference in the risk-adjusted cost of capital in the United States and Japan, and that capital cost advantages of Japanese firms, if any, arise from complex interactions between government subsidies and corporate ownerships structures (Flaherty and Itami, 1984). Similarly, relatively low wage rates in Japan have been suggested by some authors as the primary reason for the success of Japanese companies in the US market (Itami, 1978). However, recently, companies such as Honda and Nissan have commissioned plants in the USA and have been able to retain practically the same levels of cost advantages over US manufacturers as they had for their production in Japan (Allen, 1985). Overall, there is increasing evidence that while comparative advantages of countries can provide competitive advantages to firms, the realization of such benefits is not automatic but depends on complex organizational factors and processes.

Scale Economies

Scale economies, again, is a fairly well established concept, and its implications for competitive advantage are quite well understood. Microeconomic theory provides a strong theoretical and empirical basis for evaluating the effect of scale on cost reduction, and the use of scale as a competitive tool is common in practice. Its primary implication for strategy is that a firm must expand the volume of its output so as to achieve available scale benefits. Otherwise a competitor who can achieve such volume can build cost advantages, and this can lead to a vicious cycle in which the low-volume firm can progressively lose its competitive viability.

While scale, by itself, is a static concept, there may be dynamic benefits of scale through what has been variously described as the experience or learning effect. The higher volume that helps a firm to exploit scale benefits also allows it to accumulate learning, and this leads to progressive cost reduction as the firm moves down its learning curve.

The concept of the value-added chain recently popularized by Porter (1985) adds considerable richness to the analysis of scale as a source of competitive advantage. This conceptual apparatus allows a disaggregated analysis of scale benefits in different value-creating activities of the firm. The efficient scale may vary widely by activity—being higher for component production, say, than for assembly. In contrast to a unitary view of scale, this disaggregated view permits the firm to configure different elements of its value chain to attain optimum scale economies in each.

Traditionally, scale has been seen as an unmixed blessing—something that always helps and never hurts. Recently, however, many researchers have argued otherwise (e.g. Evans, 1982). It has been suggested that scale efficiencies are obtained through increased specialization and through creation of dedicated assets and systems. The same processes cause inflexibilities and limit the firm's ability to cope with change. As environmental turbulence has increased, so has the need for strategic and operational flexibility (Mascarenhas, 1982). At the extreme, this line of argument has led to predictions of a re-emergence of the craft form of production to replace the scale-dominated assembly form (Piore and Sabel, 1984). A more typical argument has been to emphasize the need to balance scale and flexibility, through the use of modern technologies such as CAD/CAM and flexible manufacturing systems (Gold, 1982).

Scope Economies

Relatively speaking, the concept of scope economies is both new and not very well understood. It is based on the notion that certain economies arise from the fact that the cost of the joint production of two or more products can be less than the cost of producing them separately. Such cost reductions can take place due to many reasons—for example resources such as information or technologies, once acquired for use in producing one item, may be available costlessly for production of other items (Baumol, Panzer and Willig, 1982).

The strategic importance of scope economies arises from a diversified firm's ability to share investments and costs across the same or different value chains that competitors, not possessing such internal and external diversity, cannot. Such sharing can take place across segments, products, or markets (Porter, 1985) and may involve joint use of different kinds of assets (see Table 2).

A diversified firm may share physical assets such as production equipment, cash, or brand names across different businesses and markets. Flexible manufacturing systems using robots, which can be used for production of different items, is one example of how a firm can exploit such scope benefits. Cross-subsidization of markets and exploitation of a global brand name are other examples of sharing a tangible asset across different components of a firm's product and market portfolios.

A second important source of scope economies is shared external relations: with customers, suppliers, distributors, governments, and other institutions. A multinational bank like Citibank can provide relatively more effective service to a multinational customer than can a bank that operates in a single country (see Terpstra, 1982). Similarly, as argued by Hamel and Prahalad (1985), companies such as Matsushita have benefited considerably from their ability to market a diverse range of products through the same distribution channel. In another variation, Japanese

Table 2
Scope Economies in Product and Market Diversification

	Sources of scope economies	
	Product diversification	Market diversification
Shared physical assets	Factory automation with flexibility to produce multiple products (Ford)	Global brand name (Coca-Cola)
Shared external relations	Using common distribution channel for multiple products (Matsushita)	Servicing multi-national customers world-wide (Citibank)
Shared learning	Sharing R&D in computer and communications businesses (NEC)	Pooling knowledge developed in different markets (Procter and Gamble)

trading companies have expanded into new businesses to meet different requirements of their existing customers.

Finally, shared knowledge is the third important component of scope economies. The fundamental thrust of NEC's global strategy is 'C&C'—computers and communication. The company firmly believes that its even strengths in the two technologies and resulting capabilities of merging them in-house to create new products gives it a competitive edge over global giants such as IBM and AT&T, who have technological strength in only one of these two areas. Another example of the scope advantages of shared learning is the case of Liquid Tide described earlier in this paper.

Even scope economies, however, may not be costless. Different segments, products or markets of a diversified company face different environmental demands. To succeed, a firm needs to differentiate its management systems and processes so that each of its activities can develop *external consistency* with the requirements of its own environment. The search for scope economies, on the other hand, is a search for *internal consistencies* within the firm and across its different activities. The effort to create such synergies may invariably result in some compromise with the objective of external consistency in each activity.

Further, the search for internal synergies also enhances the complexities in a firm's management processes. In the extreme, such complexities can overwhelm the organization, as it did in the case of EMI, the UK-based music, electronics, and leisure products company which attempted to manage its new CT scanner business within the framework of its existing organizational structure and processes (see EMI and the CT scanner, ICCH case 9–383–194). Certain parts of a company's portfolio of businesses or markets may be inherently very different from some others, and it may be best not to look for economies of scope across them. For example, is the soft drinks industry, bottling and distribution are intensely local in scope, while the tasks of creating and maintaining a brand image, or that of designing efficient bottling plants, may offer significant benefits from global integration. Carrying out both these sets of functions in-house would clearly lead to internalizing enormous differences within the company with regard to the organizing, coordinating, and controlling tasks. Instead of trying to cope with these complexities, Coca-Cola has externalized those functions which are purely local in scope (in all but some key strategic markets). In a variation of the same theme, IBM has 'externalized' the PC business by setting up an almost stand-alone organization, instead of trying to exploit scope benefits by integrating this business within the structure of its existing organization (for a more detailed discussion on multinational scope economies and on the conflicts between internal and external consistencies, see Lorange, Scott, Morton and Ghoshal, 1986).

PRESCRIPTIONS IN PERSPECTIVE

Existing literature on global strategy offers analytical insights and helpful prescriptions for almost all the different issues indicated in Table 1. Table 3 shows a selective list of relevant publications, categorized on the basis of issues that, according to this author's interpretations, the pieces primarily focus on.[4]

---

[4]From an academic point of view, strategy of the multinational corporation is a specialized and highly applied field of study. It is built on the broader field of business policy and strategy which, in turn, rests on the foundation of a number of academic disciplines such as economics, organization theory, finance theory, operations research, etc. A number of publications in those underlying disciplines, and a significant body of research carried out in the field of strategy, in general, provide interesting insights on the different issues highlighted in Table 1. However, given the objective of suggesting a limited list of further readings that *managers* may find useful, such publications have not been included in Table 3. Further, even for the more applied and prescriptive literature on global strategy, the list is only illustrative and not exhaustive.

Table 3
Selected References for Further Reading

Strategic objectives	Sources of competitive advantage		
	National differences	Scale economies	Scope economies
Achieving efficiency in current operations	Kogut (1985a),; Itami (1978); Okimoto, Sugano and Weinstein (1984)	Hout, Porter and Rudden (1982); Levitt (1983); Doz (1978); Leontiades (1984); Gluck (1983)	Hamel and Prahalad (1985); Hout, Porter and Rudden (1982); Porter (1985); Ohmae (1985)
Managing risks	Kiechel (1981); Kobrin (1982); Poynter (1985); Lessard and Lightstone (1983); Srinivasulu (1981); Herring (1983)	Evans (1982); Piore and Sabel (1984); Gold (1982); Aaker and Mascarenhas (1984)	Kogut (1985b); Lorange, Scott Morton and Ghoshal (1986)
Innovation, learning and adaptation	Westney (1985); Terpstra (1977); Ronstadt and Krammer (1982)	BCG (1982); Rapp (1973)	Bartlett and Ghoshal (1985)

Pigeon-holing academic contributions into different parts of a conceptual framework tends to be unfair to their authors. In highlighting what the authors focus on, such categorization often amounts to an implicit criticism for what they did not write. Besides, most publications cover a broader range of issues and ideas than can be reflected in any such categorization scheme. Table 3 suffers from all these deficiencies. At the same time, however, it suggests how the proposed framework can be helpful in integrating the literature and in relating the individual pieces to each other.

From Parts to the Whole

For managers, the advantage of such synthesis is that it allows them to combine a set of insightful but often partial analyses to address the totality of a multidimensional and complex phenomenon. Consider, for example, a topic that has been the staple for academics interested in international management: explaining and drawing normative conclusions from the global successes of many Japanese companies. Based on detailed comparisons across a set of matched pairs of US and Japanese firms, Itami concludes that the relative successes of the Japanese firms can be wholly explained as due to the advantages of lower wage rates and higher labor productivity. In the context of a specific industry, on the other hand, Toder (1978) shows that manufacturing scale is the single most important source of the Japanese competitive advantage. In the small car business, for example, the minimum efficient scale requires an annual production level of about 400,000 units. In the late 1970s no US auto manufacturer produced even 200,000 units of any subcompact configuration vehicle, while Toyota produced around 500,000 Corollas and Nissan produced between 300,000 and 400,000 B210s per year. Toder estimates that US manufacturers suffered a cost disadvantage of between 9 and 17 percent on account of inefficient scale alone. Add to it the effects of wage rate differentials and exchange rate movements, and Japanese success in the US auto market may not require any further explanation. Yet process-orientated scholars such as Hamel and Prahalad suggest a much more complex explanation of the Japanese tidal wave. They see it as arising out of a dynamic process of strategic evolution that exploits scope economies as a crucial weapon in the final stages. All these authors provide compelling arguments to support their own explanations, but do not consider or refute each other's hypotheses.

This multiplicity of explanations only shows the complexity of global strategic management.

However, though different, these explanations and prescriptions are not always mutually exclusive. The manager's task is to find how these insights can be combined to build a multidimensional and flexible strategy that is robust to the different assumptions and explanations.

The Strategic Trade-offs

This, however, is not always possible because there are certain inherent contradictions between the different strategic objectives and between the different sources of competitive advantage. Consider, for instance, the popular distinction between a global and a multidomestic strategy described by Hout et al. (1982). A global strategy requires that the firm should carefully separate different value elements, and should locate each activity at the most efficient level of scale in the location where the activity can be carried out at the cheapest cost. Each activity should then be integrated and managed interdependently so as to exploit available scope economies. In essence, it is a strategy to maximize efficiency of current operations.

Such a strategy may, however, increase both endogenous and exogenous risks for the firm. Global scale of certain activities such as R&D and manufacturing may result in the firm's costs being concentrated in a few countries, while its revenues accrue globally, from sales in many different countries. This increases the operating exposure of the firm to the vicissitudes of exchange rate movements because of the mismatch between the currencies in which revenues are obtained and those in which costs are incurred. Similarly, the search for efficiency in a global business may lead to greater amounts of intra-company, but inter-country, flows of goods, capital, information and other resources. These flows are visible, salient and tend to attract policy interventions from different host governments. Organizationally, such an integrated system requires a high degree of coordination, which enhances the risks of management failures. These are lessons that many Japanese companies have learned well recently.

Similarly, consideration of the learning objective will again contradict some of the proclaimed benefits of a global strategy. The implementation of a global strategy tends to enhance the forces of centralization and to shift organizational power from the subsidiaries to the headquarters. This may result in demotivation of subsidiary managers and may erode one key asset of the MNC—the potential for learning from its many environments. The experiences of Caterpillar is a case in point. An exemplary practitioner of global strategy, Cat has recently spilled a lot of red ink on its balance sheet and has lost ground steadily to its archrival, Komatsu. Many factors contributed to Caterpillar's woes, not the least of which was the inability of its centralized management processes to benefit from the experiences of its foreign subsidiaries.

On the flipside of the coin, strategies aimed at optimizing risk or learning may compromise current efficiency, Poynter (1985) has recommended 'upgrade,' i.e. increasing commitment of technology and resources in subsidiaries, as a way to overcome risk of policy interventions by host governments. Kogut (1985b), Mascarenhas (1982) and many others have suggested creating strategic and operational flexibility as a mechanism for coping with macroenvironmental risks. Bartlett and Ghoshal (1985) have proposed the differentiated network model of multinational organizations as a way to operationalize the benefits of global learning. All these recommendations carry certain efficiency penalties, which the authors have ignored.

Similar trade-offs exist between the different sources of competitive advantages. Trying to make the most of factor cost economies may prevent scale efficiency, and may impede benefiting from synergies across products or functions. Trying to benefit from scope through product diversification may affect scale, and so on. In effect these contradictions between the different strategic objectives, and between the different means for achieving them, lead to trade-offs between each cell in the framework and practically all others. These trade-offs imply that to formulate and implement a global strategy, MNC managers must consider all the issues suggested in Table 1, and must evaluate the implications of different strategic alternatives on each of these issues. Under a particular set of circumstances a particular strategic objective may dominate and a particular source of competitive advantage may play a more important role than the others (Fayerweather, 1981). The complexity of global strategic management arises from the need to understand those situational contingencies, and to adopt a strategy after evaluating the trade-offs it implies. Existing prescriptions can sensitize MNC managers to the different factors they must consider, but cannot provide ready-made and standardized solutions for them to adopt.

CONCLUSION

This paper has proposed a framework that can help MNC managers in reviewing and analyzing the strategies of their firms. It is not a blueprint for formulating strategies; it is a road map for reviewing them. Irrespective of whether strategies are analytically formulated or organizationally formed (Mintzberg, 1978), every firm has a realized strategy. To the extent that the realized strategy may differ from the intended one, managers need to review what the strategies of their firms really are. The paper suggests a scheme for such a review which can be an effective instrument for exercising strategic control.

Three arguments underlie the construct of the framework. First, in the global strategy literature, a kind of industry determinism has come to prevail not unlike the technological determinism that dominated management literature in the 1960s. The structures of industries may often have important influences on the appropriateness of corporate strategy, but they are only one of many such influences. Besides, corporate strategy may influence industry structure just as much as be influenced by it.

Second, simple schemes for categorizing strategies of firms under different labels tend to hide more than they reveal. A map for more detailed comparison of the content of strategies can be more helpful to managers in understanding and improving the competitive positions of their companies.

Third, the issues of risk and learning have not been given adequate importance in the strategy literature in general, and in the area of global strategies in particular. Both of these are important strategic objectives and must be explicitly considered while evaluating or reviewing the strategic positions of companies.

The proposed framework is not a replacement of existing analytical tools but an enhancement that incorporates these beliefs. It does not present any new concepts or solutions, but only a synthesis of existing ideas and techniques. The benefit of such synthesis is that it can help managers in integrating an array of strategic moves into an overall strategic thrust by revealing the consistencies and contradictions among those moves.

For academics this brief view of existing literature on global strategy will clearly reveal the need for more empirically grounded and systematic research to test and validate the hypotheses which currently appear in the literature as prescriptions and research conclusions. For partial analyses to lead to valid conclusions, excluded variables must be controlled for, and rival hypotheses must be considered and eliminated. The existing body of descriptive and normative research is rich enough to allow future researchers to adopt a more rigorous and systematic approach to enhance the reliability and validity of their findings and suggestions. The proposed framework, it is hoped, may be of value to some researchers in thinking about appropriate research issues and designs for furthering the field of global strategic management.

ACKNOWLEDGMENTS

The ideas presented in this paper emerged in the course of discussions with many friends and colleagues. Don Lessard, Eleanor Westney, Bruce Kogut, Chris Bartlett and Nitin Nohria were particularly helpful. I also benefited greatly from the comments and suggestions of the two anonymous referees from the *Strategic Management Journal*.

REFERENCES

Aaker, D. A. and B. Mascarenhas. 'The need for strategic flexibility,' *Journal of Business Strategy*, 5(2), Fall 1984, pp. 74–82.

Aldrich, H. E. *Organizations and Environments*, Prentice-Hall, Englewood Cliffs, NJ, 1979.

Allen, M. K. 'Japanese companies in the United States: the success of Nissan and Honda.' Unpublished manuscript, Sloan School of Management, MIT, November 1985.

Bartlett, C. A. 'Global competition and MNC managers,' ICCH Note No. 0-385-287, Harvard Business School, Boston, 1985.

Bartlett, C. A. and S. Ghoshal. 'The new global organization: differentiated roles and dispersed responsibilities,' Working Paper No. 9-786-013, Harvard Business School, Boston, October 1985.

Baumol, W. J., J. C. Panzer and R. D. Willig. *Contestable Markets and the Theory of Industry Structure*, Harcourt, Brace, Jovanovich, New York, 1982.

Boston Consulting Group, *Perspectives on Experience*, BCG, Boston, MA, 1982.

Calvet, A. L. 'A synthesis of foreign direct investment theories and theories of the multinational firm,' *Journal of International Business Studies*, Spring-Summer 1981, pp. 43–60.

Caves, R. E. 'Industrial organization, corporate strategy and structure,' *Journal of Economic Literature*, XVIII, March 1980, pp. 64–92.

Doz, Y. L. 'Managing manufacturing rationalization within multinational companies,' *Columbia Journal of World Business*, Fall 1978, pp. 82–94.

Doz, Y. L., C. A. Bartlett and C. K. Prahalad. 'Global competitive pressures and host country demands: managing tensions in MNC's, *California Management Review*, Spring 1981, pp. 63–74.

Evans, J. S. *Strategic Flexibility in Business*, Report No. 678, SRI International, December 1982.

Fayerweather, J. 'Four winning strategies for the international corporation,' *Journal of Business Strategy*, Fall 1981, pp. 25–36.

Flaherty, M. T. and H. Itami. 'Finance,' in Okimoto, D. I., T. Sugano and F. B. Weinstein (Eds.), *Competitive Edge*, Stanford University Press, Stanford, CA, 1984.

Gluck, F. 'Global competition in the 1980's,' *Journal of Business Strategy*, Spring 1983, pp. 22–27.

Gold, B. 'Robotics, programmable automation, and international competitiveness,' *IEEE Transactions on Engineering Management*, November 1982.

Hamel, G. and C. K. Prahalad. 'Do you really have a global strategy?,' *Harvard Business Review*, July-August 1985, pp. 139–148.

Hannan, M. T. and J. Freeman. 'The population ecology of organizations,' *American Journal of Sociology*, 82, 1977, pp. 929–964.

Hatsopoulos, G. N. 'High cost of capital: handicap of American industry,' Report Sponsored by the American Business Conference and Thermo-Electron Corporation, April 1983.

Hax, A. C. and N. S. Majluf. *Strategic Management: An Integrative Perspective*, Prentice-Hall, Englewood Cliffs, NJ, 1984.

Herring, R. J. (ed.), *Managing International Risk*, Cambridge University Press, Cambridge, 1983.

Hofer, C. W. and D. Schendel. *Strategy Formulation: Analytical Concepts*, West Publishing Co., St. Paul, MN, 1978.

Hout, T., M. E. Porter and E. Rudden, 'How global companies win out,' *Harvard Business Review*, September–October 1982, pp. 98–108.

Itami, H. 'Japanese-U.S. comparison of managerial productivity,' *Japanese Economic Studies*, Fall 1978.

Kiechel, W. 'Playing the global game,' *Fortune*, November 16, 1981, pp. 111–126.

Kobrin, S. J. *Managing Political Risk Assessment*, University of California Press, Los Angeles, CA, 1982.

Kogut, B. 'Normative observations on the international value-added chain and strategic groups,' *Journal of International Business Studies*, Fall 1984, pp. 151–167.

Kogut, B. 'Designing global strategies: comparative and competitive value added chains,' *Sloan Management Review*, 26(4), Summer 1985a, pp. 15–28.

Kogut, B. 'Designing global strategies: profiting from operational flexibility,' *Sloan Management Review*, Fall 1985b, pp. 27–38.

Leontiades, J. 'Market share and corporate strategy in international industries,' *Journal of Business Strategy*, 5(1), Summer 1984, pp. 30–37.

Lessard, D. and J. Lightstone. 'The impact of exchange rates on operating profits: new business and financial response,' mimeo, Lightstone-Lessard Associates, 1983.

Levitt, T. 'The globalization of markets,' *Harvard Business Review*, May–June 1983, pp. 92–102.

Lorange, P., M. S. Scott Morton and S. Ghoshal. *Strategic Control*, West Publishing Co., St. Paul, MN, 1986.

Mascarenhas, B. 'Coping with uncertainty in international business,' *Journal of International Business Studies*, Fall 1982, pp. 87–98.

Mintzberg, H. 'Patterns in strategic formation,' *Management Science*, 24, 1978, pp. 934–948.

Ohmae, K. *Triad Power: The Coming Shape of Global Competition*, Free Press, New York, 1985.

Okimoto, D. I., T. Sugano and F. B. Weinstein (Eds.). *Competitive Edge*, Stanford University Press, Stanford, CA, 1984.

Perlmutter, H. V. 'The tortuous evolution of the multinational corporation,' *Columbia Journal of World Business*, January–February 1969, pp. 9–18.

Piore, M. J. and C. Sabel. *The Second Industrial Divide: Possibilities and Prospects*, Basic Books, New York, 1984.

Porter, M. E. *Competitive Strategy*, Basic Books, New York, 1980.

Porter, M. E. 'Competition in global industries: a conceptual framework,' paper presented to the Colloquium on Competition in Global Industries, Harvard Business School, 1984.

Porter, M. E. *Competitive Advantage*, Free Press, New York, 1985.

Poynter, T. A. International Enterprises and Government Intervention, Croom Helm, London, 1985.

Prahalad, C. K. 'The strategic process in a multinational corporation.' Unpublished doctoral dissertation, Graduate School of Business Administration, Harvard University, 1975.

Rapp, W. V. 'Strategy formulation and international competition,' *Columbia Journal of World Business*, Summer 1983, pp. 98–112.

Robinson, R. D. *International Business management: A Guide to Decision Making*, Dryden Press, Illinois, 1978.

Ronstadt, R. and R. J. Krammer, 'Getting the most out of innovations abroad,' *Harvard Business Review*, March–April 1982, pp. 94–99.

Rutenberg, D. P. *Multinational Management*, Little, Brown, Boston, MA, 1982.

Srinivasula, S. 'Strategic response to foreign exchange risks,' *Columbia Journal of World Business*, Spring 1981, pp. 13–23.

Terpstra, V. 'International product policy: the role of foreign R&D,' *Columbia Journal of World Business*, Winter 1977, pp. 24–32.

Terpstra, V. *International Dimensions of Marketing*, Kent, Boston, MA, 1982.

Toder, E. J. *Trade Policy and the U.S. Automobile Industry*, Praeger Special Studies, New York, 1978.

Vernon, R. *Storm Over the Multinationals*, Harvard University Press, Cambridge, MA, 1977.

The Wall Street Journal, April 29, 1985, p. 1.

Westney, D. E. 'International dimensions of information and communications technology.' Unpublished manuscript. Sloan School of Management, MIT, 1985.

Woo, C. Y. and K. O. Cool. 'The impact of strategic management of systematic risk,' Mimeo, Krannert Graduate School of Management, Purdue University, 1985.

Chapter 2

A Note on Global Strategies

Bruce Kogut
University of Pennsylvania

Abstract *This article augments, as well as takes issues with, the recent review by Ghoshal on international competition. The central question is what changes strategically when a firm moves from domestic to overseas competition. In analyzing this question, it is shown that there exists a neglected line of relevant research by two schools of thought: the Cambridge (Massachusetts) axis and internalization theory. The recent focus of research is described as understanding the multinational corporation as a network competing on its flexibility and the transfer of acquired capabilities across borders.*

The article by Sumantra Ghoshal (1987), entitled 'Global strategy: an organizing framework,' is a well-written and fluent review of a growing literature on international competition. I would like to augment his review by describing the earlier work on foreign direct investment as an outcome of oligopolistic rivalry, as well as the work on internalization arguments. The significance of this augmentation rests in (1) giving a sense of direction to the development of research on international competition and (2) showing how some of the current parlance is derived, and in some cases better explained, in this earlier work.

In augmenting Ghoshal's review, I take the opportunity to make three critical points. The first is to address, briefly, some of his criticism of my work. The second is to show that the unique aspects to international competition are fewer than suggested. If we are to avoid the wastefulness of excessive subdivision of the strategy field, it is important to isolate the incremental difference between a domestic and international setting. The third point is to give a sense of the development of the field from concentration on the initial foreign direct investment to exploring the multinational network as a basis of competition. This history matters, because arguably Ghoshal's identification of the sense of confusion in reading the recent literature arises from neglecting the substantial contribution of earlier writers. It is easier to draw a trend line in current thinking if we look back to other recent points in time.

Whenever new subjects and concepts are proposed it seems fair to ask what is different from what we already know. Analogously, the starting question for an analysis of global strategies is what is different when we move from a domestic to an international context. The traditional answer has been simply that the world is a bigger place, and hence all economies related to the

Reproduced by permission of John Wiley and Sons Limited from *Strategic Management Journal*, Vol. 10, pp. 383–389, 1989.

size of operations are, therefore, affected. A more interesting distinction is how differences in national markets create profit opportunities and influence the competitive positioning of firms.

The distinction which I have made is between the locational structure and operating flexibility of the multinational network, which is similar to—thought less felicitous than—Porter's configuration and coordination dimensions (Kogut, 1983; Porter, 1986). It is principally the operating side which drives the incremental value of being multinational. This operating flexibility stems from the benefits of coordinating the flows within a *multinational network*. The value of such flexibility rests not only on exploiting differentials in factor, product, and capital markets, but also on the transfer of learning and innovations throughout the firm, as well as the enhanced leverage to respond to competitors' and governments' threats. This flexibility, as I have underlined elsewhere, is, however, costly and organizationally complex to achieve.[1] Firms vary widely in their recognition of competing on the multinational network, as well as in terms of their ability to do so.

The shift in thinking about international competition in terms of network flexibility is reflected, as will be described later, in the work of many researchers. In order to have a sense of the current direction it is useful to understand the contribution, and continuing merits, of the work done primarily in the 1970s. The earlier writings on the international firm were less concerned with the benefits of being multinational but more with the initial decision to invest abroad. Their primary focus was on the location of investment rather than the operating management of these investments. Prior to 1960, most scholars viewed foreign direct investment as the flow of capital from one country to the next in the anticipation of higher returns. It was Hymer's (1960) distinctive contribution to shift the analysis from countries to industries. To him—and the excellent work which followed by Kindleberger (1969), Caves (1971), Vernon (1971), Horst (1974), Knickerbocker (1976), Graham (1978), and others—international competition was simply the extension of oligopolistic rivalry across borders. The themes of this research should strike a familiar chord with strategists of the industry analysis cloth: entry barriers, competitive signalling, and preemptive investments.

Indeed, the impressive work of the early 1970s, which was largely centered around a Cambridge (Massachusetts) axis, has laid the often unacknowledged foundation to recent theoretical treatments of cross-border dumping, strategic trade theory, and foreign investment as signaling commitment. These ideas underlie the more recent writings on the importance of being able to counter competition in multiple markets (Hout, Porter, and Rudden, 1982) and cross-subsidize across markets (Hamel and Prahalad, 1985).

There are important insights in this early work which are still neglected, though they strike familiar tunes. For example, recent game theoretic treatments of reputation rely upon retaliation in order to attain cooperation. Retaliation is effective even if there is only a small chance that a firm would respond in kind to a competitive price cut. The probability of retaliation multiplied by the aggressor's market share and by the drop in price may not be offset by expected gains to the aggressor if the time horizon is sufficiently long.

Let us take a concrete example. Ford probably thinks twice before cutting price if GM has the reputation for retaliation. But what good is GM's reputation when it has no credible way to affect Toyota's home market share and prices. The cutting of price by GM in the U.S. would hurt

---

[1]Ghoshal faults my work for seeing flexibility as without costs or requiring organizational support. He also argues that operating flexibility is conceived as creating side-bets to cover contingencies. I refer the reader to one article (Kogut, 1985) in order to evaluate these claims.

(because of GM's much larger market share) itself much more than Toyota. This asymmetry in the game between GM and Toyota has been of fundamental importance. It would seem GM has had only two alternatives: watch its market share fall and Toyota's increase to the point that the latter is worried about retaliation, or try to compete on cost (possibly with the help of Korean and Japanese allies).

In short, being multinational is one way to eliminate the asymmetrical exposure when international competition is between a few players. Yet, though these issues are recognized as important (as did Knickerbocker, 1973, in the conclusion to his book), there is still surprisingly little empirical work on international industry competition. Nor is there a theoretical or empirical treatment of the question of what happens when national oligopolies, following different rules of the game (e.g. cooperative and non-cooperative agreements) collide.[2]

In the mid to late 1970s the focus of work switched from the international extension of oligopolistic competition to the benefits of reducing 'transaction costs' by internalizing trade among countries. (Transaction costs in this literature are often not equivalent to Williamson's definition, since they include strategic motivations, such as being able to price discriminate across markets.) This approach was first suggested by McManus (1972), but became the central focus only after the publication of a book by two University of Reading scholars, Buckley and Casson, in 1976. Concurrent and subsequent contributions were made by Dunning (1977), Hennart (1982), Magee (1977), Rugman (1980) and Teece (1983).

The gist of the argument is straightforward. There are potential costs to relying on markets and contracts; suppliers might cheat, the transfer of technology might be difficult to price, or the creation of forward markets to hedge price risk might be impaired. Because of these market failures there is a benefit to being multinational, due to the possibility of internalizing trade within the firm and creating internal markets. There are a number of markets where this argument is especially pertinent, e.g. mineral markets or high-technology markets.

There are some debates in this literature which have yet to be addressed in the broader transaction cost literature. Dunning (1977), for example, distinguishes between internalization and ownership advantage. Internalization falls under the problem of establishing the boundary of the firm. Ownership advantages refers to the proprietary assets of the firm and corresponds to how possession of these assets influence, or are influenced by, the strategic positioning of the firm. There is considerably more work required in flushing out these distinctions, but it is an important contribution to distinguish between the problem of transacting goods and creating and preserving intangible assets.

In part, the work of Lessard, which is admirably summarized by Ghoshal, is also related to the internalization perspective. Agmon's and Lessard's (1977) observation was that diversification by real capital investments across borders is valuable if there are impediments (i.e. the absence of capital markets) to the flow of portfolio investments. This value stems not from better management of risks, but from the reduction in risk premia attached to an internationally diversified firm as opposed to one which is wholly domestic. The benefit of diversification is incremental to being multinational relative to domestic; it is not a question of better risk management relative to that of other multinational corporations. It is, on the other hand, tough to manage the exposure created by exchange rate—as Lessard's other work (1986) has carefully analyzed—but managing better is always good, whether a firm is international or not.

---

[2]However, see the recent work of Lyons, 1984, and Casson, 1987.

   The dominant framework for the analysis of global strategies at this time was that of global integration and national adaptation.[3] Benefits of a larger market encourage, so the underlying logic suggested, standardization to capitalize on scale economies, but country differences impede such efforts. This trade-off was largely focused on end-products and the problems of market access. At the same time, the prevailing wisdom on the organizational design of the multinational was of product and area divisions, with staff functions being under corporate and divisional control.

   It was a minor but non-trivial adjustment to alter this framework so that the global integration and country adaptation trade-off may be resolved by standardizing some links of the value-added chain and differentiating other links. Not surprisingly, the differentiated links frequently entail downstream activities. In this sense the international value-added chain is simply a twist on the original integration and differentiation choice.[4] But there is an important implication of this adjustment that is not often reflected in current empirical work, namely, a standardization and national differentiation typology is too simple and inaccurate if focused only at the market for final goods.

   The fundamental change in thinking about global competition in the 1980s has been the shift in interest over the decision to invest overseas to the strategic value of operating assets in multiple countries. An important element in this shift is the distinction between increased economies due to serving a larger market and the acquisition of advantages built upon the multinational network. On the cost side these advantages are achieved through scale and scope economies, learning (inclusive of the transfer of organizational practices across borders), and exploiting options written on movements in national conditions.

   Ghoshal's Table 3 summarizes this emergent view and provides, simultaneously, a decision tool for managers. In this table the columns represent the following sources of competitive advantage: national differences, scale economies, and scope economies. The following strategic objectives are given as the rows: achieving efficiency, managing risks, and innovation, learning, and adaptation. The discussion of each of these individual categories is creative and well done.

   Yet the matrix is misleading in a few regards. For the purpose of understanding a global strategy, the question is how the expansion across national markets alters strategies in terms of costs and opportunities. There are a few unfortunate outcomes of not clearly identifying this question, one being the trite but not trivial academic concern of credit, another more substantive. The issue of credit arises because the neglect of isolating the above question allows references (often on an *ad hoc* basis) to works which are unrelated to the international setting. Once these gates are open, the logic of selection is unclear.[5]

   Substantively, the failure to isolate the question of what changes when we cross borders leads to an artificial division in the strategy field without clearly identifying why. And there is an important distinction to be made. Consider, for example, Ghoshal's argument that innovation, learning, and adaptation are similar strategic objectives to be traded off against efficiency and risk. There is the very interesting behavioral question of whether strategic planning tools oriented toward economic efficiency stamp out attention which should be paid to innovation and learning.

---

   [3]The origins of this framework are to be found. Stephen Kobrin has reminded me, in the work of John Fayerweather (1969), but its most influential expression derives from Prahalad (1975). It was expanded by Doz (1979) to include the role of governments and by Bartlett (1979) in terms of the organizational prerequisites at the country level.

   [4]For two views on this adjustment, see Kogut (1984) and Porter (1986). My article was derived from a set of 1982 teaching notes which benefited from suggestions from Don Lessard.

   [5]Clearly, for example, the origins of the idea of the firm as a learning organization are found in the writings of March and Mintzberg.

The analysis of market exploitation and market creation may require, behaviorally, different analytical approaches.

But this procedural issue of the choice of analytical heuristics should not cloud the substantive evaluation of the costs and merits of learning and innovation. It is incomplete reasoning to say that learning must be traded off against efficiency, for learning is a source of advantage in which firms frequently knowingly invest and exploit with associated efficiency and risks. The decision by aircraft manufacturers to centralize airframe assembly, but contract internationally for other parts, is based on the efficiency merits of localized learning at the cost of the risk of labor interruption.[6] It is reasonable, as well, to ask if adaptation to local managerial practices is efficient, inclusive of the revenue impact if this adaptation should be useful in the future to the rest of the corporation.

This latter point of the revenue impact of transferring future benefits back to the rest of the corporation provides insight to why this reasoning is incomplete when framed as a tradeoff, but still of merit. It is an important point that internationalization of a firm's activities is beneficial not only because unit costs fall, but also because new profit opportunities are gained and new capabilities are, potentially developed. The benefits of investing overseas can rarely be evaluated on a stand-alone project basis.

Rather, a multinational corporation can be seen as consisting of proprietary assets from which it derives current cash flows, as well as of a set of options inherent in operating in multiple environments. It is possible to analyze many questions in strategy in terms of whether the purchasing of an option is worth its potential future exercise.[7] Frequently, managers make the argument that an investment in a country is valuable because it represents a growth opportunity. The net present value looks bad, but the incremental option value should be considered.

Options can be driven by random events such as exchange rate movements which encourage a policy of multiple plants with the ability to shift production. There are other kinds of options. Some of these options are simply that innovations may differ across countries, and it is useful to have operating assets dispersed in order to exercise the right to acquire and transfer them. It might be worthwhile to build research and development or manufacturing facilities in order to ascertain, understand, and transfer such innovations as they occur.[8] It is an outright error to call the investment in such options as a trade-off with efficiency or as narrowly falling under the management of risk as side-bets. To the contrary, such investments represent the incremental value of managing foreign subsidiaries as a network instead of as a set of dyadic relationships between headquarters and subsidiaries. Thus, the recognition that multinationality can be valued as a bundle of options has significant implications for the organization and management of the international firm.

Similar observations were made in earlier texts as well. As part of the Cambridge axis, Franko (1971) and Stopford and Wells (1974) had analyzed the conflict between serving subsidiary versus network goals, especially in the context of losing flexibility as a result of joint ventures. The most explicit early description of the multinational corporation as competing on flexibility is to be found in Vernon's (1979) discussion of the global network in terms of scanning abilities. He writes of the global scanner's innovative response to a threat in some national market:

---

[6]Implicitly, an assessment of political risk and bargaining is critical in evaluating international strategies. See Doz (1979) and Kobrin (1982).

[7]See Myers (1984) for a general statement, and Kogut (1983) for an application to the multinational corporation.

[8]See Ronstadt (1978) for a discussion. Note, however, that the internalization literature is relevant to analyzing why these assets must be owned rather than relying on the market to purchase the innovation.

The firm might launch the innovative process in the market that had produced the stimulus; or, if economies of scale were important and an appropriate facility existed elsewhere in the system, in a location well removed from the prospective market. In either case, once the innovation was developed, the global scanner would be in a position to service any market in which it was aware that demand existed; and would be in a position to detect and serve new demands in other markets as they subsequently arose.

Acknowledgement of the importance of network flows can be found in textbooks as well, such as Robock, Simmonds, and Zwick (1977), Robinson (1978), and especially Franklin Root's *International Trade and Investment* (1973).[9]

Despite these observations on the multinational network, the benefits of utilizing and transferring local resources among subsidiaries only became highlighted in later work. Of course, having the potential to exercise flexibility is a far cry from having the management system to do it. The earlier work on the multinational corporation had emphasized product and area divisions which were suited to the management of dyadic relationships between headquarters and subsidiaries. The structures also presumed that subsidiaries would be implementers of corporate plans and product developments.

Competing on the basis of the multinational network may not be conducive with the previous structures. To a greater extent the fountainhead of the ideas regarding the organization of the multinational network is Perlmutter's notion of the geocentric firm (Perlmutter, 1969).[10] More recently, Bartlett (1986) and Bartlett and Ghoshal (1986) have been concerned with outlining how the management of an integrated network is critical to the exploiting of the resources of national subsidiaries for the larger system. Prahalad and Doz (1987) give an insightful analysis of managerial resolutions of the global integration and local responsiveness conflict in terms of a wider interdependence among subsidiaries. Hedlunds' (1986) heterarchy is the boldest statement of the organizational aspects of competing through multiple centers and the transfer of learning from country subsidiaries throughout the network.

From an international managerial perspective, the challenge is not simply the dyadic implementation of headquarters' desires in a local market, as specified in the important work of the 1970s and early 1980s. Rather, it is the creation of organizational structures and systems which permit the exploitation of opportunities inherent in the network of operating in different national environments. There is no argument that this is hard to do, and some firms do it better, or that the notions of centralization and decentralization fail to capture the importance of network coordination. It also may be true that it is easier to isolate the substantive strategic content of an international strategy than to define the operating systems to pull it off. But the management question should be seen as a complement, as opposed to a substitute, to the identification of the content of an international strategy.

It seems fair, to close with our initial point, to ask what is the analytical value of prefacing strategy with the word global. What is distinctive in the international context, besides larger market size, is the variance in country environments and the ability to profit through the system-wide management of this variance. The amount of empirical work done on issues of international competition, involving both management as well as industry structure issues, is impressive. It may be of benefit if, along with the conflicts, the cumulative results of a long line of research are stressed.

---

[9]Robock, Simmonds, and Zwick (1977: 400) has, moreover, a strikingly temporary discussion of the ITT's advantage over local competitors due to 'cross-fertilization' across its dispersed laboratories and factories.

[10]For an analytical treatment, see Rutenberg (1982).

ACKNOWLEDGMENTS

I would like to thank Lars Hakanson, Stephen Kobrin, Orjan Solvell, Udo Zander, and the anonymous referees for their comments on an earlier draft.

REFERENCES

Agmon, T. and D. Lessard. 'Financial factors and the international expansion of small-country firms.' In Agmon, T. and C. Kindleberger (eds.), *Multinationals from Small Countries*, MIT Press, Cambridge, 1977.

Bartlett, C 'Multinational structural evolution: the changing decision environment in international divisions,' doctoral dissertation, Harvard Business School, 1979.

Bartlett, C. 'Building and managing the transnational: the new organizational challenge.' In Porter, M. (ed.), *Competition in Global Industries*, Harvard Business School Press, Boston, 1986.

Bartlett, C and S. Ghoshal. 'Tapping your subsidiaries for global reach,' *Harvard Business Review*, November–December, 1986, pp. 87–94.

Buckley, P. J. and M. Casson, *The Future of the Multinational Enterprise*, Holmes and Meier, London, 1976.

Casson, M. *The Firm and the Market*, MIT Press, Cambridge, 1987.

Caves, R. E. 'International corporations: the industrial economics of foreign direct investment,' *Economica*, 38,, 1971, pp. 1–27.

Doz, Y. L. *Government Control and Multinational Strategic Management: Power Systems and Telecommunications Equipment*, Praeger, New York, 1979.

Doz, Y. L. 'Managing manufacturing rationalization within multinational companies,' *Columbia Journal of World Business*, Fall 1978, pp. 82–94.

Dunning, J. H. 'Trade, location of economic activity and the MNE: a search for an eclectic approach.' In Ohlin, Bertil, et al. (eds.), *The International Allocation of Economic Activity*, Holmes and Meier, London, 1977.

Fayerweather, J. *International Business Management: A Conceptual Framework*, George Allen & Unwin, London, 1969.

Franko, L. *Joint Venture Survival in Multinational Corporations*, Praeger, New York, 1971.

Ghoshal, S. 'Global strategy: an organizing framework,' *Strategic Management Journal*, 8(5), 1987, pp. 425–440.

Graham, M. E. 'Transatlantic investment by multinational firms: a rivalistic phenomenon?,' *Journal of Post-Keynsian Economics*, 1, 1978, pp. 82–99.

Hamel, G. and C. K. Prahalad. 'Do you really have a global strategy?,' *Harvard Business Review*, July–August, 1985, pp. 139–148.

Hedlung, G. 'The hypermodern MNC—a heterarchy,' *Human Resource Management*, 25, 1986, pp. 9–25.

Hennart, J. F. *A Theory of the Multinational Enterprise*, University of Michigan, Ann Arbor, 1982.

Horst, T. *At Home Abroad: A Study of the Domestic and Foreign Operations of the American Food-Processing Industry*, Ballinger, Cambridge, 1974.

Hout, T., M. E. Porter and E. Rudden, 'How global companies win out,' *Harvard Business Review*, September–October 1982, pp. 98–108.

Hymer, S. *The International Operations of National Firms: A Study of Direct Investment*, MIT Press, Cambridge, 1976; publication of Ph.D. thesis of same title, Massachusetts Institute of Technology, 1960.

Kindleberger, C. P. *American Business Abroad*, Yale University, New Haven, 1969.

Knickerbocker, F. *Oligopolistic Reaction and Multinational Enterprise*, Harvard University, Graduate School of Business Administration, Boston, 1973.

Knickerbocker, F. *Market Structure and Market Power Consequences of Foreign Direct Investment by Multinational Corporations*, Center for Multinational Studies, Washington, 1976.

Kobrin, S. *Managing Political Risk Assessment: Organizational Response to Environmental Change*, University of California Press, Berkeley, 1982.

Kogut, B. 'Foreign direct investment as a sequential process.' In Kindleberger, C. and D. Audretsch (eds.), *The Multinational Corporation in the 1980s.* MIT Press, Cambridge, 1983.

Kogut, B. 'Normative observations on the international value-added chain and strategic groups,' *Journal of International Business Studies,* Fall, 1984, pp. 151–167.

Kogut, B. 'Designing global strategies: profiting from operating flexibility,' *Sloan Management Review,* Fall, 1985, pp. 27–38.

Lessard, D. 'Finance and global competition: exploiting financial scope and coping with volatile exchange rates.' In Porter, M. (ed.), *Competition in Global Industries,* Harvard Business School, Boston, 1986.

Lyons, B. R. 'The pattern of international trade in differentiated products: an incentive for the existence of multinational firms.' In Krerzkowski, H. (ed.), *Monopolistic Competition and International Trade,* Oxford University Press, London, 1984.

Magee, S. P. 'Information and the multinational corporation: an appropriability approach.' In Bhagwati J. (ed.), *The New Economic Order: The North-South Debate,* MIT Press, Cambridge, 1977.

McManus, J. C. 'The theory of the international firm.' In Pacquet, G. (ed.), *The Multinational Firm and the National State,* Collier Macmillan Canada, Ontario, 1972.

Myers, S. 'Finance theory and financial strategy,' *Interfaces,* 14, 1984, pp. 126–137.

Perlmutter, H. 'The tortuous evolution of the multinational corporation, *Columbia Journal of World Business,* January–February, 1969, pp. 9–18.

Porter, M. E. 'Competition in global industries: a conceptual framework.' In Porter, M. (ed.), *Competition in Global Industries,* Harvard Business School Press, Boston, 1986.

Prahalad, C. K. 'The strategic process in a multinational corporation,' unpublished doctoral dissertation, Graduate School of Business Administration, Harvard University, 1975.

Prahalad C. K. and Y. Doz. *The Multinational Mission,* Free Press, New York, 1987.

Robinson, R. D. *International Business Management,* Dryden Press, Hinsdale, Illinois, 1978.

Robock, S., K. Simmonds and J. Zwick. *International Business and Multinational Enterprises,* Irwin, New York, 1977.

Ronstadt, R. 'International R&D: the establishment and evolution of research and development abroad by seven U.S. multinationals,' *Journal of International Business Studies,* 10, 1978, pp. 7–24.

Root, F. *International Trade and Investment,* Southwestern Publishing Co., Cincinnati, 1973.

Rugman, A. M. 'Internalization as a general theory of foreign direct investment: a re-appraisal of the literature,' *Weltwirtschaftliches Archiv.* 116, 1980, pp. 365–379.

Rutenberg, D. *Multinational Management,* Little, Brown, Boston, 1982.

Stopford, J. and L. Wells, *Managing the Multinational Enterprise,* Basic Books, New York, 1972.

Teece, D. 'A transaction cost theory of the multinational enterprise.' In Casson, M. (ed.), *The Growth of International Business,* Allen and Unwin. London, 1983.

Vernon, R. *Sovereignty at Bay: The Multinational Spread of US Enterprises,* Basic Books, New York, 1971.

Vernon, R. 'The product hypothesis in a new international environment,' *Oxford Bulletin of Economics and Statistics,* 41, 1979, pp. 255–267.

Chapter 3

Strategic Planning for a Global Business

Balaji S. Chakravarthy
University of Minnesota

Howard V. Perlmutter
University of Pennsylvania

Abstract *Strategic planning in a multinational corporation (MNC) has become progressively more complex over the years due to the globalization of its businesses and the increasing activism of its stakeholders. This paper reviews four generic planning systems that are available to an MNC for meeting this challenge and discusses the context in which each should be used.*

Two recent trends have made strategic planning more complex in a multinational corporation (MNC): globalization of several industries and increased activism of its stakeholders. Until a decade ago, most multinational corporations did not seriously deal with either global integration or stakeholder activism.

A globally focused firm uses its world-wide system of resources to compete in national markets (Hout, Porter, and Rudden, 1982). Various country subsidiaries consequently become highly interdependent in their operational strategies, since the minimum volume necessary to exploit scale economies and experience effects is unavailable within a single national market. In order to be a viable competitor in a global business, an MNC must ensure tight integration of its world-wide operations.

Concurrent with the above trend has been the increasing pressure on MNCs from host governments. These stakeholders are forcing MNCs to concern themselves more with issues of legitimacy, i.e., whether the actions of MNCs are consonant with the interests of the host country.

The fundamental planning challenge for an MNC is one of balancing the economic imperative of global integration with the political imperative of prudent stakeholder management (Doz, 1980). In an extreme case, the two can pull in opposite directions. Giving the subsidiary autonomy to pursue a strategy responsive to host government needs can nurture legitimacy, but it must be balanced with suitable controls to ensure proper integration of the subsidiary's strategy with that of other subsidiaries. This paper focuses on the role of strategic planning systems in bringing about such a balance.

The paper is divided into two main sections. The first section elaborates the planning challenge. The second section describes briefly the choice of strategic planning systems currently available to an MNC and assesses their relevance for a global business.

THE CHALLENGES FOR STRATEGIC PLANNING

Three important contextual factors define the business planning challenge faced by an MNC:

* the *economic imperative* that determines where the MNC should locate various elements of the value chain for a given business;
* the *political imperative* as shaped by the demands of the host countries in which the MNC operates; and,
* the MNC's own *strategic predisposition*.

The Economic Imperative

Based on the economic forces operating in an industry, Porter (1984) offers two distinct strategic options for an MNC: a global strategy (cost leadership, differentiation, and segmentation) and a country-centered strategy (national responsiveness, or protected markets). Each of these strategies is distinguished by two criteria: (1) extent of global centralization/coordination, and (2) breadth of target segments within the industry (see Chart 1).

A primary determinant of whether a firm should pursue a global or country-centered strategy is the proportion of value added in the upstream activities of the industry's value chain. In industries such as automobiles, motorcycles, chemicals, steel, and heavy electrical systems, where significant value is added in upstream activities (i.e., R&D and manufacturing), MNCs have found it advantageous to pursue a global strategy. On the other hand, in industries such as insurance and consumer packaged goods, where a substantial proportion of value is added in downstream activities (i.e., marketing, sales and service), a country-centered strategy has been more viable.

However, even within an industry, the choice of strategy depends on the segments of the value chain that a firm competes in. For example, if a firm in the aircraft industry merely sells and services aircrafts worldwide, a country-centered strategy may be appropriate to it. Similarly, if there are global customers for an insurance company's product (e.g. marine insurance), the company may have to pick a global strategy. As a corollary, a vertically integrated firm can choose to pursue different strategies for different segments of the industry's value chain.

Globalization of industries is on the rise because of the increasing potential for centralization and coordination of business activities (Porter, 1984). The move towards centralization is helped by the continuing homogenization of product needs among countries and the marketing systems and business infrastructure through which these needs are served. Cheaper and more reliable transportation has also contributed to centralization. (The lack of such transportation was a major deterrent to inter-country shipments in the past.) Greater coordination is being facilitated primarily by the international communications revolution. Integrated transmission of voice, data, and video signals worldwide is projected to become a reality in the near future. The emergence of global buyers and suppliers also calls for greater coordination between the various subsidiaries of an MNC.

The above analysis of the economic imperatives confronting an MNC would suggest that global strategies (both cost leadership and differentiation) will displace country-centered strategies in several industries. However, the new political imperatives faced by an MNC represent a counter-trend towards national responsiveness. These will be examined next.

Extent of Global Centralization/Coordination

Breadth of Target Segments Within the Industry	Global Cost Leadership	Global Differentiation	Protected Markets
Broad	Global Cost Leadership	Global Differentiation	Protected Markets
Narrow	Global Segmentation		National Responsiveness
	Global Strategy		Country-Centered Strategy

Chart 1 Strategic alternatives in a global industry. Source: Porter (1984).

The Political Imperative

Doz and Prahalad (1980) offer a useful framework for understanding the political imperatives that drive the business strategies of an MNC. They define two important determinants of business context: (1) the bargaining power of the MNC, and (2) the bargaining power of the host government. The bargaining power of the MNC is based on three sources: proprietary technology, world-wide market share (economies of scale), and product differentiation. The bargaining power of the host government is derived from its desire and ability to control market access, and the size and attractiveness of the national market that it controls.

In situations where the MNC is a technology or market leader and where the bargaining power of the host government is weak, a global integration strategy is appropriate. For example, Boeing could choose a global integration strategy in Europe because of its relative power over host governments (Doz and Prahalad, 1980). Boeing is a technology leader with a dominant share of the world market. Consequently, the host governments could not force it to adopt a more country-centered strategy.

On the other hand, in situations where the power balance is skewed in favor of the host government, a country-centered strategy is more appropriate. Examples of such an approach are provided by Honeywell in France and Chrysler in the UK (Doz and Prahalad, 1980).

The push towards country-centered strategies comes from the growing number of powerful external stakeholders. Management must not only worry abut an MNC's viability (i.e., meeting its profit objectives), but also about its legitimacy (i.e., stakeholder perceptions as to whether the firm's activities are consonant with the values of the host country), (Heenan and Perlmutter, 1979).

Home and host governments are key external stakeholders, and both have begun to regulate MNC activities with increasing sophistication. In addition to its role as a regulator, the host government can engage in other relationships with an MNC: as a co-negotiator (along with unions in labor relations), as a supplier (where public utilities and raw material industries may be state owned), as a competitor (through its public sector corporations), or even as a distributor (where channels are state owned). In coping with powerful external stakeholders such as the host government, the MNC requires strategies that are tailored to each national context.

Strategic Predisposition

The strategic predisposition of a firm is shaped by a number of factors: the circumstances of its birth, the leadership style of its CEOs, its past administrative practices, the myths and folklore that have endured in the organization, etc. Heenan and Perlmutter (1979) describe four distinct predispositions in an MNC:

• *Ethnocentrism* is a predisposition where all strategic decisions are guided by the values and interests of the parent. Such a firm is predominantly concerned with its viability worldwide and legitimacy only in its home country.

• *Polycentrism* is a predisposition where strategic decisions are tailored to suit the cultures of the various countries in which the MNC competes. A polycentric multinational is primarily concerned with legitimacy in every country that it operates in, even if that means some loss of profits.

• *Regiocentrism* is a predisposition that tries to blend the interests of the parent with that of the subsidiaries at least on a limited regional basis. A regiocentric multinational tries to balance viability and legitimacy at the regional level.

• *Geocentrism* is a predisposition that seeks to integrate diverse subsidiaries through a global systems approach to decision making. A geocentric firm tries to balance viability and legitimacy through a global networking of its businesses. On occasion, these networks may even include the firm's stakeholders and competitors. Geocentrism can be further classified as enclave or integrative geocentrism. The former deals with high priority problems of host countries in a marginal fashion; the latter recognizes that the MNC's key decisions must be separately assessed for their impact on each country.

The above predispositions are seldom found their pure form. An MNC's predominant predisposition is called its EPRG profile. An ethnocentric or polycentric EPRG profile is very common (Perlmutter, 1969), while a regiocentric or geocentric EPRG profile is relatively new among MNCs. Each EPRG profile is associated with a distinct social architecture (Perlmutter, 1984). The mission, governance structure, strategy, organization structure, and culture associated with the four EPRG profiles are described in Table 1.

The administrative systems associated with each EPRG profile reinforce one another and over a period of time define the distinct mode in which an MNC adapts to its environment. In a sense, the profile gets institutionalized and dictates the firm's behavior in a variety of functions (Table 2). In an ethnocentric multinational, for example, marketing, manufacturing, finance, and personnel decisions are typically made at headquarters with very little input from country managers.

The predisposition of an MNC can be at odds with the strategy appropriate to its economic or political imperatives. For example, an ethnocentric firm may find it difficult to adopt a nationally responsive strategy, or a polycentric firm may not be successful in implementing a global integration strategy.

STRATEGIC PLANNING SYSTEMS: CHOICES AND LIMITATIONS

The three forces described in the previous section can and often do pull in different directions. In fact, the planning challenge is to reconcile their differences. For ease of exposition, we will represent the various business contexts that an MNC can experience in a two dimensional framework (Chart 2).

The strategic planning systems that have been used in the past by large diversified corporations fall under four distinct categories: Model I, or top-down planning; Model II, or bottom-up planning; Model III, or portfolio planning; and Model IV, or dual structure planning (Chakravarthy and Lorange, 1984). The ability of each of these systems to balance viability and legitimacy in the distinct business contexts defined by Chart 2 are discussed below.

Model I: Planning for Cell 4

Model I, a top down approach to planning, seeks to provide the MNC with a global competitive advantage through tight integration of its worldwide activities.

A Model I company is typically organized into several product groups worldwide. It is the responsibility of each product group manager to ensure the needed global integration through an elaborate formal plan that is monitored for progress each month at all levels of management. This planning system is associated with a large and powerful planning staff at the headquarters, who carefully scrutinize and independently double check all strategic plans proposed by the national unit managers.

The legitimacy issue is dealt with in such a system through additional "citizenship costs" incurred by each subsidiary (Doz and Prahalad, 1980). In other words, the MNC using a Model I

Table 1
Orientation of the Firm Under Different EPRG Profiles

Orientation of the firm	EPRG profile			
	Ethnocentric	Polycentric	Regiocentric	Geocentric
1. Mission	Profitability (viability)	Public acceptance (legitimacy)	Both profitability and public acceptance (viability and legitimacy)	Both profitability and public acceptance (viability and legitimacy)
2. Governance • Direction of goal setting	Top down	Bottom up (each subsidiary decides upon local objectives)	Mutually negotiated between region and its subsidiaries	Mutually negotiated at all levels of the corporation
• Communication	Hierarchical, with headquarters giving high volume of orders, commands and advice	Little communication to and from headquarters and between subsidiaries	Both vertical and lateral communication within region	Both vertical and lateral communication within the company
• Allocation of resources	Investment opportunities decided at headquarters	Self-supporting subsidiaries, no cross-subsidies	Regions allocate resources, under guidelines from headquarters	World wide projects, allocation influenced by local and headquarters' managers
3. Strategy	Global integrative	National responsiveness	Regional integrative and national responsiveness	Global integrative and national responsiveness
4. Structure	Hierarchical product divisions	Hierarchical area divisions, with autonomous national units	Products and regional organizations tied through a matrix	A network of organizations, (including some stakeholders and competitor organizations)
5. Culture	Home country	Host country	Regional	Global

Source: 1. Perlmutter (1984).
2. Heenan and Perlmutter (1979).

Table 2

EPRG Profile in Different Functional Areas

Functional area	EPRG profile			
	Ethnocentric	Polycentric	Regiocentric	Geocentric
Technology				
Production technology	Mass production	Batch production	Flexible manufacturing	Flexible manufacturing
Marketing				
Product planning	Product development determined primarily by the needs of home country customers	Local product development based on local needs	Standardize within region, but not across	Global product, with local variations
Marketing mix decisions	Made at headquarters	Made in each country	Made regionally	Made jointly with mutual consultation
Finance				
Objective	Repatriation of profits to home country	Retention of profits in host country	Redistribution within region	Redistribution globally
Financing relations	Home country institutions	Host country institutions	Regional institutions	Other global institutions
Personnel practices				
Perpetuation	People of home country developed for key positions everywhere in the world	People of local nationality developed for key positions in their own country	Regional people developed for key positions anywhere in the region	Best people everywhere in the world developed for key position everywhere in the world
Evaluation and control	Home standards applied for persons and performance	Determined locally	Determined regionally	Standards which are universal, weighted to suit local conditions

Source: Heenan & Perlmutter (1979).
Perlmutter (1984).

35

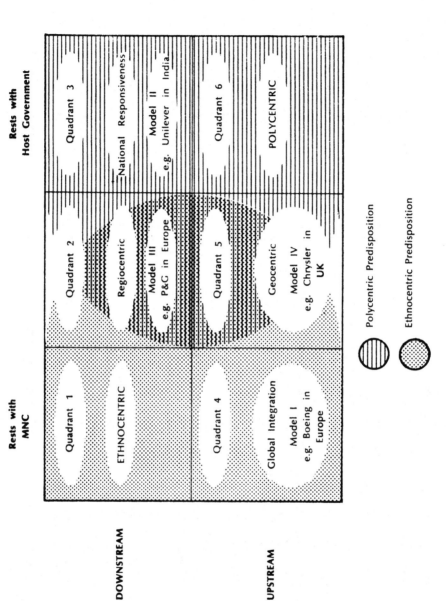

Chart 2 A framework for choosing strategic planning systems.

planning system chooses to pay the penalty for non-conformance with the host government's demands in the form of higher import duties and taxes. For a period under Harold Geneen, ITT was a company that followed such a system of planning (Kotter, Schlesinger and Sathe, 1979).

The business context to which this system is best suited is cell 4. Cell 4 represents a business context where global integration is desirable and possible. The relatively high value that is added upstream suggests that the pooling of R&D and manufacturing activities among the MNC's various subsidiaries can result in important cost savings. A centrally coordinated strategic plan can facilitate the proper scheduling of these activities. Moreover, given that the locus of relative power rests with the MNC, it will face few obstacles from the host government for such an integration. Boeing's aircraft business in Europe falls in this cell. Other examples are IBM or AT&T (eventually) in world markets. This is not to suggest that these companies are restricted only to a Model I planning system, but to point out that given their contexts, they can use such a system.

It must be noted, however, that the locus of relative power can shift back to the host government if there are other eager competitors who are willing to collaborate with it. In fact, like in the case of Honeywell in France, the host government can provide suitable incentives to attract a "weak" MNC. This can mean a loss of market for a Model I MNC. A Model I planning approach must be tempered, therefore, with some sensitivity to the needs of the host country.

Model II: Planning for Cell 3

A firm using a Model II planning system is typically organized by geographic areas (as opposed to product groups as in Model I). The smallest geographic unit is a national unit. Each national unit is delegated the responsibility for balancing its legitimacy and viability goals within broad guidelines issued by headquarters. The subsidiaries behave as if they are national companies. There are very few functional interdependencies across national units, and headquarters seldom resort to cross-subsidies. Typically, monitoring and control are financially oriented in a Model II planning system. The headquarters has a very thin corporate planning staff who act primarily as consolidators of national unit business plans.

Theoretically, a Model II planning system can be very responsive to the needs of the host government, but at costs in the duplication of resources and limits to the economic advantages of multinationality. A Model II firm has competitive advantages over a national firm only in a few domains: pooling of financial risks, sharing of R&D costs, coordination of export marketing, and some skill transfers among subsidiaries. If Model I was overly focused on the economic imperative, Model II is especially partial to the political imperative.

Model II is best suited to a cell 3 business. Cell 3 represents a business where the economic imperative (high value added downstream) and the political imperative both point to a national responsiveness strategy. Unilever's operations in India are a case in point. The subsidiary sells consumer products, toiletries and animal feed, none of which lies in the core of essential industrial sectors as defined by the Indian government. Consequently, Unilever can operate in India only on the government's terms. In such a setting, a Model II planning process is quite appropriate. The parent exercises largely financial control and provides the subsidiary with technical and managerial assistance and with help in its export efforts when sought.

Model III: Portfolio Planning

Models I and II are suitable only for select business segments of an MNC and cannot be used consistently throughout the firm. Model I presumes that national stakeholders can be appeased by paying suitable citizenship costs. As the recent woes of Union Carbide in Bhopal, India, would point out, citizenship costs currently are being measured by more exacting world standards. Consequently, a planning orientation like Model I that completely ignores legitimacy issues can eventually hurt even the firm's viability.

On the other hand, a planning orientation that is predominantly responsive to national interests ignores the many advantages of multinationality. Given the trend towards globalization in many industries, a Model II planning orientation can hurt the competitive position of an MNC in world markets.

Instead of selecting one of the two pure archetypes discussed above, a diversified MNC can use both planning systems to suit its different business contexts. This approach is also called portfolio planning. An MNC using a Model III planning system is typically organized in global product divisions like a Model I firm. However, unlike a Model I firm, it uses a top-down or bottom-up planning process, depending on the context of each of its businesses. This is a popular approach among MNCs. According to a recent survey, over fifty percent of all US-based diversified MNCs use this system of planning (Haspeslagh, 1982).

The attractiveness of an industry environment and the competitive strengths of the firm in that industry are normally the two determinants of whether the business will be subjected to a Model I or Model II planning system. A business in a growing national market where the company is trying to build market share will typically employ Model II planning, while a business in a maturing or mature national market where the company has a strong competitive position will generally use a Model I planning process. This is consistent with the emphasis on marketing (country-centered strategy) in the first business as the MNC tries to build market share, and on manufacturing and distribution (global integration strategy) in the second business as it seeks to improve operational efficiency.

Portfolio planning is best suited to a cell 1 or cell 2 business context. In either case, given the MNC's relative power over its host countries, it is free to attempt at least limited coordination among groups of countries in a region. Each such region is treated as a planning unit in a Model III system.

The Model III planning approach is most effective only when the planning challenge can be neatly compartmentalized as either integrative (regional integration) or adaptive (national responsiveness), (Lorange, 1980). This is indeed possible in several business contexts. The economic forces faced by a firm need not always be in conflict with the political forces. As Porter (1984) points out:

> Some economic forces favor standardization (e.g., scale economies) but others favor country-centered strategies (e.g., product heterogeneity and transport costs). Similarly, there are political forces working towards a country-centered strategy (e.g., local content rules and local ownership laws) and political forces favoring global strategies (export subsidies, R&D support for targeted industries), (1984: 30).

Designing a planning system that simultaneously encourages adaptation and integration within a region is, however, difficult. For example, in industries like telecommunications, a global integration strategy can optimally exploit special upstream resources like R&D and manufacturing; however, given the salience of this industry to national economies, host governments are likely to insist on a country-centered strategy.

Moreover, the assumption of Model III that a country unit can be initially subjected to a country-centered strategy (Model II) and then switched to a regional integration strategy (Model I), may be untenable in countries where such integration implies retrenchment in investment.

This is especially true in countries where the MNC has several business interests. The host country can use its leverage in one business to extract concessions in another, where the MNC supposedly has more power over the host country. A sequential attention to the legitimacy and viability needs of a business, as proposed in Model III, needs to be replaced therefore with a system that can ensure simultaneous attention to these needs. Model IV on Dual Structure Planning is such a system.

Model IV: Dual Structure Planning

A cell 5 or cell 6 business context is the most difficult since it simultaneously requires a global integration and national responsiveness orientation. For example, Chrysler's operations in the UK should be responsive to the host government, while at the same time derive global integrative advantages to compete successfully with other international auto manufacturers.

In order to use a dual structure planning system, the MNC must be organized in a matrix structure, with product and area as its two dimensions. A planning system can then be designed to stress adaptation along one dimension and integration along the other (Lorange, 1976). If, for example, the corporation wants the subsidiary to be country-centered, it should use an adaptive orientation for strategies formulated by the business side of the matrix, and use the area dimension of the matrix for integration. In other words, while national unit managers have leeway in adapting the company's businesses to their local environments, they would still be answerable for profit performance set through the budgeting process. Conversely, to implement a global business strategy, the MNC should allow adaptation on the area dimension at the national unit level while ensuring integration through the product dimension of the matrix. Thus, the integrative side of the matrix becomes in effect the operating structure, while the adaptive dimension becomes the strategic structure (Lorange, 1984).

The relative emphasis on adaptation or integration within a national market can be altered by moving key managers to the appropriate side of the matrix, and by altering the planning, control, and reward systems used in that country (Prahalad, 1976). The planning system acts like a lens to focus the matrix structure toward a national responsive or global integrative orientation as required from country to country. It also leads to a more balanced orientation within each country than that provided by a Model III, especially if the MNC's culture encourages healthy confrontation between the two sides of the matrix. An example of a company that uses a dual structure planning is IBM. It is most useful to firms that are not widely diversified and that derive their competitive advantage from a common product-market, technology, or operation base.

A Model IV planning system can theoretically provide the simultaneous balance required between legitimacy and viability. The relative power difference between the two dimensions of the global matrix can be set at different equilibrium levels to suit each business context. However, fine tuning a global matrix structure through a Model IV planning system requires the simultaneous support of several other administrative systems including staffing, control, and reward systems (Doz and Prahalad, 1981). The orchestration of all of these systems can easily become an administrative nightmare (Davis and Lawrence, 1977). A recent survey showed that less than 5 percent of all MNCs attempted such a planning system (Haspeslagh, 1982).

CONCLUSIONS

The discussion in the previous sections showed how currently available planning systems are not quite suited to the needs of a global business. One way of dealing with this problem would be for the MNC to position itself in quadrants where the economic and political pressures are not conflicting. It can also attempt to rectify power imbalances with the host government by manipulating the resource dependencies of the subsidiary. However, as was pointed out earlier, current trends suggest that increasing numbers of global businesses will face the simultaneous challenge of global integration and national responsiveness. A hybrid of Model III and Model IV will be the best initial option for meeting this twin challenge.

A Hybrid Planning System

The Model IV planning system proposed in the previous section can theoretically help balance the visibility and legitimacy goals of an MNC. However, as mentioned earlier, dual structure planning is relatively new. Instead of attempting a company wide Model IV planning approach, it is perhaps more prudent to first attempt Model IV planning only within select regions where there are strong pressures for both legitimacy and viability (Chakravarthy, 1984). Other regions can be managed using a Model III planning system.

In such a system, the headquarters must help balance the region's orientation towards integration and national responsiveness by maintaining a counterbalancing functional and administrative view. In other words, if the region seems to be veering off to a nationally responsive orientation, staff advisors at the headquarters must be managers who are biased towards global integration. Finally, the monitoring, control, and reward systems must acknowledge performance towards the goals of all major stakeholders of the firm, and not merely those of the stockholders of the parent company. The proposed hybrid system is discussed at length in a follow-up paper.

Strategic Predisposition

The major bottleneck we anticipate in implementing the hybrid planning system discussed above is the predominant ethnocentric predisposition exhibited by most MNCs. An ethnocentric firm essentially focuses on bottom line profits, and treats all political imperatives as unnecessary constraints. Even a polycentric firm pursues a country-centered strategy vigorously only when it is dictated by an economic imperative (cell 3 in Chart 2), and not as enthusiastically when imposed by a political imperative (cells 1 and 2 in Chart 2). The governing management paradigm in most MNCs seems to be overly biased towards viability (Perlmutter, 1984).

On the other hand, most host governments expect the MNC to treat political imperatives as goals and economic imperatives (reasonable profits) as constraints. The mindsets of the MNC managers and their international stakeholders would seem to be irreconcilably different. Unless an MNC begins to change its predisposition, it is headed on a collision course with its stakeholders, regardless of the planning system that it uses.

The real challenge for an MNC is then to alter its predisposition to a more regiocentric or geocentric orientation (Perlmutter, 1984). On occasion, the MNC may have to seek the cooperation of select competitors and important stakeholders in order to proactively simplify the environment in which it competes. Cooperation and competition are both accepted strategies under a geocentric predisposition.

The most important instrument available for changing the predisposition of an MNC is human resource management. Very few managers have personally internalized and resolved the tension between maximizing the firm's profit goals and emphasizing the needs of the host government. It is important, therefore, that the personnel policies of an MNC ensure: (1) that the proper mix of attitudes is nurtured through job rotation, promotion, and placement; and (2) that job assignments are carefully made in keeping with the manager's attitudes. The critical determinant of an MNC's successful adaptation to its environment is its ability to nurture relevant attitudes in its managerial work force.

REFERENCES

Chakravarthy, B. S., "Strategic Adaptation to Deregulation: Toward a Conceptual Framework," Working Paper WP 84-07, Reginald Jones Center, The Wharton School, 1985.

Chakravarthy, B. S., "Strategic Self-Renewal: A Planning Framework for Today," *The Academy of Management Review*, 1984, 9(3), 536–547.

Chakravarthy, B. S. and P. Lorange, "Managing Strategic Adaptation: Options in Administrative Systems Design," *Interfaces*, 1984, 14(1), 34–46.

Davis, S. and P. Lorange, *Matrix*, Reading, Mass: Addison-Wesley, 1977.

Doz, Y. L., "Strategic Management in Multinational Companies," *Sloan Management Review*, 1980, 21(2), 27–46.

Doz, Y. L., and C. K. Prahalad, "Headquarters Influence and Strategic Control in MNCs," *Sloan Management Review*, Fall, 1981, 15–29.

Haspeslagh, P., "Portfolio Planning: Uses and Limits," *Harvard Business Review*, 1982, 60(1), 58–73.

Heenan, D. A. and H. V. Perlmutter, *Multinational Organizational Development: A Social Architecture Perspective*, Reading, Mass: Addison-Wesley, 1979.

Hout, T., M. E. Porter, and E. Rudden, "How Global Companies Win Out," *Harvard Business Review*, 1982, 60(5), 98–108.

Kotter, J. P., L. A. Schlesinger, and V. Sathe, *Organization: Text, Cases and Readings*, Homewood, Ill: Richard D. Irwin, 1979, 271–310.

Lorange, P., "A Framework for Strategic Planning in Multinational Corporations," *Journal of Long Range Planning*, June 1976, 276–288.

Lorange, P., *Corporate Planning: An Excessive View Point*, Englewood Cliffs, N.J.: Prentice-Hall, 1980.

Lorange, P., "Organizational Structure and Management Processes: Implications for Effective Strategic Management," in W. Guth (Ed.), *Handbook of Strategic Management*, New York: Warren, Gorham, and Lamont, 1984.

Perlmutter, H. V., "The Tortuous Evolution of the Multinational Corporation," *Columbia Journal of World Business*, January–February, 1969, 9–18.

Perlmutter, H. V., "Building the Symbiotic Societal Enterprise: A Social Architecture for the Future," *World Futures, 1984*, 19(3/4), 271–284.

Porter, M. E., "Competition in Global Industries: A Conceptual Framework," Paper presented at the Prince Bertil Symposium on Strategies for Global Competition, Stockholm School of Economics, November 7–9, 1984.

Prahalad, C. K., "Strategic Choices in Diversified MNCs," *Harvard Business Review*, 1976, 54(4), 67–78.

Chapter 4

Defining and Measuring the International Strategic Focus of Multinational Corporations

Franklin R. Root
University of Pennsylvania

Kanoknart Visudtibhan
The George Washington University

Abstract *In this paper we review several approaches to the definition and measurement of international business strategy from the perspective of the international strategic focus concept. To help remedy the lack of empirical studies of strategic focus, we undertook a small pilot study, comprising 25 multinational corporations in the pharmaceutical and food-processing industries. Our study demonstrates the importance of the level of analysis (corporate, business, or functional) and the distinction between pure and mixed forms of international strategic focus.*

INTRODUCTION

The international strategy of multinational companies (MNCs) has occupied several researchers (Kogut, 1985; Doz, 1986; Ghoshal, 1987; and others). Nonetheless, there is no widely-accepted definition of international business strategy, let alone a common typology classifying the strategies of MNCs. One approach to the study of international business strategy is from the perspective of a firm's *strategic focus*. Specifically, the concepts of *global focus* and *multidomestic focus* are used to distinguish two categories of strategy followed by MNCs.

In this paper we first take inventory of the current state of knowledge about international strategy from the perspective of the strategic focus of MNCs. How is strategic focus defined? At which levels of analysis? After taking up these questions, we then offer empirical measurements of international strategic focus. We end our paper with a discussion of the implications of our study for researchers and managers.

DEFINING INTERNATIONAL STRATEGIC FOCUS

The use of strategic focus to explain MNC strategies derives from the distinctive character such firms, in particular, give to their cross-national operations. When companies become multinational, they experience a higher degree of "strategic tension" (Doz, Bartlett, and Pralahad, 1981). On the one hand, their drive for growth and economic success pulls them toward the exploitation of global economies of scope and scale through operations that are integrated across countries. On the other hand, their need for acceptance (legitimacy) in host countries pulls them toward more responsiveness to individual national policies and differences, possibly forsaking global economies of scope and scale. Researchers have used several terminologies to label these two extremes of strategic focus. Examples are *unification* versus *fragmentation* (Fayerweather, 1969; Kobrin, 1986) *worldwide integration* versus *national responsiveness* (Doz, 1980), *worldwide focus* versus *host-country focus* (Doz, Bartlett, and Pralahad, 1981), *global focus* versus *multidomestic focus* (Porter, 1985), and *global standardization* versus *differentiation* (Robock and Simmonds, 1989).

The conceptual foundation underlying the approach to international strategy as a response to economic and political imperatives owes much to the work of Fayerweather (1969). His framework was later adopted by Pralahad and Doz who used it to address organizational and strategic processes as well as the structural design of MNCs. They have identified several forces driving companies toward either extreme of strategic focus. However, they have not offered a precise definition of the strategic focus concept itself.

Table 1 lists definitions of global focus proposed by several researchers. Observe that these definitions differ on the scope of activities. For instance, Kobrin emphasizes one particular activity (manufacturing), Daft emphasizes two activities (product design and manufacturing), and Lessard includes all activities in the value-added chain. Despite these differences in scope, all the definitions of global focus imply an interdependence among an MNC's activities in various countries. In sum, researchers commonly view an integrated system of MNC operations as a necessary basis for international economies of scale or specialization. Most, if not all, of these definitions also imply that managers in globally-focused firms perceive competition to take place in a *single* world market.

It is widely accepted in the strategic management literature that strategy can be addressed at the corporate, business and functional levels. To comprehend fully an MNC's strategy, therefore, one needs to take into account these different levels. Several studies have directly or indirectly

Table 1
Selected Definitions of Global Focus

Researcher	Definitions
Porter (1980)	The strategy that targets a particular segment of the industry in which the firm competes on a worldwide basis
Doz (1980)	Specialization of plants across borders to make an integrated multinational product
Davidson (1984)	Firms with high degrees of internationalization anticipate fewer competitors and the potential benefits of developing global markets
Lessard (1984)	Firms obtain benefits associated with scale and learning by integrating, coordinating and transferring knowledge across national boundaries at virtually all levels of the value-added chain
Shanks (1985)*	Firms that concentrate different functions in different countries
Kobrin (1986)	Cross-border rationalization of manufacturing operations or sourcing abroad
Daft (1988)	The standardization of product design and advertising strategies throughout the world
Allio (1989)	Companies exploit the similarities among countries to enhance competitive advantage. Businesses are managed with a single integrated strategy, even if it serves different markets.

Source: Compiled by authors.
*In Freeman (1985).

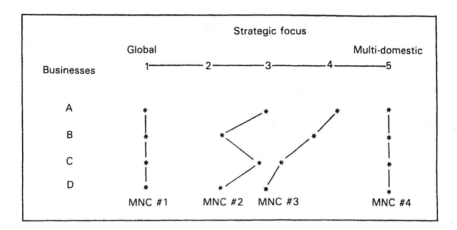

Figure 1 MNC corporate profiles of strategic focus at the business level.

discussed this issue. For example, when examining international strategic focus at the business level in their 1983 study, Hamel and Pralahad recognized that strategic focus may not be consistent across functions within a single business. Tracing competitive advantage to a firm's individual value-added activities, Porter (1986) asserts that managers must decide where and how to perform each activity in the value chain and how to coordinate similar activities in different countries.

Figure 1 depicts hypothetical corporate profiles of strategic focus in four MNCs at the business level. In the cases of MNCs #1 and #4, we can induce that they are respectively global and multidomestic in their *corporate* strategic focus because the focuses of their individual businesses are uniform. But in the cases of MNCs #2 and #3, we *cannot* induce the corporate strategic focus because the focuses of their individual businesses are different.

Profiles may also be drawn at the functional level. A multinational company operating in (say) four businesses may have value-added profiles for each business as shown in Figure 2. Clearly, Business #1 has a global focus and Business #4 a multidomestic focus, but the profiles of Businesses #2 and #3 are difficult to label.

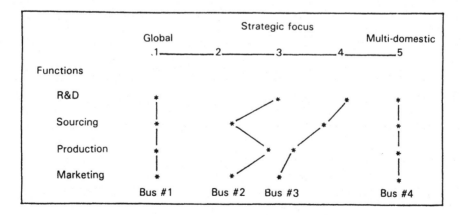

Figure 2 MNC business profiles of strategic focus at the functional level.

Ambiguous profiles such as those of MNCs #2 and #3 in Figure 1 and Businesses #2 and #3 in Figure 2 call into question the approach to international strategy in terms of the two extreme focuses.

MEASURING INTERNATIONAL STRATEGIC FOCUS

The usefulness of the international strategic focus concept depends on our ability to operationalize it. The challenge is to transform the foregoing pictorial representations into a meaningful measurement of strategic focus while preserving distinctions among the three levels of analysis. We know of no empirical attempts to do this. To help fill this gap, we offer here a small, exploratory investigation.

We define international strategic focus as the *governing perception* held by MNC corporate managers of the geographical boundaries of the markets in which their companies compete at the present time and in the foreseeable future. These *market-boundary* perceptions determine how corporate managers view the role of country subsidiaries. We hypothesize that when managers perceive their firms as competing in single world markets, they create systems that integrate manufacturing and marketing/distribution activities across countries with associated intra-corporate product transfers. In contrast, when managers perceive their firms as competing in many autonomous national markets, they create systems that allow their businesses to adapt to each market's distinctive features, becoming locally competitive with no or modest intra-corporate transfers. The primary purpose of our study, then, is to establish whether or not the market-boundary perceptions of MNC managers are consistent with the observed pattern of their firm's intra-corporate flows across countries.

Twenty-five U.S. MNCs drawn from the pharmaceutical and food-processing industries constitute our research sample. We selected these industries because they are recognized as representing the two extremes of international strategic focus. Global integration is commonly viewed as the dominant focus of pharmaceutical MNCs; and domestic orientation as that of food-processing MNCs (Hamel and Pralahad, 1983; Guisinger and Associates, 1985). Because we confined our study to these two industries only, we did not investigate the association between industry characteristics and strategic focus, leaving that question for later research.

A short questionnaire (shown in the Appendix) was answered by 15 pharmaceutical and 10 food-processing MNCs. Their responses provided information for each MNC on its two principal lines of business (as measured by corporate sales), the perception of the MNC manager or managers of the strategic focus of their principal lines of business, the country locations and value-added functions of its foreign subsidiaries, and the pattern of its intra-corporate product transfers.

Table 2 shows the location, value-added activities and intracompany exports and imports of a principal business perceived as multidomestic by a responding MNC manager. Each subsidiary is highly self-sufficient: it manufactures products for the local market using local raw materials and intermediate products. Consequently, there are hardly any flows of product between a subsidiary and the parent company or other subsidiaries. The manager rated this business 5 on the 5-point scale (see Appendix).

In contrast, Table 3 indicates a pattern of interdependence among the subsidiaries and the parent company on both the demand and supply sides. Only three subsidiaries in the Asia/Pacific region and one in Latin America sell only locally; the other subsidiaries export to sister subsidiaries within and/or outside their regions, and four subsidiaries (one-third of the total) export to the U.S. parent. All subsidiaries import raw materials, intermediate products or final products

Table 2

Value-Added Functions and Intra-Corporate Product Transfers of a Business Perceived as Multidomestic by the Company Manager

Country	Principal functions of subsidiaries						Direction of intracompany exports and imports					
							Export to			Import from		
								Foreign controlled subsidiaries			Foreign controlled subsidiaries	
	R&D	Supply of raw materials	Manufacture of intermediate products	Assembly of final products	Marketing and distribution	Sell only locally	US parent	Within region	Outside region	US parent	Within region	Outside region
Canada	×	×	×	×	×	×						
Region 1												
#1	×	×	×	×	×	×	×[1]					
#2	×	×	×	×	×	×						
Region 2												
#1	×			×	×	×		×[1]			×	
#2		×	×	×	×	×		×[1]				
#3	×			×	×	×						
Region 3												
#1	×	×	×	×	×	×		×[1]				
#2	×	×	×	×	×	×						
#3	×	×	×	×	×	×						

Note. Region 1 is Latin America, Region 2 is Western Europe, and Region 3 is Asia/Pacific. #1, #2, etc. are individual countries.
[1] One of 25 firms.

Table 3

Value-Added Functions and Intra-Corporate Product Transfers of a Business Perceived as Global by the Company Manager

Country	Principal functions of subsidiaries					Sell only locally	Direction of intracompany exports and imports					
	R&D	Supply of raw materials	Manufacture of intermediate products	Assembly of final products	Marketing and distribution		Export to			Import from		
							US parent	Foreign controlled subsidiaries		US parent	Foreign controlled subsidiaries	
								Within region	Outside region		Within region	Outside region
Canada				X	X				X	X		X
Region 1												
#1			X	X	X			X		X		X
#2		X	X	X	X			X	X	X		X
#3			X	X				X	X	X		X
#4					X	X	X			X	X	X
Region 2												
#1	X			X	X	X		X[1]	X[1]	X	X	X
#2				X	X			X	X	X	X	
#3			X				X	X	X	X		
#4					X		X	X	X	X	X	
Region 3												
#1	X			X	X			X			X	
#2		X	X	X	X	X				X		X
#3	X		X	X	X	X						
#4					X	X				X		X

Note. Region 1 is Latin America, Region 2 is Western Europe, and Region 3 is Asia/Pacific. #1, #2, etc. are individual countries.
[1] One of 25 firms.

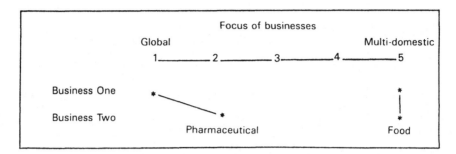

Figure 3 Average profiles of strategic focus for the pharmaceutical and food-processing industries. *Average score. *Source*: Mail survey of 25 companies.

from sister subsidiaries or the parent company. The responding manager rated this business *1* on the 5-point scale (see Appendix).

We found that the association of managerial perceptions of strategic focus and intracorporate product transfers was the same as depicted in Tables 2 and 3 for 22 of the 25 sample companies. Hence, we concluded that the market-boundary perception of MNC managers (as measured by a 5-point scale) is a reliable indicator of strategic focus at the business level. Figure 3 shows the mathematical average score of managers' responses for all sample MNCs in the two industries by principal lines of business. It confirms that the pharmaceutical industry has a global strategic focus while the food-processing industry has a multidomestic strategic focus.

The different strategic focuses of these two industries is also evident at the level of value-added activities. Figure 4 reveals that individual value-added activities may have different strategic focuses in the same industry. It also shows that the downstream value-added activities of the pharmaceutical industry become increasingly less global (more multidomestic) so that the profile slopes downward from left to right. In contrast, the profile of the food-processing industry is a vertical line except for R&D.

To conclude, measuring the strategic focus of an MNC is a challenging task. In particular, the focus becomes problematic when an MNC operates in several lines of business. One way to handle such diversity is to define an MNC's strategic focus as the *average* of the scale values of its different businesses weighted by the percentage of corporate sales of each business. Algebraically,

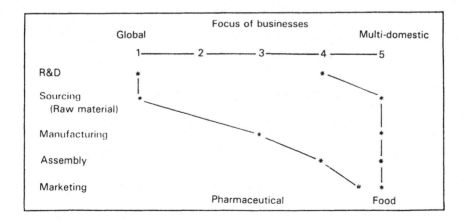

Figure 4 Average profiles of strategic focus along the value-added chain for the pharmaceutical and food-processing industries. *Average of two principal businesses. *Source*: Mail survey of 25 companies.

Table 4
Classification of MNCs into Strategic Focus Groups According to the Average
of the Scale Values of Their Two Principal Lines of Business Weighted by Corporate Sales

Industry	Number of company	Focus		
		Global	Mixed	Multi-domestic
Pharmaceutical	15	9 (60%)	4 (27%)	2 (13%)
Food-processing	10	—	2 (20%)	8 (80%)

$$\text{Focus} = \sum_{i=1}^{N} (\text{Percentage Corporate Sales}_i)(\text{Scale Value}_i)$$

where i = individual businesses and N = number of lines of business in the company. Using this formula for two lines of business, we classified the 25 sample companies into a global focus group (scale value is less than 2.33), a multidomestic group (scale value is greater than 3.67), and a mixed group (scale values ranging from 2.34 to 3.66). Table 4 shows the results.

It may be argued that the percentage of foreign sales rather than corporate sales should be used to weight scale values. However, several executives indicated that in general they pay more attention to the business that contributes a large percentage of corporate sales unless its foreign sales exceed its domestic sales. Table 5 offers a classification of the sample companies using the percentage of foreign sales as a weight. Although the number of firms in each cell changes slightly, the pattern remains the same.

IMPLICATIONS FOR RESEARCHERS AND MANAGERS

Our empirical study demonstrates that an MNC's strategic focus can be measured along a global/multidomestic continuum. But it also demonstrates that researchers need to take into account multiple levels of analysis. When strategic focus is simultaneously considered at the corporate, business, and functional levels, it becomes evident that researchers can no longer think in terms of two focal extremes. Also, the definition of strategic focus in terms of managerial market-boundary perceptions highlights the *dynamic* nature of the strategic focus concept: When managers alter their market-boundary perceptions of a function, a business or the entire corporation,

Table 5
Classification of MNCs into Strategic Focus Groups According to the Average
of the Scale Values of Their Two Principal Lines of Business Weighted by Foreign Sales

Industry	Number of company	Focus		
		Global	Mixed	Multi-domestic
Pharmaceutical	15	8 (47%)	5 (33%)	3 (20%)
Food-processing	10	—	3 (30%)	7 (70%)

then they will initiate changes in the ways in which their companies integrate (or don't integrate) operations across countries. Researchers need to investigate, therefore, the process through which managerial market-boundary perceptions are formed and reformed over time.

The measurement of the degree of interdependence *within* MNCs is critical to our understanding of the international strategic focus concept. Our study shows the close association between the cross-national pattern of intra-corporate transfers and managerial perceptions of strategic focus. Using multiple measures will help clarify interdependence. Kobrin (1988) has suggested an index using flows of exports and imports, but only an industry index can be so calculated because of the lack of data at the company level. Gladwin and Wasilewski (1986) have proposed a model that looks at organizational design in different contexts of environmental interdependence, but they offer no measure of interdependence.

We believe that the approach and results of our study are important for managers responsible for international strategic planning. They offer managers a tool to map the profiles of value activities and businesses: What are the geographical market-boundaries of individual functions and businesses? How does an investment or disinvestment decision alter the geographical interdependence of an MNC's operations? In an increasingly turbulent global competitive environment, the mapping of strategic focus profiles can help managers better assess the impact of current and prospective changes in that environment on corporate strategy.

REFERENCES

Allio, Robert J. (1989). Formulating Global Strategy. *Planning Review.* March/April:22–28.

Babbie, Earl R. (1973). *Survey Research Methods.* California: Wadsworth Publishing Company, Inc.

Daft, Richard L. (1988). *Management.* New York: The Dryden Press.

Davidson, William (1982). *Global Strategic Management.* New York: John Wiley.

Doz, Ives L. (1978). Managing manufacturing rationalization within multinational companies. *Columbia Journal of World Business.* Fall: 82–94.

——. (1980). Strategic management in multinational corporations. *Sloan Management Review.* 21(2): 27–46.

——. (1986). *Strategic Management in Multinational Companies.* New York: Pergamon Press.

——. Christopher A. Bartlett & C. K. Prahalad. (1981). Global competitive pressures and host country demands: managing tensions in MNCs. *California Management Review.* Spring: 63–74.

Fayerweather, John (1969). *International Business Management.* New York: McGraw-Hill Book Company.

Freeman, David H. (1985). Managing information systems at the multinational. *Infosystems.* January: 52–53.

Ghoshal, Sumantra. (1987). Global strategy: an organizational framework. *Strategic Management Journal.* 8(5): 425–440.

Gladwin, Thomas N. & Nikolai Wasilewski. (1986). Environmental interdependence and organizational design: the case of MNCs. *Advances in Strategic Management.* 4: 229–277.

Guisinger, Stephen E. & Associates. (1985). *Investment Incentives and Performance Requirements.* New York: Praeger.

Hamel, Gary & Prahalad, C. K. (1983). Managing strategic responsibility in the MNC. *Strategic Management Journal.* 4: 341–351.

Kobrin, Stephen. (1986). Strategic integration in fragmented environments: social and political assessment by subsidiaries of multinational firms. In D. Schendel, N. Hood and J. E. Vahline (editors) *Strategies in Global Competition.* New York: John Wiley and Sons, Ltd.

——. (1988). *Measuring Global Integration.* Paper presented in IBEAR Conference. University of Southern California. April.

Kogut, Bruce. (1985). Designing global strategies: comparative and competitive value-added chains. *Sloan Management Review.* 26(4): 15–28.

——. (1984). Normative observations on the international value-added chain and strategic groups. *Journal of International Business Studies.* Fall: 151–167.

Lessard, Donald. (1984). *Notes on Global Strategy.* Sloan School of Management. MIT.

Porter, Michael E. (1980). *Competitive Strategy: Techniques for Analyzing Industries and Competitors.* New York: The Free Press.

———. (1985). *Competitive Advantage: Creating and Sustaining Superior Performance.* New York: The Free Press.

———. (1986). Changing patterns of international competition. *California Management Review.* Winter.

Prahalad, C. K. (1976). Strategic choice in diversified MNCs. *Harvard Business Review.* July–August: 67–78.

Robock, Stephan H. and Kenneth Simmonds. (1989). *International Business and Multinational Enterprises.* (Fourth edition). Boston: Richard D. Irwin, Inc.

APPENDIX

Selected Questions from the Questionnaire Survey

Patterns of Multinational Operations

1. Please identify two individual businesses of your corporation that account for the highest sales of your total corporate sales, and indicate their respective percentage shares of total corporate sales and their shares of foreign sales in 1986.

SIC code (if known)	Product or product line	% share of corporate sales	% share of foreign sales
#1 _____	_____	_____	_____
#2 _____	_____	_____	_____

2. Please indicate the strategic focus of each of your two businesses identified in the previous question by circling a number on each of the following five-point scales that associates best with its position (1 – strong global focus; 5 – strong host-country focus).

Definition of terms:

Global focus implies (in its extreme expression) that the business is competing in a single world market with fully integrated manufacturing and marketing/distribution activities across countries.

Host-country focus implies (in its extreme expression) that there is no global market but only a set of national markets, and that each country requires a full adaptation of the business to the country's unique features.

Business #1

    1 _____ 2 _____ 3 _____ 4 _____ 5
Global   Host-country
 focus   focus

Business #2

    1 _____ 2 _____ 3 _____ 4 _____ 5
Global   Host-country
 focus   focus

For business #1, please provide information on the geographical locations of *controlled* foreign subsidiaries (50% or more of equity owned by your corporation) and their principal functions (value-added or major activities of the business). Please indicate appropriate entries with checkmarks.

For each country location of *controlled* foreign subsidiaries in business #1, please indicate below with checkmarks the direction of its intracompany exports and imports. (Disregard any exports or imports with *independent* parties.)

Principal Functions of Subsidiaries

Direction of Intracompany Exports and Imports

Country locations of controlled subsidiaries	R&D	Supply of raw materials	Manufacture of intermediate products	Assembly of final products	Marketing and distribution	Sell only locally	Export to			Import from		
							US parent	Foreign controlled subsidiaries		US parent	Foreign controlled subsidiaries	
								Within region	Outside region		Within region	Outside region
Canada												
Latin America												
a.												
b.												
c.												
d.												
e.												
Western Europe												
a.												
b.												
c.												
d.												
e.												
Asia-Pacific												
a.												
b.												
c.												
d.												
e.												

For business #2, please provide information on the geographical locations of *controlled* foreign subsidiaries (50% or more of equity owned by your corporation) and their principal functions (value-added or major activities of the business). Please indicate appropriate entries with checkmarks.

For each country location of *controlled* foreign subsidiaries in business #2, please indicate below with checkmarks the direction of its intracompany exports and imports. (Disregard any exports or imports with *independent* parties.)

Principal Functions of Subsidiaries | Direction of Intracompany Exports and Imports

Country locations of controlled subsidiaries	R&D	Supply of raw materials	Manufacture of intermediate products	Assembly of final products	Marketing and distribution	Sell only locally	Export to US parent	Export to Foreign controlled subsidiaries Within region	Export to Foreign controlled subsidiaries Outside region	Import from US parent	Import from Foreign controlled subsidiaries Within region	Import from Foreign controlled subsidiaries Outside region
Canada												
Latin America												
a.												
b.												
c.												
d.												
e.												
Western Europe												
a.												
b.												
c.												
d.												
e.												
Asia-Pacific												
a.												
b.												
c.												
d.												
e.												

Part One

Review and Questions

Review

The papers in Part One introduce concepts and relationships as well as theories that are helpful in the design and assessment of international or global strategies. Ghoshal offers an "organizing framework," or map, of global management that is intended to guide teaching and research and to help managers relate and synthesize different perspectives and prescriptions. His underlying premise is that simple categorical schemes, such as global versus multidomestic strategies, are not very useful in understanding the corporate-level strategy of large multinational corporations (MNCs).

The framework postulates three broad strategic objectives of MNCs: (1) obtaining efficiency in current operations, (2) managing risks, and (3) innovation, learning, and adaptation. To achieve these objectives, MNC managers can tap three sources of competitive advantage: (1) national differences, (2) scale economies, and (3) scope economies. The strategic task of managing globally is to use all three sources in moving toward the three objectives. The complexity of global strategic management stems from the need to understand situational contingencies and to evaluate trade-offs among the strategic objectives and among the sources of competitive advantage.

Kogut argues that the central question on global strategies is, What changes strategically when a firm moves from domestic to international competition? He asserts that ideas about global competition shifted in the 1980s from interest in investing abroad to interest in operating assets in multiple countries. It is mainly this operating side that drives the incremental value of being multinational. The flexibility that comes from the coordination of flows within a multinational network gives MNCs the capability of exploiting differentials in factor, product, and capital markets; of transferring learning and innovation throughout the firm; and of using network leverage to respond to the threats of competitors and governments. Kogut draws a distinction between greater economies of scale due to serving large global markets and the acquisition of advantages built on multinational networks. He perceives the MNC as consisting of proprietary assets from which it derives current cash flows as well as a set of options inherent in multi-environment operations. In sum, Kogut highlights the MNC network, which is largely only implicit in Ghoshal's framework.

Chakravarthy and Perlmutter see the fundamental challenge for international managers to be the ability to balance between the *economic imperative* of global integration to achieve viability and the *political imperative* of prudent stakeholder management (particularly of host governments) to achieve legitimacy. The planning challenge is also defined by the strategic predisposition of the individual MNC, namely, ethnocentric, polycentric, regiocentric, or geocentric.

To these authors, the primary determinant for whether a multinational firm pursues a global or country-centered strategy is the proportion of value added in the upstream activities of its industry's value chain. A large proportion of upstream activities points to a global strategy. However, the choice of strategy also depends on the *segments* of the value chain in which the firm chooses to compete. A global strategy is also appropriate when the bargaining power of the MNC is strong in relation to that of host governments. Using the value chain and power dimensions, the authors then construct four models of strategic planning.

The approach of Chakravarthy and Perlmutter complements that of Ghoshal and that of Kogut by introducing the political (legitimacy) issue confronting international managers.

After a review of several definitions of *global focus*, Root and Visudtibhan conclude that all of the definitions state or imply an interdependence among an MNC's activities in different countries. Most also state or imply that managers in globally focused firms perceive competition as taking place in single, world markets. The authors then offer their own interpretation of *international strategic focus* as the governing perception held by MNC corporate managers of the geographical boundaries of the markets in which their firms compete. The outcome of a *global* strategic focus is a high degree of interdependence among the firm's operations in different countries.

This hypothesis is supported by an empirical investigation that shows a strong positive association between managers' perceptions of strategic focus and the actual cross-national intracorporate product flows of their firms at the business level. At the very least, the perceptions that MNC managers have of market boundaries are consistent with the observed pattern of interdependence among the parent company and its foreign subsidiaries as measured by product flows on both demand and supply sides. From a dynamic perspective, it is postulated that changes in managers' perceptions of market boundaries will initiate changes in the ways their companies do or do not integrate operations across countries.

The empirical investigation also demonstrates that the determination of an MNC's strategic focus must take into account the corporate, business, and functional levels. Managers can no longer think in terms of the two focal extremes, but instead will need to map strategic focus profiles at different levels. This effort, in turn, should improve managers' assessment of changes in the global competitive environment in terms of impact on corporate strategy. In short, the empirical investigation relates to several of the concepts and themes developed in the other three papers in Part One.

Questions

1. Why, according to Ghoshal, is there need for an "organizing framework" for global strategy?
2. What is the "efficiency" perspective on strategic management?
3. What are economies of scale? What is their *strategic* importance?
4. What are economies of scope? What is their *strategic* importance?
5. What are some inherent contradictions (trade-offs) among Ghoshal's different strategic objectives? Among his different sources of competitive advantage?
6. According to Kogut, how does the multinational network become the basis of international competition?
7. What is the *economic imperative* facing MNCs? What is the *political imperative*?
8. Why should a high proportion of a firm's value added being located in upstream activities encourage a global strategy?

9. What are the sources of the bargaining power of MNCs toward national host governments? Of national host governments toward MNCs?
10. What is the meaning of each of the four strategic predispositions of an MNC?
11. What is the distinction between global strategic focus and multidomestic strategic focus?
12. Why may it be impossible to induce an MNC's *corporate* strategic focus from the focuses of its individual businesses? The strategic focus of an individual business from its value-added profile?
13. What is the significance of the *market boundary perceptions* held by MNC managers?
14. How can the mapping of strategic focus profiles help MNC managers better assess current and prospective changes in the global competitive environment in terms of impact on corporate strategy?

Part Two
Creating Strategies for International Competitive Advantage

Chapter 5

Changing Patterns of International Competition

Michael E. Porter
Harvard Business School

When examining the environmental changes facing firms today, it is a rare observer who will conclude that international competition is not high on the list. The growing importance of international competition is well recognized both in the business and academic communities, for reasons that are fairly obvious when one looks at just about any data set that exists on international trade or investment. Exhibit 1, for example, compares world trade and world GNP. Something interesting started happening around the mid-1950s, when the growth in world trade began to significantly exceed the growth in world GNP. Foreign direct investment by firms in developing countries began to grow rapidly a few years later, about 1963.[1] This period marked the beginning of a fundamental change in the international competitive environment that by now has come to be widely recognized. It is a trend that is causing sleepless nights for many business managers.

There is a substantial literature on international competition, because the subject is far from a new one. A large body of literature has investigated the many implications of the Heckscher-

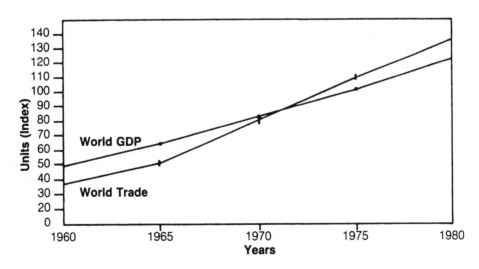

Exhibit 1 Growth of world trade.

Ohlin model and other models of international trade which are rooted in the principle of compara-tive advantage.[2] The unit of analysis in this literature is the country. There is also considerable literature on the multinational firm, reflecting the growing importance of the multinational since the turn of the century. In examining the reasons for the multinational, I think it is fair to characterize this literature as resting heavily on the multinational's ability to exploit intangible assets.[3] The work of Hymer and Caves among others has stressed the role of the multinational in transferring know-how and expertise gained in one country market to others at low cost, and thereby offsetting the unavoidable extra costs of doing business in a foreign country. A more recent stream of literature extends this by emphasizing how the multinational firm internalizes transactions to circumvent imperfections in various intermediate markets, most importantly the market for knowledge.

There is also a related literature on the problems of entry into foreign markets and the life cycle of how a firm competes abroad, beginning with export or licensing and ultimately moving to the establishment of foreign subsidiaries. Vernon's product cycle of international trade com-bines a view of how products mature with the evolution in a firm's international activities to predict the patterns of trade and investment in developed and developing countries.[4] Finally, many of the functional fields in business administration research have their branch of literature about international issues—e.g., international marketing, international finance. This literature concentrates, by and large, on the problems of doing business in a foreign country.

As rich as it is, however, I think it is fair to characterize the literature on international competition as being limited when it comes to the choice of a firm's international strategy. Though the literature provides some guidance for considering incremental investment decisions to enter a new country, it provides at best a partial view of how to characterize a firm's overall international strategy and how such strategy should be selected. Put another way, the literature focuses more on the problem of becoming a multinational than on strategies for established multinationals. Although the distinction between domestic firms and multinationals is seminal in a literature focused on the problems of doing business abroad, the fact that a firm is multinational says little if anything about its international strategy except that it operates in several countries.

Broadly stated, my research has been seeking to answer the question: what does international competition mean for competitive strategy? In particular, what are the distinctive questions for competitive strategy that are raised by international as opposed to domestic competition? Many of the strategy issues for a company competing internationally are very much the same as for one competing domestically. A firm must still analyze its industry structure and competitors, under-stand its buyer and the sources of buyer value, diagnose its relative cost position, and seek to establish a sustainable competitive advantage within some competitive scope, whether it be across-the-board or in an industry segment. These are subjects I have written about extensively.[5] But there are some questions for strategy that are peculiar to international competition, and that add to rather than replace those listed earlier. These questions all revolve, in one way or another, around how a firm's activities in one country affect or are affected by what is going on in other countries—the connectedness among country competition. It is this connectedness that is the focus of this article and of a broader stream of research recently conducted under the auspices of the Harvard Business School.[6]

PATTERNS OF INTERNATIONAL COMPETITION

The appropriate unit of analysis in setting international strategy is the industry, because the industry is the arena in which competitive advantage is won or lost. The starting point for understanding international competition is the observation that its pattern differs markedly from industry to industry. At one end of the spectrum are industries that I call *multidomestic,* in which competition in each country (or small group of countries) is essentially independent of competition in other countries. A multidomestic industry is one that is present in many countries (e.g., there is a consumer banking industry in Sri Lanka, one in France, and one in the U.S.), but in which competition occurs on a country-by-country basis. In a multidomestic industry, a multinational firm may enjoy a competitive advantage from the one-time transfer of know-how from its home base to foreign countries. However, the firm modifies and adapts its intangible assets to employ them in each country and the outcome is determined by conditions in each country. The competitive advantages of the firm, then, are largely specific to each country. The international industry becomes a collection of essentially domestic industries—hence the term "multidomestic." Industries where competition has traditionally exhibited this pattern include retailing, consumer packaged goods, distribution, insurance, consumer finance, and caustic chemicals.

At the other end of the spectrum are what I term *global* industries. The term global—like the word "strategy"—has become overused and perhaps under-understood. The definition of a global industry employed here is an industry in which a firm's competitive position in one country is significantly influenced by its position in other countries.[7] Therefore, the international industry is not merely a collection of domestic industries but a series of linked domestic industries in which the rivals compete against each other on a truly worldwide basis. Industries exhibiting the global pattern today include commercial aircraft, TV sets, semiconductors, copiers, automobiles, and watches.

The implications for strategy of the distinction between multidomestic and global industries are quite profound. In a multidomestic industry, a firm can and should manage its international activities like a portfolio. Its subsidiaries or other operations around the world should each control all the important activities necessary to do business in the industry and should enjoy a high degree of autonomy. The firm's strategy in a country should be determined largely by the circumstances in that country; the firm's international strategy is then what I term a "country-centered strategy."

In a multidomestic industry, competing internationally is discretionary. A firm can choose to remain domestic or can expand internationally if it has some advantage that allows it to overcome the extra costs of entering and competing in foreign markets. The important competitors in multidomestic industries will either be domestic companies or multinationals with stand-alone operations abroad—this is the situation in each of the multidomestic industries listed earlier. In a multidomestic industry, then, international strategy collapses to a series of domestic strategies. The issues that are uniquely international revolve around how to do business abroad, how to select good countries in which to compete (or assess country risk), and mechanisms to achieve the one-time transfer of know-how. These are questions that are relatively well developed in the literature.

In a global industry, however, managing international activities like a portfolio will undermine the possibility of achieving competitive advantage. In a global industry, a firm must in some way integrate its activities on a worldwide basis to capture the linkages among countries. This will require more than transferring intangible assets among countries, though it will include it. A firm may choose to compete with a country-centered strategy, focusing on specific market segments or countries when it can carve out a niche by responding to whatever local country differences are present. However, it does so at some considerable risk from competitors with global strategies. All the important competitors in the global industries listed earlier compete worldwide with coordinated strategies.

In international competition, a firm always has to perform some functions in each of the countries in which it competes. Even though a global competitor must view its international activities as an overall system, it has still to maintain some country perspective. It is the balancing of these two perspectives that becomes one of the essential questions in global strategy.[8]

CAUSES OF GLOBALIZATION

If we accept the distinction between multidomestic and global industries as an important taxonomy of patterns of international competition, a number of crucial questions arise. When does an industry globalize? What exactly do we mean by a global strategy, and is there more than one kind? What determines the type of international strategy to select in a particular industry?

An industry is global if there is some competitive advantage to integrating activities on a worldwide basis. To make this statement operational, however, we must be very precise about what we mean by "activities" and also what we mean by "integrating." To diagnose the sources of competitive advantage in any context, whether it be domestic or international, it is necessary to adopt a disaggregated view of the firm. In my newest book, *Competitive Advantage.* I have developed a framework for doing so, called the value chain.[9] Every firm is a collection of discrete activities performed to do business that occur within the scope of the firm—I call them value activities. The activities performed by a firm include such things as salespeople selling the product, service technicians performing repairs, scientists in the laboratory designing process techniques, and accountants keeping the books. Such activities are technologically and in most cases physically distinct. It is only at the level of discrete activities, rather than the firm as a whole, that competitive advantage can be truly understood.

A firm may possess two types of competitive advantage: low relative cost or differentiation—its ability to perform the activities in its value chain either at lower cost or in a unique way relative to its competitors. The ultimate value a firm creates is what buyers are willing to pay for what the firm provides, which includes the physical product as well as any ancillary services or benefits. Profit results if the value created through performing the required activities exceeds the collective cost of performing them. Competitive advantage is a function of either providing comparable buyer value to competitors but performing activities efficiently (low cost), or of performing activities at comparable cost but in unique ways that create greater buyer value than competitors and, hence, command a premium price (differentiation).

The value chain, shown in Figure 1, provides a systematic means of displaying and categorizing activities. The activities performed by a firm in any industry can be grouped into the nine generic categories shown. The labels may differ based on industry convention, but every firm performs these basic categories of activities in some way or another. Within each category of activities, a firm typically performs a number of discrete activities which are particular to the industry and to the firm's strategy. In service, for example, firms typically perform such discrete activities as installation, repair, parts distribution, and upgrading.

The generic categories of activities can be grouped into two broad types. Along the bottom are what I call *primary* activities, which are those involved in the physical creation of the product or service, its delivery and marketing to the buyer, and its support after sale. Across the top are what I call *support* activities, which provide inputs or infrastructure that allow the primary activities to take place on an ongoing basis.

Procurement is the obtaining of purchased inputs, whether they be raw materials, purchased services, machinery, or so on. Procurement stretches across the entire value chain because it supports every activity—every activity uses purchased inputs of some kind. There are typically many different discrete procurement activities within a firm, often performed by different people. Technology development encompasses the activities involved in designing the product as well as in creating and improving the way the various activities in the value chain are performed. We

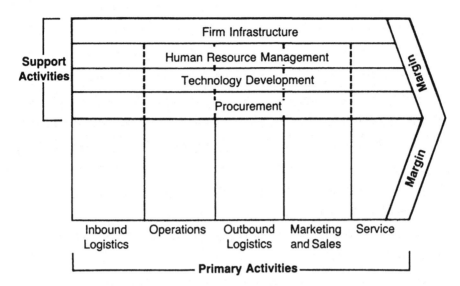

Figure 1 The value chain.

tend to think of technology in terms of the product or manufacturing process. In fact, every activity a firm performs involves a technology or technologies which may be mundane or sophisticated, and a firm has a stock of know-how about how to perform each activity. Technology development typically involves a variety of different discrete activities, some performed outside the R&D department.

Human resource management is the recruiting, training, and development of personnel. Every activity involves human resources, and thus human resources management activities cut across the entire chain. Finally, firm infrastructure includes activities such as general management, accounting, legal, finance, strategic planning, and all the other activities decoupled from specific primary or support activities but that are essential to enable the entire chain's operation.

Activities in a firm's value chain are not independent, but are connected through what I call linkages. The way one activity is performed frequently affects the cost or effectiveness of other activities. If more is spent on the purchase of a raw material, for example, a firm may lower its cost of fabrication or assembly. There are many linkages that connect activities, not only within the firm but also with the activities of its suppliers, channels, and ultimately its buyers. The firm's value chain resides in a larger stream of activities that I term the value system. Suppliers have value chains that provide the purchased inputs to the firm's chain; channels have value chains through which the firm's product or service passes; buyers have value chains in which the firm's product or service is employed. The connections among activities in this vertical system also become essential to competitive advantage.

A final important building block in value chain theory, necessary for our purposes here, is the notion of *competitive scope*. Competitive scope is the breadth of activities the firm employs together in competing in an industry. There are four basic dimensions of competitive scope:

- *segment* scope, or the range of segments the firm serves (e.g., product varieties, customer types);
- *industry* scope, or the range of industries the firm competes in with a coordinated strategy;
- *vertical* scope, or what activities are performed by the firm versus suppliers and channels; and

- *geographic* scope, or the geographic regions the firm operates in with a coordinated strategy.

Competitive scope is vital to competitive advantage because it shapes the configuration of the value chain, how activities are performed, and whether activities are shared among units. International strategy is an issue of geographic scope, and can be analyzed quite similarly to the question of whether and how a firm should compete locally, regionally, or nationally within a country. In the international context, government tends to have a greater involvement in competition and there are more significant variations among geographic regions in buyer needs, although these differences are matters of degree.

International Configuration and Coordination of Activities

A firm that competes internationally must decide how to spread the activities in the value chain among countries. A distinction immediately arises between the activities labeled downstream on Figure 2, and those labeled upstream activities and support activities. The location of downstream activities, those more related to the buyer, is usually tied to where the buyer is located. If a firm is going to sell in Japan, for example, it usually must provide service in Japan and it must have salespeople stationed in Japan. In some industries it is possible to have a single sales force that travels to the buyer's country and back again; some other specific downstream activities such as the production of advertising copy can also sometimes be done centrally. More typically, however, the firm must locate the capability to perform downstream activities in each of the countries in which it operates. Upstream activities and support activities, conversely, can at least conceptually be decoupled from where the buyer is located.

This distinction carries some interesting implications. The first is that downstream activities create competitive advantages that are largely country-specific: a firm's reputation, brand name, and service network in a country grow out of a firm's activities in that country and create entry/mobility barriers large'y in that country alone. Competitive advantage in upstream and support

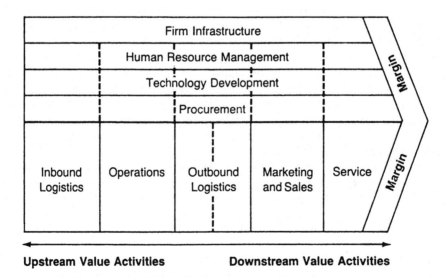

Figure 2 Upstream and downstream activities.

activities often grows more out of the entire system of countries in which a firm competes than from its position in any one country, however.

A second implication is that in industries where downstream activities or buyer-tied activities are vital to competitive advantage, there tends to be a more multidomestic pattern of international competition. In industries where upstream and support activities (such as technology development and operations) are crucial to competitive advantage, global competition is more common. In global competition, the location and scale of these potentially footloose activities is optimized from a worldwide perspective.[10]

The distinctive issues in international, as contrasted to domestic, strategy can be summarized in two key dimensions of how a firm competes internationally. The first is what I term the *configuration* of a firm's activities worldwide, or where in the world each activity in the value chain is performed, including in how many places. The second dimension is what I term *coordination,* which refers to how like activities performed in different countries are coordinated with each other. If, for example, there are three plants—one in Germany, one in Japan, and one in the U.S.—how do the activities in those plants relate to each other?

A firm faces an array of options in both configuration and coordination for each activity. Configuration options range from concentrated (performing an activity in one location and serving the world from it—e.g., one R&D lab, one large plant) to dispersed (performing every activity in each country). In the latter case, each country would have a complete value chain. Coordination options range from none to very high. For example, if a firm produces its product in three plants, it could, at one extreme, allow each plant to operate with full autonomy—e.g., different product standards and features, different steps in the production process, different raw materials, different part numbers. At the other extreme, the plants could be tightly coordinated by employing the same information system, the same production process, the same parts, and so forth. Options for coordination in an activity are typically more numerous than the configuration options because there are many possible levels of coordination and many different facets of the way the activity is performed.

Figure 3 lists some of the configuration issues and coordination issues for several important categories of value activities. In technology development, for example, the configuration issue is where R&D is performed: one location? two locations? and in what countries? The coordination issues have to do with such things as the extent of interchange among R&D centers and the location and sequence of product introduction around the world. There are configuration issues and coordination issues for every activity.

Figure 4 is a way of summarizing these basic choices in international strategy on a single diagram, with coordination of activities on the vertical axis and configuration of activities on the horizontal axis. The firm has to make a set of choices for each activity. If a firm employs a very dispersed configuration—placing an entire value chain in every country (or small group of contiguous countries) in which it operates, coordinating little or not at all among them—then the firm is competing with a country-centered strategy. The domestic firm that only operates in one country is the extreme case of a firm with a country-centered strategy. As we move from the lower left-hand corner of the diagram up or to the right, we have strategies that are increasingly global.

Figure 5 illustrates some of the possible variations in international strategy. The purest global strategy is to concentrate as many activities as possible in one country, serve the world from this home base, and tightly coordinate those activities that must inherently be performed near the buyer. This is the pattern adopted by many Japanese firms in the 1960s and 1970s, such as Toyota. However, Figures 4 and 5 make it clear that there is no such thing as one global strategy. There are many different kinds of global strategies, depending on a firm's choices about configuration and coordination throughout the value chain. In copiers, for example, Xerox has until

Value Activity	Configuration Issues	Coordination Issues
Operations	• Location of production facilities for components and end products	• Networking of international plants • Transferring process technology and production know-how among plants
Marketing and Sales	• Product line selection • Country (market) selection	• Commonality of brand name worldwide • Coordination of sales to multinational accounts • Similarity of channels and product positioning worldwide • Coordination of pricing in different countries
Service	• Location of service organization	• Similarity of service standards and procedures worldwide
Technology Development	• Number and location of R&D centers	• Interchange among dispersed R&D centers • Developing products responsive to market needs in many countries • Sequence of product introductions around the world
Procurement	• Location of the purchasing function	• Managing suppliers located in different countries • Transferring market knowledge • Coordinating purchases of common items

Figure 3 Configuration and coordination issues by category of activity.

recently concentrated R&D in the U.S. but dispersed other activities, in some cases using joint-venture partners to perform them. On dispersed activities, however, coordination has been quite high. The Xerox brand, marketing approach, and servicing procedures have been quite standardized worldwide. Canon, on the other hand, has had a much more concentrated configuration of activities and somewhat less coordination of dispersed activities. The vast majority of support activities and manufacturing of copiers have been performed in Japan. Aside from using the Canon brand, however, local marketing subsidiaries have been given quite a bit of latitude in each region of the world.

A global strategy can now be defined more precisely as one in which a firm seeks to gain competitive advantage from its international presence through either concentrating configuration, coordination among dispersed activities, or both. Measuring the presence of a global industry empirically must reflect both dimensions and not just one. Market presence in many countries and some export and import of components and end products are characteristic of most global industries. High levels of foreign investment or the mere presence of multinational firms are not reliable measures, however, because firms may be managing foreign units like a portfolio.

Configuration/Coordination and Competitive Advantage

Understanding the competitive advantages of a global strategy and, in turn, the causes of industry globalization requires specifying the conditions in which concentrating activities globally and coordinating dispersed activities leads to either cost advantage or differentiation. In each case, there are structural characteristics of an industry that work for and against globalization.

The factors that favor concentrating an activity in one or a few locations to serve the world are as follows:

- economies of scale in the activity;
- a proprietary learning curve in the activity;
- comparative advantage in where the activity is performed; and
- coordination advantages of co-locating linked activities such as R&D and production.

The first two factors relate to *how many* sites an activity is performed at, while the last two relate to *where* these sites are. Comparative advantage can apply to any activity, not just production. For example, there may be some locations in the world that are better places than others to do research on medical technology or to perform software development. Government can promote the concentration of activities by providing subsidies or other incentives to use a particular country as an export base, in effect altering comparative advantage—a role many governments are playing today.

There are also structural characteristics that favor dispersion of an activity to many countries, which represent concentration costs. Local product needs may differ, nullifying the advantages of scale or learning from one-site operation of an activity. Locating a range of activities in a country

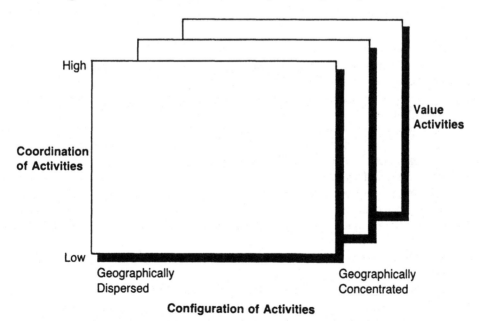

Figure 4 The dimensions of international strategy.

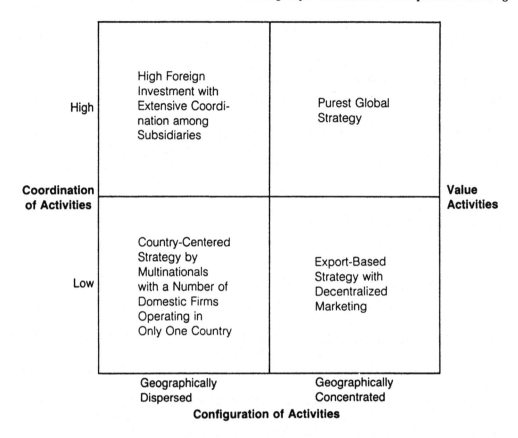

Figure 5 Types of international strategy.

may facilitate marketing in that country by signaling commitment to local buyers and/or providing greater responsiveness. Transport, communication, and storage costs may make it inefficient to concentrate the activity in one location. Government is also frequently a powerful force for dispersing activities. Governments typically want firms to locate the entire value chain in their country, because this creates benefits and spillovers to the country that often go beyond local content. Dispersion is also encouraged by the risks of performing an activity in one place: exchange-rate risks, political risks, and so on. The balance between the advantages of concentrating and dispersing an activity normally differ for each activity (and industry). The best configuration for R&D is different from that for component fabrication, and this is different from that for assembly, installation, advertising, and procurement.[11]

The desirability of coordinating like activities that are dispersed involves a similar balance of structural factors. Coordination potentially allows the sharing of know-how among dispersed activities. If a firm learns how to operate the production process better in Germany, transferring that learning may make the process run better in plants in the United States and Japan. Differing countries, with their inevitably differing conditions, provide a fertile basis for comparison as well as opportunities for arbitraging knowledge, obtained in different places about different aspects of the business. Coordination among dispersed activities also potentially improves the ability to reap economies of scale in activities if subtasks are allocated among locations to allow some specialization—e.g., each R&D center has a different area of focus. While there is a fine line between such forms of coordination and what I have termed configuration, it does illustrate how the way a network of foreign locations is managed can have a great influence on the ability to reap the benefits of any given configuration of activities. Viewed another way, close coordination is frequently a partial offset to dispersing an activity.

Coordination may also allow a firm to respond to shifting comparative advantage, where shifts in exchange rates and factor costs are hard to forecast. Incrementally increasing the production volume at the location currently enjoying favorable exchange rates, for example, can lower overall costs. Coordination can reinforce a firm's brand reputation with buyers (and hence lead to differentiation) through ensuring a consistent image and approach to doing business on a world-wide basis. This is particularly likely if buyers are mobile or information about the industry flows freely around the world. Coordination may also differentiate the firm with multinational buyers if it allows the firm to serve them anywhere and in a consistent way. Coordination (and a global approach to configuration) enhances leverage with local governments if the firm is able to grow or shrink activities in one country at the expense of others. Finally, coordination yields flexibility in responding to competitors, by allowing the firm to differentially respond across countries and to respond in one country to a challenge in another.

Coordination of dispersed activities usually involves costs that differ by form of coordination and industry. Local conditions may vary in ways that may make a common approach across countries suboptimal. If every plant in the world is required to use the same raw material, for example, the firm pays a penalty in countries where the raw material is expensive relative to satisfactory substitutes. Business practices, marketing systems, raw material sources, local infra-structures, and a variety of other factors may differ across countries as well, often in ways that may mitigate the advantages of a common approach or of the sharing of learning. Governments many restrain the flow of information required for coordination or may impose other barriers to it. The transaction costs of coordination, which have recently received increased attention in domestic competition, are vitally important in international strategy.[12] International coordination involves long distances, language problems, and cultural barriers to communication. In some industries, these factors may mean that coordination is not optimal. They also suggest that forms of coordination which involve relatively infrequent decisions will enjoy advantages over forms of coordination involving on-going interchange.

There are also substantial organizational difficulties involved in achieving cooperation among subsidiaries, which are due to the difficulty in aligning subsidiary managers' interests with those of the firm as a whole. The Germans do not necessarily want to tell the Americans about their latest breakthroughs on the production line because it may make it harder for them to outdo the Americans in the annual comparison of operating efficiency among plants. These vexing organi-zational problems mean that country subsidiaries often view each other more as competitors than collaborators.[13] As with configuration, a firm must make an activity-by-activity choice about where there is net competitive advantage from coordinating in various ways.

Coordination in some activities may be necessary to reap the advantages of configuration in others. The use of common raw materials in each plant, for example, allows worldwide purchasing. Moreover, tailoring some activities to countries may allow concentration and standardization of other activities. For example, tailored marketing in each country may allow the same product to be positioned differently and hence sold successfully in many countries, unlocking possibilities for reaping economies of scale in production and R&D. Thus coordination and configuration interact.

Configuration/Coordination and the Pattern of International Competition

When benefits of configuring and/or coordinating globally exceed the costs, an industry will globalize in a way that reflects the net benefits by value activity. The activities in which global competitors gain competitive advantage will differ correspondingly. Configuration/coordination determines the ongoing competitive advantages of a global strategy which are additive to competitive advantages a firm derives/possesses from its domestic market positions. An initial transfer of knowledge from the home base to subsidiaries is one, but by no means the most important, advantage of a global competitor.[14]

An industry such as commercial aircraft represents an extreme case of a global industry (in the upper right-hand corner of Figure 4). The three major competitors in this industry—Boeing, McDonnell Douglas, and Airbus—all have global strategies. In activities important to cost and differentiation in the industry, there are compelling net advantages to concentrating most activities and coordinating the dispersed activities extensively.[15] In R&D, there is a large fixed cost of developing an aircraft model ($1 billion or more) which requires worldwide sales to amortize. There are significant economies of scale in production, a steep learning curve in assembly (the learning curve was born out of research in this industry), and apparently significant advantages of locating R&D and production together. Sales of commercial aircraft are infrequent (via a highly skilled sales force), so that even the sales force can be partially concentrated in the home country and travel to buyers.

The costs of a concentrated configuration are relatively low in commercial aircraft. Product needs are homogeneous, and there are the low transport costs of delivering the product to the buyer. Finally, worldwide coordination of the one dispersed activity, service, is very important—obviously standardized parts and repair advice have to be available wherever the plane lands.

As in every industry, there are structural features which work against a global strategy in commercial aircraft. These are all related to government, a not atypical circumstance. Government has a particular interest in commercial aircraft because of its large trade potential, the technological sophistication of the industry, its spillover effects to other industries, and its implications for national defense. Government also has an unusual degree of leverage in the industry: in many instances, it is the buyer. Many airlines are government owned, and a government official or appointee is head of the airline.

The competitive advantages of a global strategy are so great that all the successful aircraft producers have sought to achieve and preserve them. In addition, the power of government to intervene has been mitigated by the fact that there are few viable worldwide competitors and that there are enormous barriers to entry created in part by the advantages of a global strategy. The result has been that firms have sought to assuage government through procurement. Boeing, for example, is very careful about where it buys components. In countries that are large potential customers, Boeing seeks to develop suppliers. This requires a great deal of extra effort by Boeing both to transfer technology and to work with suppliers to assure that they meet its standards. Boeing realizes that this is preferable to compromising the competitive advantage of its strongly integrated worldwide strategy. It is willing to employ one value activity (procurement) where the advantages of concentration are modest to help preserve the benefits of concentration in other activities. Recently, commercial aircraft competitors have entered into joint ventures and other coalition arrangements with foreign suppliers to achieve the same effect, as well as to spread the risk of huge development costs.

The extent and location of advantages from a global strategy vary among industries. In some industries, the competitive advantage from a global strategy comes in technology development, although firms gain little advantage in the primary activities so that these are dispersed around the world to minimize concentration costs. In other industries such as cameras or videocassette recorders, a firm cannot succeed without concentrating production to achieve economies of scale, but instead it gives subsidiaries much local autonomy in sales and marketing. In some industries, there is no net advantage to a global strategy and country-centered strategies dominate—the industry is multidomestic.

Segments or stages of an industry frequently vary in their pattern of globalization. In aluminum, the upstream (alumina and ingot) stages of the industry are global businesses. The downstream stage, semifabrication, is a group of multidomestic businesses because product needs vary by country, transport costs are high, and intensive local customer service is required. Scale economies in the value chain are modest. In lubricants, automotive oil tends to be a country-centered business while marine motor oil is a global business. In automotive oil, countries have varying driving standards, weather conditions, and local laws. Production involves blending various kinds of crude oils and additives, and is subject to few economies of scale but high shipping costs. Country-centered competitors such as Castrol and Quaker State are leaders in most countries. In the marine segment, conversely, ships move freely around the world and require the same oil everywhere. Successful competitors are global.

The ultimate leaders in global industries are often first movers—the first firms to perceive the possibilities for a global strategy. Boeing was the first global competitor in aircraft, for example, as was Honda in motorcycles, and Becton Dickinson in disposable syringes. First movers gain scale and learning advantages which are difficult to overcome. First mover effects are particularly important in global industries because of the association between globalization and economies of scale and learning achieved through worldwide configuration/coordination. Global leadership shifts if industry structural change provides opportunities for leapfrogging to new products or new technologies that nullify past leaders' scale and learning—again, the first mover to the new generation/technology often wins.

Global leaders often begin with some advantage at home, whether it be low labor cost or a product or marketing advantage. They use this as a lever to enter foreign markets. Once there, however, the global competitor converts the initial home advantage into competitive advantages that grow out of its overall worldwide system, such as production scale or ability to amortize R&D costs. While the initial advantage may have been hard to sustain, the global strategy creates new advantages which can be much more durable.

International strategy has often been characterized as a choice between worldwide standardization and local tailoring, or as the tension between the economic imperative (large-scale efficient facilities) and the political imperative (local content, local production). It should be clear from the discussion so far that neither characterization captures the richness of a firm's international strategy choices. A firm's choice of international strategy involves a search for competitive advantage from configuration/coordination throughout the value chain. A firm may standardize (concentrate) some activities and tailor (disperse) others. It may also be able to standardize and tailor at the same time through the coordination of dispersed activities, or use local tailoring of some activities (e.g., different product positioning in each country) to allow standardization of others (e.g., production). Similarly, the economic imperative is not always for a global strategy—in some industries a country-centered strategy is the economic imperative. Conversely, the political imperative is to concentrate activities in some industries where governments provide strong export incentives and locational subsidies.

Global Strategy vs. Comparative Advantage

Given the importance of trade theory to the study of international competition, it is useful to pause and reflect on the relationship of the framework I have presented to the notion of comparative advantage. Is there a difference? The traditional concept of comparative advantage is that factor-cost or factor-quality differences among countries lead to production of products in countries with an advantage which export them elsewhere in the world. Competitive advantage in this view, then, grows out of *where* a firm performs activities. The location of activities is clearly one source of potential advantage in a global firm. The global competitor can locate activities wherever comparative advantage lies, decoupling comparative advantage from its home base or country of ownership.

Indeed, the framework presented here suggests that the comparative advantage story is richer than typically told, because it not only involves production activities (the usual focus of discussions) but also applies to other activities in the value chain such as R&D, processing orders, or designing advertisements. Comparative advantage is specific to the *activity* and not the location of the value chain as a whole.[16] One of the potent advantages of the global firm is that it can spread activities among locations to reflect different preferred locations for different activities, something a domestic or country-centered competitor does not do. Thus components can be made in Taiwan, software written in India and basic R&D performed in Silicon Valley, for example. This international specialization of activities within the firm is made possible by the growing ability to coordinate and configure globally.

At the same time as our framework suggests a richer view of comparative advantage, however, it also suggests that many forms of competitive advantage for the global competitor derive less from *where* the firm performs activities than from *how* it performs them on a worldwide basis; economies of scale, proprietary learning, and differentiation with multinational buyers are not tied to countries but to the configuration and coordination of the firm's worldwide system. Traditional sources of comparative advantage can be very elusive and slippery sources of competitive advantage for an international competitor today, because comparative advantage frequently shifts. A country with the lowest labor cost is overtaken within a few years by some other country—facilities located in the first country then face a disadvantage. Moreover, falling direct labor as a percentage of total costs, increasing global markets for raw materials and other inputs, and freer flowing technology have diminished the role of traditional sources of comparative advantage.

My research on a broad cross-section of industries suggests that the achievement of sustainable world market leadership follows a more complex pattern than the exploitation of comparative advantage per se. A competitor often starts with a comparative advantage-related edge that provides the basis for penetrating foreign markets, but this edge is rapidly translated into a broader array of advantages that arise from a global approach to configuration and coordination as described earlier. Japanese firms, for example, have done a masterful job of converting temporary labor-cost advantages into durable systemwide advantages due to scale and proprietary knowhow. Ultimately, the systemwide advantages are further reinforced with country-specific advantages such as brand identity as well as distribution channel access. Many Japanese firms were fortunate enough to make their transitions from country-based comparative advantage to global competitive advantage at a time when nobody paid much attention to them and there was a buoyant world economy. European and American competitors were willing to cede market share in "less desirable" segments such as the low end of the producer line, or so they thought. The Japanese translated these beachheads into world leadership by broadening their lines and reaping advantages in scale and proprietary technology. The Koreans and Taiwanese, the latest low labor cost entrants to a number of industries, may have a hard time replicating Japan's success, given slower growth, standardized products, and now alert competitors.

Global Platforms

The interaction of the home-country conditions and competitive advantages from a global strategy that transcend the country suggest a more complex role of the country in firm success than implied by the theory of comparative advantage. To understand this more complex role of the country, I define the concept of a *global platform*. A country is a desirable global platform in an industry if it provides an environment yielding firms domiciled in that country an advantage in competing globally in that particular industry.[17] An essential element of this definition is that it hinges on success *outside* the country, and not merely country conditions which allow firms to successfully master domestic competition. In global competition, a country must be viewed as a platform and not as the place where all a firm's activities are performed.

There are two determinants of a good global platform in an industry, which I have explored in more detail elsewhere.[18] The first is comparative advantage, or the factor endowment of the country as a site to perform particular activities in the industry. Today, simple factors such as low-cost unskilled labor and natural resources are increasingly less important to global competition compared to complex factors such as skilled scientific and technical personnel and advanced infrastructure. Direct labor is a minor proportion of cost in many manufactured goods and auto-mation of non-production activities is shrinking it further, while markets for resources are in-creasingly global, and technology has widened the number of sources of many resources. A country's factor endowment is partly exogenous and partly the result of attention and investment in the country.

The second determinant of the attractiveness of a country as a global platform in an industry are the characteristics of a country's demand. A country's demand conditions include the size and timing of its demand in an industry, factors recognized as important by authors such as Linder and Vernon.[19] They also include the sophistication and power of buyers and channels and the product features and attributes demanded. Local demand conditions provide two potentially pow-erful sources of competitive advantage to a global competitor based in that country. The first is *first-mover advantages* in perceiving and implementing the appropriate global strategy. Pressing local needs, particularly peculiar ones, lead firms to embark early to solve local problems and gain proprietary know-how. This is then translated into scale and learning advantages as firms move early to compete globally. The other potential benefit of local demand conditions is a baseload of demand for product varieties that will be sought after in international markets. These two roles of the country in the success of a global firm reflect the interaction between conditions of local supply, the composition and timing of country demand, and economies of scale and learning in shaping international success.

The two determinants interact in important and sometimes counterintuitive ways. Local de-mand and needs frequently influence private and social investment in endogenous factors of production. A nation with oceans as borders and dependence on sea trade, for example, is more prone to have universities and scientific centers dedicated to oceanographic education and re-search. Similarly, factor endowment seems to influence local demand. The per capita consump-tion of wine is highest in wine-growing regions, for example.

Comparative disadvantage in some factors of production can be an advantage in global compe-tition when combined with pressing local demand. Poor growing conditions have led Israeli farmers to innovate in irrigation and cultivation techniques, for example. The shrinking role in competition of simple factors of production relative to complex factors such as technical person-nel seem to be enhancing the frequency and importance of such circumstances. What is important today is unleashing innovation in the proper direction, instead of passive exploitation of static cost advantages in a country which can shift rapidly and be overcome. International success today is a dynamic process resulting from continued development of products and processes. The forces which guide firms to undertake such activity thus become central to international competition.

A good example of the interplay among these factors is the television set industry. In the U.S., early demand was in large screen console sets because television sets were initially luxury items kept in the living room. As buyers began to purchase second and third sets, sets became smaller and more portable. They were used increasingly in the bedroom, the kitchen, the car, and elsewhere. As the television set industry matured, table model and portable sets became the universal product variety. Japanese firms, because of the small size of Japanese homes, cut their teeth on small sets. They dedicated most of their R&D to developing small picture tubes and to making sets more compact. In the process of naturally serving the needs of their home market, then, Japanese firms gained early experience and scale in segments of the industry that came to dominate world demand. U.S. firms, conversely, cut their teeth on large-screen console sets with fine furniture cabinets. As the industry matured, the experience base of U.S. firms was in a segment that was small and isolated to a few countries, notably the U.S. Japanese firms were able to penetrate world markets in a segment that was both uninteresting to foreign firms and in which they had initial scale, learning, and labor cost advantages. Ultimately the low-cost advantage disappeared as production was automated, but global scale and learning economies took over as the Japanese advanced product and process technology at a rapid pace.

The two broad determinants of a good global platform rest on the interaction between country characteristics and firms' strategies. The literature on comparative advantage, through focusing on country factor endowments, ignoring the demand side, and suppressing the individual firm, is most appropriate in industries where there are few economies of scale, little proprietary technology or technological change, or few possibilities for product differentiation.[20] While these industry characteristics are those of many traditionally traded goods, they describe few of today's important global industries.

THE EVOLUTION OF INTERNATIONAL COMPETITION

Having established a framework for understanding the globalization of industries, we are now in a position to view the phenomenon in historical perspective. If one goes back far enough, relatively few industries were global. Around 1880, most industries were local or regional in scope.[21] The reasons are rather self-evident in the context of our framework. There were few economies of scale in production until fuel-powered machines and assembly-line techniques emerged. There were heterogeneous product needs among regions within countries, much less among countries. There were few if any national media—the *Saturday Evening Post* was the first important national magazine in the U.S. and developed in the teens and twenties. Communicating between regions was difficult before the telegraph and telephone, and transportation was slow until the railroad system became well developed.

These structural conditions created little impetus for the widespread globalization of industry. Those industries that were global reflected classic comparative advantage considerations—goods were simply unavailable in some countries (who then imported them from others) or differences in the availability of land, resources, or skilled labor made some countries desirable suppliers to others. Export of local production was the form of global strategy adapted. There was little role or need for widespread government barriers to international trade during this period, although trade barriers were quite high in some countries for some commodities.

Around the 1880s, however, were the beginnings of what today has blossomed into the globalization of many industries. The first wave of modern global competitors grew up in the late 1800s and early 1900s. Many industries went from local (or regional) to national in scope, and some began globalizing. Firms such as Ford, Singer, Gillette, National Cash Register, Otis, and Western Electric had commanding world market shares by the teens, and operated with integrated worldwide strategies. Early global competitors were principally American and European companies.

Driving this first wave of modern globalization were rising production scale economies due to advancements in technology that outpaced the growth of the world economy. Product needs also became more homogenized in different countries as knowledge and industrialization diffused. Transport improved, first through the railroad and steamships and later in trucking. Communication became easier with the telegraph then the telephone. At the same time, trade barriers were either modest or overwhelmed by the advantages of the new large-scale firms.

The burst of globalization soon slowed, however. Most of the few industries that were global moved increasingly towards a multidomestic pattern—multinationals remained, but between the 1920s and 1950 they often evolved towards federations of autonomous subsidiaries. The principal reason was a strong wave of nationalism and resulting high tariff barriers, partly caused by the world economic crisis and world wars. Another barrier to global strategies, chronicled by Chandler[22] was a growing web of cartels and other interfirm contractual agreements. These limited the geographic spread of firms.

The early global competitors began rapidly dispersing their value chains. The situation of Ford Motor Company was no exception. While in 1925 Ford had almost no production outside the U.S., by World War II its overseas production had risen sharply. Firms that became multinationals during the interwar period tended to adopt country-centered strategies. European multinationals, operating in a setting where there were many sovereign countries within a relatively small geographical area, were quick to establish self-contained and quite autonomous subsidiaries in many countries. A more tolerant regulatory environment also encouraged European firms to form cartels and other cooperative agreements among themselves, which limited their foreign market entry.

Between the 1950s and the late 1970s, however, there was a strong reversal of the interwar trends. As Exhibit 1 illustrated, there have been very strong underlying forces driving the globalization of industries. The important reasons can be understood using the configuration/coordination dichotomy. The competitive advantage of competing worldwide from concentrated activities rose sharply, while concentration costs fell. There was a renewed rise in scale economies in many activities due to advancing technology. The minimum efficient scale of an auto assembly plant more than tripled between 1960 and 1975, for example, while the average cost of developing a new drug more than quadrupled.[23] The pace of technological change has increased, creating more incentive to amortize R&D costs against worldwide sales.

Product needs have continued to homogenize among countries, as income differences have narrowed, information and communication has flowed more freely around the world, and travel has increased.[24] Growing similarities in business practices and marketing systems (e.g., chain stores) in different countries have also been a facilitating factor in homogenizing needs. Within countries there has been a parallel trend towards greater market segmentation, which some observers see as contradictory to the view that product needs in different countries are becoming similar. However, segments today seem based less on country differences and more on buyer differences that transcend country boundaries, such as demographic, user industry, or income groups. Many firms successfully employ global focus strategies in which they serve a narrow segment of an industry worldwide, as do Daimler-Benz and Rolex.

Another driver of post-World War II globalization has been a sharp reduction in the real costs of transportation. This has occurred through innovations in transportation technology including increasingly large bulk carriers, container ships, and larger, more efficient aircraft. At the same time, government impediments to global configuration/coordination have been falling in the postwar period. Tariff barriers have gone down, international cartels and patent-sharing agreements have disappeared, and regional economic pacts such as the European Community have emerged to facilitate trade and investment, albeit imperfectly.

The ability to coordinate globally has also risen markedly in the postwar period. Perhaps the most striking reason is falling communication costs (in voice and data) and reduced travel time for individuals. The ability to coordinate activities in different countries has also been facilitated by growing similarities among countries in marketing systems, business practices, and infrastructure—country after country has developed supermarkets and mass distributors, television advertising, and so on. Greater international mobility of buyers and information has raised the payout to coordinating how a firm does business around the world. The increasing number of firms who are multinational has created growing possibilities for differentiation by suppliers who are global.

The forces underlying globalization have been self-reinforcing. The globalization of firms' strategies has contributed to the homogenization of buyer needs and business practices. Early global competitors must frequently stimulate the demand for uniform global varieties; for example, as Becton Dickinson did in disposable syringes and Honda did in motorcycles. Similarly, globalization of industries begets globalization of supplier industries—the increasing globalization of automotive component suppliers is a good example. Pioneering global competitors also stimulate the development and growth of international telecommunications infrastructures as well as the creation of global advertising media—e.g., *The Economist* and *The Wall Street Journal*.

STRATEGIC IMPLICATIONS OF GLOBALIZATION

When the pattern of international competition shifts from multidomestic to global, there are many implications for the strategy of international firms. While a full treatment is beyond the scope of this paper, I will sketch some of the implications here.[25]

At the broadest level, globalization casts new light on many issues that have long been of interest to students of international business. In areas such as international finance, marketing, and business-government relations, the emphasis in the literature has been on the unique problems of adapting to local conditions and ways of doing business in a foreign country in a foreign currency. In a global industry, these concerns must be supplemented with an overriding focus on the ways and means of international configuration and coordination. In government relations, for example, the focus must shift from stand-alone negotiations with host countries (appropriate in multidomestic competition) to a recognition that negotiations in one country will both affect other countries and be shaped by possibilities for performing activities in other countries. In finance, measuring the performance of subsidiaries must be modified to reflect the contribution of one subsidiary to another's cost position or differentiation in a global strategy, instead of viewing each subsidiary as a stand-alone unit. In battling with global competitors, it may be appropriate in some countries to accept low profits indefinitely—in multidomestic competition this would be unjustified.[26] In global industries, the overall system matters as much or more than the country.

Of the many other implications of globalization for the firm, there are two of such significance that they deserve some treatment here. The first is the role of *coalitions* in global strategy. A coalition is a long-term agreement linking firms but falling short of merger. I use the term coalition to encompass a whole variety of arrangements that include joint ventures, licenses, supply agreements, and many other kinds of interfirm relationships. Such interfirm agreements have been receiving more attention in the academic literature, although each form of agreement has been looked at separately and the focus has been largely domestic.[27] International coalitions, linking firms in the same industry based in different countries, have become an even more important part of international strategy in the past decade.

International coalitions are a way of configuring activities in the value chain on a worldwide basis jointly with a partner. International coalitions are proliferating rapidly and are present in many industries.[28] There is a particularly high incidence in automobiles, aircraft, aircraft engines, robotics, consumer electronics, semiconductors and pharmaceuticals. While international coalitions have long been present, their character has been changing. Historically, a firm from a developed country formed a coalition with a firm in a lesser-developed country to perform marketing activities in that country. Today, we observe more and more coalitions in which two firms from developed countries are teaming up to serve the world, as well as coalitions that extend beyond marketing activities to encompass activities throughout the value chain.[29] Production and R&D coalitions are very common, for example.

Coalitions are a natural consequence of globalization and the need for an integrated worldwide strategy. The same forces that lead to globalization will prompt the formation of coalitions as firms confront the barriers to establishing a global strategy of their own. The difficulties of gaining access to foreign markets and in surmounting scale and learning thresholds in production, technology development, and other activities have led many firms to team up with others. In many industries, coalitions can be a transitional state in the adjustment of firms to globalization, reflecting the need of firms to catch up in technology, cure short-term imbalances between their global production networks and exchange rates, and accelerate the process of foreign market entry. Many coalitions are likely to persist in some form, however.

There are benefits and costs of coalitions as well as difficult implementation problems in making them succeed (which I have discussed elsewhere). How to choose and manage coalitions is among the most interesting questions in international strategy today. When one speaks to managers about coalitions, almost all have tales of disaster which vividly illustrate that coalitions often do not succeed. Also, there is the added burden of coordinating global strategy with a coalition partner because the partner often wants to do things its own way. Yet, in the face of copious corporate experience that coalitions do not work and a growing economics literature on transaction costs and contractual failures, we see a proliferation of coalitions today of the most difficult kind—those between companies in different countries.[30] There is a great need for researching in both the academic community and in the corporate world about coalitions and how to manage them. They are increasingly being forced on firms today by new competitive circumstances.

A second area where globalization carries particular importance is in *organizational structure*. The need to configure and coordinate globally in complex ways creates some obvious organizational challenges.[31] Any organization structure for competing internationally has to balance two dimensions; there has to be a *country* dimension (because some activities are inherently performed in the country) and there has to be a *global* dimension (because the advantages of global configuration/coordination must be achieved). In a global industry, the ultimate authority must represent the global dimension if a global strategy is to prevail. However, within any international firm, once it disperses any activities there are tremendous pressures to disperse more. Moreover, forces are unleashed which lead subsidiaries to seek growing autonomy. Local country managers will have a natural tendency to emphasize how different their country is and the consequent need for local tailoring and control over more activities in the value chain. Country managers will be loath to give up control over activities or how they are performed to outside forces. They will also frequently paint an ominous picture of host government concerns about local content and requirements for local presence. Corporate incentive systems frequently encourage such behavior by linking incentives narrowly to subsidiary results.

In successful global competitors, an environment is created in which the local managers seek to exploit similarities across countries rather than emphasize differences. They view the firm's global presence as an advantage to be tapped for their local gain. Adept global competitors often go to great lengths to devise ways of circumventing or adapting to local differences while preserving the advantages of the similarities. A good example is Canon's personal copier. In Japan, the typical paper size is bigger than American legal size and the standard European size. Canon's personal copier will not handle this size—a Japanese company introduced a product that did not meet its home market needs in the world's largest market for small copiers! Canon gathered its marketing managers from around the world and cataloged market needs in each country. They found that capacity to copy the large Japanese paper was only needed in Japan. In consultation with design and manufacturing engineers, it was determined that building this feature into the personal copier would significantly increase its complexity and cost. The decision was made to omit the feature because the price elasticity of demand for the personal copier was judged to be high. But this was not the end of the deliberations. Canon's management then set out to find a way to make the personal copier saleable in Japan. The answer that emerged was to add another feature to the copier—the ability to copy business cards—which both added little cost and was particularly valuable in Japan. This case illustrates the principle of looking for the similarities in needs among countries and in finding ways of creating similarities, not emphasizing the differences.

Such a change in orientation is something that typically occurs only grudgingly in a multinational company, particularly if it has historically operated in a country-centered mode (as has been the case with early U.S. and European multinationals). Achieving such a reorientation requires first that managers recognize that competitive success demands exploiting the advantages of a global strategy. Regular contact and discussion among subsidiary managers seems to be a prerequisite, as are information systems that allow operations in different countries to be compared.[32] This can be followed by programs for exchanging information and sharing know-how and then by more complex forms of coordination. Ultimately, the reconfiguring of activities globally may then be accepted, even though subsidiaries may have to give up control over some activities in the process.

THE FUTURE OF INTERNATIONAL COMPETITION

Since the late 1970s, there have been some gradual but significant changes in the pattern of international competition which carry important implications for international strategy. Our framework provides a template with which we can examine these changes and probe their significance. The factors shaping the global configuration of activities by firms are developing in ways which contrast with the trends of the previous thirty years. Homogenization of product needs among countries appears to be continuing, though segmentation within countries is as well. As a result, consumer packaged goods are becoming increasingly prone toward globalization, though they have long been characterized by multidomestic competition. There are also signs of globalization in some service industries as the introduction of information technology creates scale economies in support activities and facilitates coordination in primary activities. Global service firms are reaping advantages in hardware and software development as well as procurement.

In many industries, however, limits have been reached in the scale economies that have been driving the concentration of activities. These limits grow out of classic diseconomies of scale that arise in very large facilities, as well as out of new, more flexible technology in manufacturing and other activities that is often not as scale sensitive as previous methods. At the same time, though, flexible manufacturing allows the production of multiple varieties (to serve different countries) in a single plant. This may encourage new movement towards globalization in industries in which product differences among countries have remained significant and have blocked globalization in the past.

There also appear to be some limits to further decline in transport costs, as innovations such as containerization, bulk shops, and larger aircraft have run their course. However, a parallel trend toward smaller, lighter products and components may keep some downward pressure on transport costs. The biggest change in the benefits and costs of concentrated configuration has been the

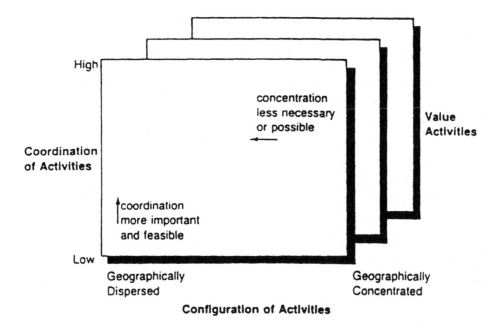

Figure 6 Future trends in international competition.

sharp rise in protectionism in recent years and the resulting rise in nontariff barriers, harkening back to the 1920s. As a group, these factors point to less need and less opportunity for highly concentrated configurations of activities.

When we examine the coordination dimension, the picture looks starkly different. Communication and coordination costs are dropping sharply, driven by breathtaking advances in information systems and telecommunication technology. We have just seen the beginning of developments in this area, which are spreading throughout the value chain.[33] Boeing, for example, is employing computer-aided design technology to jointly design components on-line with foreign suppliers. Engineers in different countries are communicating via computer screens. Marketing systems and business practices continue to homogenize, facilitating the coordination of activities in different countries. The mobility of buyers and information is also growing rapidly, greasing the international spread of brand reputations and enhancing the importance of consistency in the way activities are performed worldwide. Increasing numbers of multinational and global firms are begetting globalization by their suppliers. There is also a sharp rise in the computerization of manufacturing as well as other activities throughout the value chain, which greatly facilitates coordination among dispersed sites.

The imperative of global strategy is shifting, then, in ways that will require a rebalancing of configuration and coordination. Concentrating activities is less necessary in economic terms, and less possible as governments force more dispersion. At the same time, the ability to coordinate globally throughout the value chain is increasing dramatically through modern technology. The need to coordinate is also rising to offset greater dispersion and to respond to buyer needs.

Thus, today's game of global strategy seems increasingly to be a game of coordination—getting more and more dispersed production facilities, R&D laboratories, and marketing activities to truly work together. Yet, widespread coordination is the exception rather than the rule today in many multinationals, as I have noted. The imperative for coordination raises many questions for organizational structure, and is complicated even more when the firm has built its global system using coalitions with independent firms.

Japan has clearly been the winner in the postwar globalization of competition. Japan's firms not only had an initial labor cost advantage but the orientation and skills to translate this into more durable competitive advantages such as scale and proprietary technology. The Japanese context also offered an excellent platform for globalization in many industries, given postwar environmental and technological trends. With home market conditions favoring compactness, a lead in coping with high energy costs, and a national conviction to raise quality, Japan has proved a fertile incubator of global leaders. Japanese multinationals had the advantage of embarking on international strategies in the 1950s and 1960s when the imperatives for a global approach to strategy were beginning to accelerate, but without the legacy of past international investments and modes of behavior.[34] Japanese firms also had an orientation towards highly concentrated activities that fit the strategic imperative of the time. Most European and American multinationals, conversely, were well established internationally before the war. They had legacies of local subsidiary autonomy that reflected the interwar environment. As Japanese firms spread internationally, they dispersed activities only grudgingly and engaged in extensive global coordination. European and country-centered American companies struggled to rationalize overly dispersed configurations of activities and to boost the level of global coordination among foreign units. They found their decentralized organization structures—so fashionable in the 1960s and 1970s—to be a hindrance to doing so.

As today's international firms contemplate the future, Japanese firms are rapidly dispersing activities, due largely to protectionist pressures but also because of the changing economic factors I have described. They will have to learn the lessons of managing overseas activities that many European and American firms learned long ago. However, Japanese firms enjoy an organizational style that is supportive of coordination and a strong commitment to introducing new technologies such as information systems that facilitate it. European firms must still overcome their country-centered heritage. Many still do not compete with truly global strategies and lack modern technology. Moreover, the large number of coalitions formed by European firms must overcome the barriers to coordination if they are not to prove ultimately limiting. The European advantage may well be in exploiting an acute and well-developed sensitivity to local market conditions as well as a superior ability to work with host governments. By using modern flexible manufacturing technology and computerizing elsewhere in the value chain, European firms may be able to serve global segments and better differentiate products.

Many American firms tend to fall somewhere in between the European and Japanese situations. Their awareness of international competition has risen dramatically in recent years, and efforts at creating global strategies are more widespread. The American challenge is to catch the Japanese in a variety of technologies, as well as to learn how to gain the benefits of coordinating among dispersed units instead of becoming trapped by the myths of decentralization. The changing pattern of international competition is creating an environment in which no competitor can afford to allow country parochialism to impede its ability to turn a worldwide position into a competitive edge.

REFERENCES

1. United Nations Center on Transnational Corporations, *Salient Features and Trends in Foreign Direct Investment* (New York, NY: United Nations, 1984).
2. For a survey, see R. E. Caves and Ronald W. Jones, *World Trade and Payments*, 4th ed. (Boston, MA: Little Brown, 1985).

3. There are many books on the theory and management of the multinational, which are too numerous to cite here. For an excellent survey of the literature, see R. E. Caves, *Multinational Enterprise and Economic Analysis* (Cambridge, England: Cambridge University Press, 1982).

4. Raymond Vernon, "International Investment and International Trade in the Product Cycle." *Quarterly Journal of Economics.* Vol. 80 (May 1966): 190–207. Vernon himself, among others, has raised questions about how general the product cycle pattern is today.

5. Michael E. Porter, *Competitive Strategy: Techniques for Analyzing Industries and Competitors* (New York, NY: The Free Press, 1980); Michael E. Porter, "Beyond Comparative Advantage," Working Paper, Harvard Graduate School of Business Administration, August 1985.

6. For a description of this research, see Michael E. Porter, ed., *Competition in Global Industries* (Boston, MA: Harvard Business School Press, forthcoming).

7. The distinction between multidomestic and global competition and some of its strategic implications were described in T. Hout, Michael E. Porter, and E. Rudden. "How Global Companies Win Out," *Harvard Business Review* (September/October 1982), pp. 98–108.

8. Howard V. Perlmutter, "The Tortuous Evolution of the Multinational Corporation," *Columbia Journal of World Business* (January/February 1969), pp. 9–18. Perlmutter's concept of ethnocentric, polycentric, and geocentric multinationals takes the *firm* not the industry as the unit of analysis and is decoupled from industry structure. It focuses on management attitudes, the nationality of executives, and other aspects of organization. Perlmutter presents ethnocentric, polycentric, and geocentric as stages of an organization's development as a multinational, with geocentric as the goal. A later paper (Yoram Wind, Susan P. Douglas, and Howard V. Perlmutter, "Guidelines for Developing International Marketing Strategies," *Journal of Marketing,* Vol. 37 (April 1973: 14–23) tempers this conclusion based on the fact that some companies may not have the required sophistication in marketing to attempt a geocentric strategy. Products embedded in the lifestyle or culture of a country are also identified as less susceptible to geocentrism. The Perlmutter et al. view does not link management orientation to industry structure and strategy. International strategy should grow out of the net competitive advantage in a global industry of different types of worldwide coordination. In some industries, a country-centered strategy, roughly analogous to Perlmutter's polycentric idea, may be the best strategy irrespective of company size and international experience. Conversely, a global strategy may be imperative given the competitive advantage that accrues from it. Industry and strategy should define the organization approach, not vice versa.

9. Michael E. Porter, *Competitive Advantage: Creating and Sustaining Superior Performance* (New York, NY: The Free Press, 1985).

10. Buzzell (Robert D. Buzzell, "Can You Standardize Multinational Marketing," *Harvard Business Review* [November/December 1980], pp. 102–113); Pryor (Millard H. Pryor, "Planning in a World-Wide Business, *Harvard Business Review*, Vol. 23 [January/February 1965]); and Wind, Douglas, and Perlmutter (op. cit.) point out that national differences are in most cases more critical with respect to marketing than with production and finance. This generalization reflects the fact that marketing activities are often inherently country-based. However, this generalization is not reliable because in many industries, production and other activities are widely dispersed.

11. A number of authors have framed the globalization of industries in terms of the balance between imperatives for global integration and imperatives for national responsiveness, a useful distinction. See, C. K. Prahalad, "The Strategic Process in a Multinational Corporation," unpublished DBA dissertation, Harvard Graduate School of Business Administration, 1975; Yves Doz, "National Policies and Multinational Management," an unpublished DBA dissertation. Harvard Graduate School of Business Administration, 1976; and Christopher A. Bartlett, "Multinational Structural Evolution: The Changing Decision Environment in the International Division," unpublished DBA dissertation, Harvard Graduate School of Business Administration, 1979. I link the distinction here to where and how a firm performs the activities in the value chain internationally.

12. See, for example, Oliver Williamson, *Markets and Hierarchies* (New York, NY: The Free Press, 1975). For an international application, see Mark C. Casson, "Transaction Costs and the Theory of the Multinational Enterprise," in Alan Rugman, ed., *New Theories of the Multinational Enterprise* (Lon-

don: Croom Helm, 1982); David J. Teece, "Transaction Cost Economics and the Multinational Enterprise: An Assessment," *Journal of Economic Behavior and Organization* (forthcoming, 1986).

13. The difficulties in coordinating are internationally parallel to those in coordinating across business units competing in different industries with the diversified firm. See Michael E. Porter, *Competitive Advantage: Creating and Sustaining Superior Performance* (New York, NY: The Free Press, 1985), Chapter 11.

14. Empirical research has found a strong correlation between R&D and advertising intensity and the extent of foreign direct investment (for a survey, see Caves, 1982, op cit.). Both these factors have a place in our model of the determinants of globalization, but for quite different reasons. R&D intensity suggests scale advantages for the global competitor in developing products or processes that are manufactured abroad either due to low production scale economies or government pressures, or which require investments in service infrastructure. Advertising intensity, however, is much closer to the classic transfer of marketing knowledge to foreign subsidiaries. High advertising industries are also frequently those where local tastes differ and manufacturing scale economies are modest, both reasons to disperse many activities.

15. For an interesting description of the industry, see the paper by Michael Yoshino in Porter, ed., op. cit., (forthcoming).

16. It has been recognized that comparative advantage in different stages in a vertically integrated industry sector such as aluminum can reside in different countries. Bauxite mining will take place in resource-rich countries, for example, while smelting will take place in countries with low electrical power cost. See R. E. Caves and Ronald W. Jones, op. cit. The argument here extends this thinking *within* the value chain of any stage and suggests that the optimal location for performing individual activities may vary as well.

17. The firm need not necessarily be owned by investors in the country, but the country is its home base for competing in a particular country.

18. See Porter, *Competitive Advantage*, op. cit.

19. See S. Linder, *An Essay on Trade and Transformation* (New York, NY: John Wiley, 1961); Vernon, op. cit., (1966); W. Gruber, D. Mehta, and R. Vernon, "R&D Factor in International Trade and International Investment of United States Industries," *Journal of Political Economics*, 76/1 (1967):20–37.

20. Where it does recognize scale economies, trade theory views them narrowly as arising from production in one country.

21. See Alfred Chandler in Porter, ed., op. cit. (forthcoming) for a penetrating history of the origins of the large industrial firm and its expansion abroad, which is consistent with the discussion here.

22. Ibid.

23. For data on auto assembly, see "Note on the World Auto Industry in Transition," Harvard Business School Case Services (#9-382-122).

24. For a supporting view, see Theodore Levitt, "The Globalization of Markets," *Harvard Business Review* (May/June 1983), pp. 92–102.

25. The implications of the shift from multidomestic to global competition were the theme of a series of papers on each functional area of the firm prepared for the Harvard Business School Colloquium on Competition in Global Industries. See Porter, ed., op. cit. (forthcoming).

26. For a discussion, see Hout, Porter, and Rudden, op. cit. For a recent treatment, see Gary Hamel and C. K. Prahalad, "Do You Really Have a Global Strategy," *Harvard Business Review* (July/August 1985), pp. 139–148.

27. David J. Teece, "Firm Boundaries, Technological Innovation, and Strategic Planning," in L. G. Thomas, ed., *Economics of Strategic Planning* (Lexington, MA: Lexington Books, 1985).

28. For a treatment of coalitions from this perspective, see Porter, Fuller, and Rawlinson, in Porter, ed., op. cit., (forthcoming).

29. Hladik's recent study of international joint ventures provides supporting evidence. See K. Hladik, "International Joint Ventures: An Empirical Investigation into the Characteristics of Recent U.S. Foreign Joint Venture Partnerships," unpublished Doctoral dissertation, Business Economics Program, Harvard University, 1984.

30. For the seminal work on contractual failures, see Williamson, op. cit.

31. For a thorough and sophisticated treatment, see Christopher A. Bartlett's paper in Porter, ed., op. cit., (forthcoming).

32. For a good discussion of the mechanisms for facilitating international coordination in operations and technology development, see M. T. Flaherty in Porter, ed., op. cit. (forthcoming). Flaherty stresses the importance of information systems and the many dimensions that valuable coordination can take.

33. For a discussion, see Michael E. Porter and Victor Millar, "How Information Gives You Competitive Advantage," *Harvard Business Review* (July/August 1985), pp. 149-160.

34. Prewar international sales enjoyed by Japanese firms were handled largely through trading companies. See Chandler, op. cit.

Chapter 6

Globalization Versus Regionalization: Which Way for the Multinational?

Allen J. Morrison
University of Western Ontario

David A. Ricks and Kendall Roth
University of South Carolina

Increasingly, managers are confronted by calls for dramatic change in the way their businesses should compete internationally. Nowhere is this more apparent than in so-called "global" industries, where managers have been urged to introduce offshore manufacturing, cut costs through worldwide economies of scale, standardize products internationally, and subsidize national market-share battles through international cash flows or other support activities. These actions form the basis of "global strategies" that have been suggested as the emerging pattern of international competition.

Two fundamental assumptions drive this thinking. The first is that a sizable number of competitors are indeed using global strategies to compete; the second is that performance can be improved by pursuing global strategies, particularly in an industry that has global structural characteristics. For managers in global industries the message has been, "Either quickly adopt a global strategy or see your competitiveness diminish."

In fact, some observers have gone so far as to suggest that the imperatives to globalize are so great and the benefits so pronounced that globalization is fast becoming the strategic norm rather than the exception. Although such comments are directed toward managers in the front-line global industries (for example, semiconductors, aircraft parts, pharmaceuticals, and heavy machinery), they are also being heard by senior managers in numerous other industries that are beginning to face greater and greater levels of international competition.

RESEARCH ASSISTANCE

Three years ago, we started a major research project to examine these assumptions with the objective of giving managers some assistance as they face the turbulent decade of the 1990s. Our study involved an extensive examination of the organizational strategy and design of 115 medium and large multinational corporations and 103 affiliated subsidiaries in the United States, Canada,

Reprinted, by permission of publisher, from *Organizational Dynamics*, Winter/1991 © 1991. American Management Association, New York. All rights reserved.

the U.K., France, Germany, and Japan. The study methodology is more fully described in the box on page 96.

The results presented here, which focus on the way international companies are currently responding to global competitive dynamics, suggest that managers should view with skepticism much of the current discussion on the topic. We suggest that, instead of developing global organizational responses to international competition, managers should reassess their strategies with the objective of strengthening regional competitiveness. Such a response, however, requires considerable organizational change. Our analysis highlights the critical tasks that parent corporations and their subsidiaries must undertake to facilitate this change.

ONGOING CHALLENGES: ENVIRONMENTAL VOLATILITY

With few exceptions, there was widespread concurrence among the study's participants that environmental change had accelerated during the last half of the 1980s. To many managers, fundamental international changes—economic, political, technological, and social—were occurring in an independent manner, seemingly independent of each other. As a result, managers were often perplexed in their attempts to sort out opportunities from threats in the competitive environment. Corporate managers in particular faced myriad perspectives generated by far-flung operations in which managers must deal with their own unique challenges.

Managers have historically coped with uncertainty and complexity by constructing mental frameworks for interpreting phenomena. For U.S. managers, conventional wisdom held that the U.S. market was of paramount importance and that business practices successful at home would be successful overseas. Using this reasoning, many companies entered foreign markets either by exporting or by establishing overseas subsidiaries as "miniature replicas" of the U.S. parent. A miniature replica, which is a scaled-down version of the parent, basically produces the same products as those produced by the parent but in lower volumes for the smaller "domestic" market. Consider the following examples.

- *In home appliances, General Electric established its Camco subsidiary in Canada in 1976 by merging the appliance divisions of GSW and GE Canada and subsequently acquiring Westinghouse's Canadian major appliance operations.* Protected by Canadian tariff barriers averaging 12 percent and aided by considerable corporate resources, Camco established production facilities for refrigerators, ranges, dishwashers, stoves, and washers and dryers to serve Canadian demand. Although the scale of these facilities did not render them internationally cost-efficient, Camco has gone on to become Canada's largest major appliance manufacturer.

- *In health-care products, the Kendall Healthcare Products Company established a German subsidiary to manufacture and market a wide line of products developed in the United States.* A broad range of the parent's urological products, critical-care products, and vascular-care products are locally manufactured for German consumption. Localized manufacturing has historically made sense, given that product standards have varied considerably from country to country and that the German health-care system has been a major customer of the firm's products.

- *In consumer electronics, Matsushita Electric Industrial Company paid $108 million in 1974 for an ailing Motorola television manufacturing facility in Illinois.* Under the Quasar Electronics name, Matsushita channelled funds and designs to the upgraded, miniature replica of the parent with the objective of producing television sets in the United States that were similar in quality and price to those developed on Japan.

The management of international operations through either exports or miniature replicas was relatively easy for the parent. Minimal strategic input from local managers was required beyond the local market, thus reassuring head-office managers and encouraging their continued preoccupation with home-country competition. However, this arrangement often resulted in limited communication between parent and subsidiary and certainly restricted corporate advancement opportunities for the overseas managers. The end result in many companies was a perpetuation of the norm that international operations should be treated as appendages to home-country operations.

UNRAVELLING HOME-COUNTRY ORIENTATION: THE RISE OF GLOBAL MANIA

When this home-country orientation began to unravel in the late 1970s, the greatest effect was felt by U.S. managers. As U.S. economic dominance declined, many American managers began to realize that international markets were critically important and that, if they were to compete effectively, new international strategies would be required. This ushered in a new era of what we refer to as "global mania."

An interest in global management began to pick up in the early 1980s and was accelerated, in part, by the declining competitiveness of the United States vis-à-vis Japan. Within the emerging mind-set, managers began to perceive the world differently. Home-country competitive pressures, for example, were put in the context of broader international pressures.

Managers began to see a link between what happened at home and what happened overseas. As an indicator of the globalization of competition, experts pointed to a real shrinkage in differences from country to country—a shrinkage brought on by rising monetary interdependence, transportation and communication efficiencies, various GATT (General Agreement on Tariffs and Trade) rulings, and so on.

By the mid-1980s, numerous academic articles were lauding the merits of pursuing global strategies. Key—and often strategic—industries were identified as having global structural characteristics. These characteristics included low tariff and nontariff barriers to trade, high factor-cost differentials (i.e., in land, labor, and capital costs) between host countries, the possibility of achieving major economies of scale through worldwide production runs, and standardized product demand. Businesses were urged to respond by integrating operations around the world and by developing highly standardized products and marketing approaches.

To support these recommendations, observers noted that such companies as Caterpillar Inc., L. M. Ericsson, and Honda Motor Co., Ltd., had been highly rewarded for pursuing global integration strategies. Other observers pointed to the increasingly "stateless" world of manufacturing, in which dozens of the world's largest corporations generated more than half their sales outside their home country. Examples included ICI, which generated 78 percent of its sales outside the U.K.; Sony Corp., which produced 66 percent of total sales from outside Japan; and IBM, which received almost 63 percent of sales from activities not based in the United States.

The notion of a global strategy has had considerable appeal for corporate managers, largely because such strategies are best managed through tight central control. These strategies, like miniature replica strategies, let corporate managers ultimately determine what is produced and where it is produced. In other words, the center would continue to dominate the periphery. The global "solution" was also a concrete step—and concrete steps were called for in an era of cutthroat international competition.

However, despite the advice calling for pursuit of global strategies, our research failed to uncover widespread support for such an organizational response. The managers in our study generally did not see the world as an undifferentiated global marketplace. Interestingly, competitors in the U.S. regarded the U.S. as *preeminently* important in matters of investment, product development, position, and so on. A similar though somewhat less pronounced pattern was observed for British, German, French, Canadian, and Japanese firms with respect to their home markets.

Thus, though managers sensed that markets were becoming more competitive internationally, their loyalties remained primarily home-based. Even though they recognized that considerable international opportunities were slipping away, the vast majority of managers did not consider globalization the preferred approach for pursuing them. These managers simply viewed the advantages of globalization as being much more theoretical than real, particularly in view of some common problems that included the following:

- *Industry standards remain diverse.* In spite of talk about the convergence of standards—in the European television industry, for example—there are currently seven different technical standards governing such matters as voltage and broadcasting frequencies. To meet this diverse set of standards, Toshiba Corporation in 1981 acquired the assets of a local British consumer electronics firm and began manufacturing television sets for the European market. From a centralized plant in Plymouth, the company now produces 110 models of television sets from 14" to 28" in size, "custom" manufactured for local country needs within Europe.
- *Customers continue to demand locally differentiated products.* In many industries in Europe, North America, and Japan, subsidiaries continue to focus on reformulations, blending, and packaging activities, In the pharmaceutical industry, for example, differences in standards, tastes, and perceived needs remain a major obstacle to globalization. Prescription dosages for many products can vary up to 100 percent between Europe and Japan. Medical training and health-care delivery systems, which vary considerably from country to country, significantly influence the types of prescriptions written and the delivery of both ethical and over-the-counter drugs. In response, Parke-Davis in France and both American Cyanamid Co. and Pfizer Inc. in Germany continue to focus much of their efforts on reformulating dosages and repackaging them.
- *Being an insider remains critically important.* In theory, one advantage of a global strategy is that world-scale production maximizes production efficiencies and underwrites heavy product-development expenses. The result is supposed to be a standardized, low-cost product that, when combined with local marketing input, produces a competitive advantage for the global competitor. In reality, however, such advantages have taken on mythical proportions.

  The example of Inmos provides a case in point. Formed in 1978, the semiconductor manufacturer based in Bristol, U.K. is now a subsidiary of S.G.S.-Thomson Microelectronics, Inc. Inmos produces a variety of fast static RAMs, high-performance microprocessors (transputers), and graphics components for the worldwide market. Inmos's products are intended for global customers, and some 90 percent of its revenues are generated outside the U.K.

  However, it has observed a definite bias in the industry in favor of hardware developed in Silicone Valley. Moreover, it has found that Japanese and, particularly, U.S. customers are often skeptical of European products—and that such skepticism is more psychological than based on rational assessments of the technology and costs involved. As a result, Inmos has joined with a host of other European and Japanese semiconductor producers to consider manufacturing locally in the United States. Being perceived as an insider is still a critical concern for many firms.

- *Global organizations are difficult to manage.* To effectively implement a global strategy, managers must find ways to coordinate far-flung operations. To do this, they must denationalize operations and replace home-country loyalties with a system of common corporate values and loyalties. This is particularly challenging because globalization by definition involves exposure to and linkages with broadly divergent national cultures. Globalization is also based on huge world-scale plants in which acculturation and communication become real challenges. Production economies also reach upper limits with size—limits that of course often restrict the benefits of globalization.

   Many companies face clear, often insurmountable operational obstacles to globalization. At Cyanamid's German subsidiary, for example, a critical shortage of labor makes it nearly impossible to run a plant 24 hours a day. Furthermore, the labor laws that forbid many women in Germany from working at night compound the staffing problem. Language is another simple, though very real, obstacle to globalization.

   In Germany, Cyanamid has determined that implementing a global strategy, which would require the insertion of technical product information into packages, would mean the proliferation of centralized packaging. To speed the packaging function and to give medical practitioners in the field timely backup support, the company estimates that it would need staff members with technical fluency in approximately 12 to 15 languages at global headquarters.

   They argue further that German law outlaws global market-share battles in which profits are artificially generated in one market to support operations in another. Clearly, the promises of globalization must be viewed in the context of very real organizational obstacles and costs to be overcome.

- *Globalization often circumvents subsidiary competencies.* Many global strategies are based on rationalizing operations so that subsidiaries contribute a portion of a finished product's value-added content. Subsidiaries, which in the past functioned as miniature replicas, face a role change that often involves a reduction in their strategic autonomy.

   A case in point is Alkaril Chemicals, Ltd. of Canada, which was recently acquired by Rhone-Poulenc. Alkaril had considerable skills in developing low-volume, specialty chemicals. For surfactants in particular, the company had developed a noteworthy reputation for customized product formulation and flexible production. With the acquisition, Alkaril has been left wondering what role it will play in Rhone-Poulenc's broader strategy, which emphasizes rationalized production and greater economies of scale.

   Although subsidiaries have typically responded promptly to corporate initiatives, globalization is being resisted by many subsidiary managers who fear the loss of autonomy and personal contribution that comes with globalization. Unless they handle this situation delicately, corporations risk losing many of the top managers who ran miniature replica subsidiaries. Another very real risk is that subsidiary managers may take initiatives that restrict the parent from making future moves to rationalize operations.

THE REGIONAL ALTERNATIVE

The move toward the globalization of competition was paralleled in the latter half of the 1980s by a dramatic upsurge in regional competitive pressures. Although regional pressures come from a variety of sources, the most important developments are in the formalization of trading blocks. In North America, the Free Trade Agreement between Canada and the United States is having a far-reaching impact on the business environment. This agreement, which was signed on January 2, 1988, promises to remove all tariffs for a wide variety of industries by 1998. Although trade barriers will remain in place in the areas of agriculture, culture, and maritime-related industries, virtually every other industry faces liberalized trade.

Within the European Community, 1992 looms as a pivotal year in eliminating trade barriers among the 12 member-nations. The goal of Europe 1992, as specified first in the 1985 White Paper and reaffirmed in the 1987 Single European Act, is to sweep away the nontariff barriers that restrict the flow of goods, services, and capital throughout the trading block. Three categories of barriers are to be either eliminated or reduced: fiscal, physical, and technical barriers.

In 1989, 21 of the 22 richest industrialized nations in world—the exception being Japan—belonged to regional trading groups. Japan, as the dominant economic power of the Pacific Rim, has long attempted to strengthen its position in the region. The countries of the Pacific Rim now have the fastest-growing economies in the world, caused in part by the huge influx of Japanese investment.

Many Japanese companies, aided by the strong yen, have transferred whole manufacturing bases to such countries as Thailand and Singapore. Production in these newly industrialized economies is now increasingly being referred to as "JapaNIEs" manufacturing. Japanese economic aid to the region has shown similar growth; in 1989 it was almost 14 times greater than that supplied by the United States.

With all this investment, trade has skyrocketed. Trade within Pacific Asia is now growing at an annual rate of 30 percent and promises to surpass Pacific Asia-North American levels of $250 billion by 1991. Fearful of being left out of the development of the region, Australia and Thailand have proposed the establishment of formal Asian-Pacific consultative bodies with many similarities to the Canada-U.S. Free Trade Agreement and the Europe 1992 phenomenon.

The rise of regional trading blocks has led many companies to reassess the anticipated rise of globalization. Some are taking their cues from governments that established free-trade associations at least in part to encourage and control the economic adjustments that ultimately result in improved global competitiveness. Increasingly, regionalization is being viewed by managers as a stepping-stone to more effective global competition. This view is ably summarized by Wisse Dekker, chairman of the Supervisory Board of N. V. Philips, in an interview with Nan Stone that was reported in the *Harvard Business Review* (May-June, 1989, pp. 90-95):

> [We] need a single European market with common technical standards. Without it, we cannot achieve the optimum scale and the lower unit costs we need to be competitive worldwide.

This reasoning was shared by many managers in our study—namely, that regional strategies are increasingly providing the primary determinant of competitive advantage. In fact, according to the majority of companies surveyed, the evolution to true global competition is currently on hold. Instead of globalization, managers are finding that regional competitive pressures are taking on an ever-greater importance by introducing a set of distinct opportunities and threats.

REGIONAL COMPETITION

A consequence of regionalization pressures, our research found, is that home-oriented parents and subsidiaries—whether in Europe, North America, or Japan—were pressured to become more regionally focused or face a competitive disadvantage, even in so-called global industries. Similarly, companies that had attempted to pursue global strategies were coming under intense pressure to scale back their efforts to meet regional competitive conditions.

Under a regional strategy, companies extend home-country loyalties to the entire region. Local markets are intentionally linked within the region where competitive strategies are formulated. It is within the region that top managers determine investment locations, product mix, competitive positioning, and performance appraisals. Managers are given the opportunity to solve regional challenges regionally.

The importance of responding to the upsurge in regional pressures was not going unnoticed in the companies we studied—witness the following examples:

- *Thomson Consumer Electronics, Inc. has been trying for several years to regionalize its strategy for its television sets.* To do so it has established four Thomson factories in Europe: EWD in Germany, Seipel in France, Cedosa in Spain, and Ferguson in the U.K. Each of these factories assembles specific types of television sets for the European market. EWD, for example, has a European mandate to produce high-feature, large television sets; Cedosa of Spain focuses on low-cost, small-screen sets. The marketing and distribution of the sets is handled by a separate Thomson division that has a similar regional mandate.

  In North America, Thomson manufactures television sets under the RCA and GE name-plates. In spite of sourcing some common low-cost components from the Far East, the North American and European operations are run separately. Thomson has established a network of regional suppliers and subassemblers—largely in Mexico—to maintain the regional integrity of North American operations.
- *Warner Lambert Co. has had operations in Europe since the 1920s through its Parke-Davis subsidiary.* The company currently has manufacturing facilities in the U.K., France, Italy, Spain, Germany, Belgium, and Ireland. Historically, these plants have focused on blending and packaging to meet local needs.

  In 1987, discussions were begun under the direction of the parent to dramatically restructure operations to maximize regional responsiveness. After three years of often heated discussions, a plan was adopted to cut the number of manufacturing units to less than half of 1990 levels and to specialize in each unit. Instead of producing a large number of products for each local market, each plant would produce fewer products for the entire European market.

To the majority of the companies studied, regionalization represented a compromise between the traditional strategies adopted by miniature replica subsidiaries and the global strategies currently being advocated. Regional production facilities have often proved to be as scale-efficient as global facilities while being more forgiving of the need to tailor key product features for local markets. Regional plants also avoid many of the very real staffing, communication, and motivational problems of huge global facilities.

By shifting operations and decision making to the region, the company is also better able to maintain an insider advantage. Many of the Japanese regional investments in the automobile and consumer electronics industries have, for example, been based on the objective of developing insider market advantages. Finally, regionalization allows corporations to more effectively leverage subsidiary competencies by encouraging affiliate involvement in activities that extend beyond local markets.

The regionalization of competition is occurring irrespective of the often very real opportunities to globalize certain aspects of company operations. Indeed, many of the companies studied were sourcing raw materials and commodity components across regions; others were sharing R&D between laboratories across regions. What regionalization does suggest is that even companies in so-called global industries should move to exploit strengths and determine competitive strategies separately on a region-by-region basis. To do so may require some macro, transregional facilitation, but strategic decision making should not unilaterally emanate from world headquarters.

NEW ORGANIZATIONAL CHALLENGES

The move toward regional competition brings with it significant changes in the tasks and responsibilities of both home-country and subsidiary managers. For many companies, the organizational obstacles are extensive, suggesting a bumpy road to change.

The challenge is all the more daunting in view of the sheer magnitude of overseas investment and the weak understanding of many company managers of the opportunities and threats at hand. In 1987, for example, the value of goods and services produced by American firms in the European Community exceeded $235 billion, a figure four times the value of U.S. exports to the region. The gap continues to widen, and similar trends have been observed in North America and Japan.

For the parent, often far removed from distant markets and operations, several tasks and responsibilities become critical. That is, the parent needs to:

- *Stay abreast of local market conditions.* In many instances, subsidiary managers felt that the parent dangerously misunderstood local or regional market conditions. Adjectives such as "naive" or "simplistic" were commonly used by subsidiary managers in describing their parents' understanding of local or regional conditions. A frequently stated belief was that the parent typically overestimates the similarities between markets and consequently pushes too hard and too fast for global consolidation. Subsidiaries often act in conjunction with one another to convince the parent to proceed more cautiously.

- *Stay abreast of subsidiary strengths and weaknesses.* Many of the subsidiary managers who participated in this study commented that the parent often has only superficial understanding of the strengths and weaknesses of their operations. Though it was not unusual for a parent to know the product/market mix and sales levels of a subsidiary, it was far less common for the parent to understand the subsidiary's competitiveness on a product-by-product basis. Parents too often assumed that the subsidiary was uncompetitive outside local markets— even though, in many cases, the subsidiary could have competed on equal ground with the parent in terms of product development and cost competitiveness.

- *Prepare to shift autonomy to regional managers.* For many a corporate parent, regionalization involves a greater leap of faith than it does for a subsidiary; after all, the parent is removed from decision making, while the subsidiary remains a central participant in the process. Our research found that the adjustment to regional decision making was easiest for European managers and most difficult for Japanese managers. The Japanese difficulties stemmed from two sources: a fairly thin cadre of Japanese managers with international training and experience, and a legacy of tight top-to-bottom control that seriously frustrated non-Japanese managers.

  In one instance, the general manager of European operations for one of Japan's largest consumer electronics companies commented that he constantly felt like an outsider in the corporation. As a non-Japanese, he felt that his opportunities for further advancement were nil and that his contributions to corporate thinking were largely ignored. Unless this kind of situation changes, Japanese ability to respond to mounting regional pressures will be severely hampered.

  North American corporate managers also face serious challenges. One recent assessment of corporate preparedness for Europe 1992 ranked Canadian managers at 39 and U.S. managers at 38 out of a possible maximum score of 100. Not surprisingly, European managers fared significantly better. American corporate managers have also been criticized for their lack of preparedness in penetrating the Japanese market and the Pacific Asian market.

For the subsidiary, a different set of tasks is important. Subsidiaries need to:

- *Prepare to take strategic initiatives.* Our research found that subsidiaries can and often do influence their future roles under regionalization. Take the example of Motorola Canada. Like managers at other subsidiaries, managers at Motorola Canada were somewhat apprehensive about the risks associated with the expected rationalization of operations that would come under the Canada-U.S. Free Trade Agreement. Although the subsidiary is U.S.-owned, it employs about 2,500 people—virtually all of whom are Canadians. These people feared that, under free trade, many of their jobs would become redundant.

   In an effort to maintain some control over developments, managers began as far back as the late 1970s to take several important initiatives. First, they beefed up their R&D group; then they began looking for new products that would complement existing offerings while providing export potential independent of the parent. What resulted was a series of products—including land-mobile radios and systems, modems, and data multiplexers—for which the subsidiary was given product mandates. Such mandates have given the subsidiary considerable influence in corporate decision making while providing the parent with new sales and manufacturing resources.

   In the case of Motorola, the Canadian subsidiary was granted product mandates that allowed it access to the parent's worldwide distribution system. However, in the drive toward globalization, only a tiny fraction of the subsidiary's export sales went outside the region. To have attempted to develop, manufacture, and market universal products to worldwide customers would probably have overwhelmed the subsidiary at a time when it was struggling to gain credibility in the eyes of its parent. The more realistic initiative taken was to move regionally before pursuing a global presence.

- *Exploit existing competencies/build new strengths.* Subsidiary managers need to look for opportunities to position themselves as "natural leaders" in selected products within the region. This implies a gradual build-up of competencies through small studies, pilot production in existing facilities, and so on. With expertise comes the influence that determines the strategy's position within the region.

   The case of Cyanamid Canada is illustrative in this regard. Since 1907, Cyanamid has had Canadian operations that have benefited from high Canadian tariffs. In the early 1980s, however, the parent undertook a number of initiatives to strengthen itself as a company involved in biotechnology and specialty chemicals. What followed was a series of divestitures that caused the subsidiary to lose more than half its employees. With the movement toward free trade, concern mounted in the subsidiary that operations would be cut further as the parent rationalized operations on a regional basis.

   In spite of these troubling conditions, however, subsidiary managers clearly believed that much could be done to reverse the situation. The feeling was that the subsidiary's competitive advantage lay in producing smaller-run products that required high levels of technological input.

   Consequently, beginning in 1988, Cyanamid Canada began focusing efforts on reaching out to new technologies in highly specialized fields where it could best exploit its unique strengths; this resulted in two recent acquisitions of Canadian biotechnology companies. Both acquisitions provided the subsidiary with considerable control over operations and an opportunity to strengthen its competencies in ways that will ensure its position in the ongoing restructuring of the parent's operations.

- *Manage structural mechanisms more effectively.* Although there was a strong awareness of changing parent and subsidiary roles in all the companies we studied, many subsidiary managers were concerned about how to proceed with the necessary changes. At some subsidiaries, a damaging "us versus them" attitude had emerged. In these subsidiaries, managers often attempted to quietly sabotage change, frequently by entrenching the subsidiary through long-term supply or service contracts. These elaborate measures often severely tied the parents' hands and proved costly to both parent and subsidiary. In many of these organizations, morale was low and prospects for the future bleak.

Instead of avoiding inevitable integration, successful subsidiaries moved to preempt change through the artful use of a variety of structural mechanisms. These integrative mechanisms included a variety of such tools as personal contact between managers and the use of committees, tasks forces, and boards of directors. Knowing how and when to use appropriate structural mechanisms can maximize subsidiary influence while facilitating integration at multiple levels in the organization.

Structural mechanisms play a vital role because the move to a regional organization is a time-consuming and strenuous process. It was not uncommon for negotiations concerning a move toward regionalization to take three years or more; in many of the companies studied, negotiations that began in the mid-1980s were still ongoing five years later. Negotiations typically involved regular meetings of subsidiary managers and corporate executives and often served as the springboard for establishing more formal, regional decision-making bodies.

CONCLUSIONS: CAPABILITY AND FLEXIBILITY ARE THE KEYS

Few companies remain untouched by the complex environmental changes sweeping the world. In responding to these changes, however, managers have been urged to abandon the dated "miniature replica" approaches in favor of full-fledged global strategies. Although a global strategy promises in theory to be highly efficient, we found in this study that globalization is no panacea. In fact, global imperatives are being eclipsed by an upsurge in regional pressures. Companies are finding that the implementation of global strategies is often prohibitively costly in terms of morale, internal opposition, and lost opportunities to exploit key subsidiary strengths. As a consequence, both parents and subsidiaries are finding that regional strategies represent a safer, more manageable option.

In the course of our study, we also found that management of the regionalization process is often as important as design of the strategy. Flexibility is critical for both parents and subsidiaries as they negotiate roles and tasks in the restructuring of operations.

Here, however, managers are finding that flexibility is only as good as the competencies within the organization. As competitive pressures heat up, organizations that effectively nurture and exploit distinctive competencies stand the greatest chance of success .We suggest that regionalization provides a controlled approach to change and that it builds upon the distinctive competencies of the entire organization while responding to the legitimate pressures for greater integration.

Study Methodology

In this two-phase research project, the first phase involved classifying the international and competitive strategies of U.S.-based corporations (head-office division or stand-alone, single-industry corporations) in global industries.

The global industries were identified through a three-stage process described in Allen J. Morrison's *Competition in Global Industries: How U.S. Businesses Compete* (Quorum Books,

1990). The stages included (1) a review of the literature that has previously identified global industries, (2) a verification of the existence of at least one global competitor in the industry, and (3) an examination of the industry's trade ratio.

The data for the first phase of this research were collected through a combination of questionnaire surveys, secondary data analysis, and in-depth interviews. The survey consisted of a rather detailed instrument containing questions focused on competitive positioning, investment, political and integration activities, and assessments of environmental imperatives and performance.

The data from the questionnaires were analyzed by using a variety of univariate and multivariate procedures. These were complemented by the use of extensive secondary data involving randomly selected businesses in the sample. Post-tests involving in-depth interviews with top executives from nine different corporations in seven of the eleven S.I.C. code industries were also conducted at head offices throughout the United States.

For the second phase of the study, the strategies of affiliated subsidiaries were studied with the objective of better understanding their changing role in the implementation of global and regional strategies. In this phase, 103 responses to a questionnaire were received. Interviews were conducted with senior managers in 31 of the responding subsidiaries.

SELECTED BIBLIOGRAPHY

For a more complete discussion of the "miniature replica" model of subsidiary strategy, see Rod White and Thomas Poynter's "Strategies for Foreign-Owned Subsidiaries in Canada" (*Business Quarterly*, Summer 1984) and Harold Crookell's "Specialization and International Competitiveness" (*Business Quarterly*, Fall 1984).

To review some current discussions on the need to become global competitors, see Barrie James's "Reducing the Risks of Globalization" (*Long-Range Planning*, Vol. 23, No. 1, 1990, p. 80), "The Stateless Corporation" (*Business Week*, May 14, 1990), and "How to Go Global—and Why" (*Fortune*, August 28, 1989).

Several articles treat this topic more systematically and comprehensively. One of the first discussions of a global strategic option was outlined by C. K. Prahalad in "The Strategic Process in a Multinational Corporation," (Boston: unpublished doctoral dissertation, Harvard Graduate School of Business Administration, 1976) and later adapted by Yves Doz in "Strategic Management in Multinational Companies" (*Sloan Management Review*, Winter 1980, pp. 27–46) and by Thomas Hout, Michael Porter, and Eileen Rudden in their "How Global Companies Win Out," (*Harvard Business Review*, September-October 1982, pp. 98–108). Treatments of a more rigorous nature may be found in Sumantra Ghoshal's "Global Strategy: An Organizing Framework" (*Strategic Management Journal*, Vol. 8, No. 5, 1987, pp. 425–440), Bruce Kogut's "Designing Global Strategies: Comparative and Competitive Value-Added Chains" (*Sloan Management Review*, Summer 1985, pp. 15–28, 1985), and "A Note on Global Strategies" (*Strategic Management Journal*, Vol. 10, No. 4, 1989, pp. 383–389).

The trend toward scaling back global strategies to a more regional focus is corroborated by a recent Conference Board study, "'Building Global Teamwork for Growth and Survival" (Research Bulletin No. 228, 1989, p. 13), which found that companies are shifting up to regional strategies as a logical outgrowth of EC developments on their country-by-country businesses. Global companies were in turn shifting down to regional strategies after finding their "global businesses too cumbersome or insensitive to specific market needs."

Chapter 7

How to Take Your Company to the Global Market

George S. Yip
Visiting Associate Professor, Georgetown University

Pierre M. Loewe
Vice-President, MAC Group, Cambridge, Massachusetts

Michael Y. Yoshino
Professor, Harvard University

Abstract *Deciding how to deal with the globalization of markets poses tough issues and choices for managers. There are both external business forces and internal organizational factors to consider. External business forces revolve around the interaction of industry drivers of globalization and the different ways in which a business can be global. Understanding this interaction is key to formulating the right global strategy. Internal organizational factors play a major role in determining how well a company can implement global strategy. This paper provides a systematic approach to developing and implementing a global strategy.*

Most managers have to face the increasing globalization of markets and competition. That fact requires each company to decide whether it must become a worldwide competitor to survive.[1]

This is not an easy decision. Take the division of a multibillion-dollar company, a company that's very sophisticated and has been conducting international business for more than fifty years. The division sells a commodity product, for which it is trying to charge 40% more in Europe than it does in the United States. The price was roughly the same in the United States and in Europe when the dollar was at its all-time high. The company built a European plant which showed a greater return on investment with that European price. But the dollar has fallen and, if the company drops its European price to remain roughly the same as the US price, the return on the plant becomes negative, and some careers are in serious jeopardy. So it is attempting to maintain a 40% European price premium by introducing minor upgrades to the European product.

But its multinational customers will have none of it. They start buying the product in the United States and transshipping it to Europe. When the company tries to prevent them from transshipping, they go to a broker, who does the work for them; they still save money.

The manufacturer doesn't have a choice. It's working in a global market. And it's going to have to come up with a global price. But management is fighting a losing battle because it is unwilling to make the hard strategic and organizational changes necessary to adapt to global market conditions.

European and Japanese corporations also face these kinds of organizational roadblocks. Large European firms, for example, historically have been more multinational than US companies. Their international success is due, in part, to decentralized management. The companies simply reproduced their philosophy and culture everywhere, from India to Australia to Canada. They set up mini-headquarters operations in each country and became truly multinational with executives of different nationalities running them.

Now they are having problems running operations on a worldwide basis because these multinational executives are fighting the global imperative. In one European company, for example, the manager running a Latin American division has built an impenetrable wall around himself and his empire. He's done very well, and everyone has allowed him to do as he pleases. But the company's global strategy requires a new way of looking at Latin America. The organization needs to break down his walls of independence. So far, that's proved next to impossible.

Japanese companies face a different set of problems. On the whole, they have followed a basic, undifferentiated marketing strategy: make small Hondas, and sell them throughout the world. Then make better Hondas, ending up with the $30,000 Honda Acura. It's incremental, and it has worked.

Now, however, the Japanese must create various manufacturing centers around the globe and they're facing many difficulties. They have a coordinated marketing strategy and have built up infrastructures to coordinate marketing, which requires one particular set of skills. But now they've begun to establish three or four major manufacturing operations around the world, and they need a different set of skills to integrate these manufacturing operations. In addition, many Japanese companies are trying to add some elements of a multinational strategy back into their global one.

American multinationals have tended to take a different path. The huge domestic market, combined with cultural isolation, has fostered an "us-them" mentality within organizations. This split has made it difficult to fully adapt to the needs of international business. Until recently, overseas posts have been spurned. A marketing manager for new products in a United States consumer products company told us that running the sizable United Kingdom business would be a step down for him. As a result of others' similar views, many American firms face two conflicting challenges today. They need to complete their internationalization by increasing their adaptation to local needs, while at the same time they need to make their strategies more global.

But some companies are better off not trying to compete globally because of the difficulties of their internal situation. The CEO of one midwest manufacturer decided that his company had to go global to survive. He gave marching orders. And the organization marched. Unfortunately, they started marching over a global cliff. For example, they set up a small operation in Brazil since they had targeted South America as part of their global strategy. But the executives they appointed to run the operation had never been outside the United States before, and the company started losing money. Company analysis found that going global was just too unnatural to its cultural system and that a viable strategic alternative was to stay in the United States and play a niche strategy.

Most international companies have grappled with the types of problems we have been describing, and have tried to find a solution. This paper provides a framework for thinking through this complex and important issue. In particular the framework addresses the dual challenge of formulating and implementing a global strategy. Readers may find the framework a convenient way to analyze globalization issues.

THE DUAL CHALLENGE

Managers who want to make their businesses global face two major challenges. First, they need to figure out what a global strategy is. Then, when they know what to do, they have to get their organizations to make it happen.

DIFFERENT WAYS OF BEING GLOBAL

Developing a global strategy is complicated by the fact that there are at least five major dimensions of globalization. These are:

- Playing big in major markets.
- Standardizing the core product.
- Concentrating value-adding activities in a few countries.
- Adopting a uniform market positioning and marketing mix.
- Integrating competitive strategy across countries.

Each of these can offer significant benefits:

Playing Big in Major Markets

Playing big in major markets—countries that account for a sizable share of worldwide volume or where changes in technology or consumer tastes are most likely to start—brings these benefits:

- Larger volume over which to amortize development efforts and investments in fixed assets.
- Ability to manage countries as one portfolio, including being able to exploit differences in position along the product life cycle.
- Learning from each country.
- Being at the cutting edge of the product category by participating in the one or two major countries that lead development.

Standardizing the Core Product

The local managers of multinational subsidiaries face strong pressures to adapt their offerings to local requirements. This gets the company laudably close to the customer. But the end result can be such great differences among products offered in various countries that the overall business garners few benefits of scale.

The core product can be standardized while customizing more superficial aspects of the offering. McDonald's has done well with this approach—Europeans and Japanese may think they are eating the same hamburgers as Americans, but the ingredients have been adapted for their tastes. A French McDonald's even serves alcohol. But the core formula remains the same.

Concentrating Value-adding Activities in a Few Countries

Instead of repeating every activity in each country, a pure global strategy provides for concentration of activities in just a few countries. For example, fundamental research is conducted in just one country, commercial development in two or three countries, manufacturing in a few countries, and core marketing programs developed at regional centers, while selling and customer service take place in every country in the network. The benefits include gaining economies of scale and leveraging the special skills or strengths of particular countries. For example, the lower wage rates and higher skills in countries such as Malaysia or Hong Kong have encouraged many electronics firms to centralize worldwide assembly operations in these countries.

Adopting a Uniform Market Positioning and Marketing Mix

The more uniform the market positioning and marketing mix, the more the company can save in the cost of developing marketing strategies and programs. As one company told us, "Good ideas are scarce. By taking a uniform approach we can exploit those ideas in the maximum number of countries." Another benefit is internal focus. A company may struggle with numerous brand names and positionings around the world, while its rivals single-mindedly promote just one or two brands. There also are marketing benefits to a common brand name as international travel and cross-border media continue to grow. In consolidating its various names around the world, Exxon rapidly achieved global focus and recognition. Coca-Cola, Levis, and McDonald's are other companies that have successfully used a single-brand strategy. Mercedes, BMW, and Volvo not only use the same brand name throughout the world, but also have consistent images and positionings in different countries.

Integrating Competitive Moves Across Countries

Instead of making competitive decisions in a country without regard to what is happening in other countries, a global competitor can take an integrated approach. Tyrolia, the Austrian ski-binding manufacturer, attacked Salomon's stronghold position in its biggest market, the United States. Rather than fighting Tyrolia only in the US, Salomon retaliated in the countries where Tyrolia generated a large share of its sales and profits—Germany and Austria. Taking a global perspective, Salomon viewed the whole world—not just one country—as its competitive battleground.

Another benefit of integrating competitive strategy is the ability of a company to cross-subsidize. This involves utilizing cash generated in a profitable, high-market-share country to invest aggressively in a strategically important but low-market-share country. The purpose is, of course, to optimize results worldwide.

INDUSTRY DRIVERS OF GLOBALIZATION

How can a company decide whether it should globalize a particular business? What sort of global strategy should it pursue? Managers should look first to the business's industry. An industry's potential for globalization is driven by market, economic, environmental and competitive factors (see Chart 1).[2] Market forces determine the customers' receptivity to a global product; economic factors determine whether pursuing a global strategy can provide a cost advantage; environmental factors show whether the necessary supporting infrastructure is there; and competitive factors provide a spur to action.

The automotive industry provides a good example of all four forces. People in the industry now talk of "world cars." A number of *market factors* are pushing the industry toward globalization, including a mature market, similar demand trends across countries (such as quality/reliability and fuel efficiency), shortening product life cycles (e.g., twelve years for the Renault 5, eight for the Renault 18, and five each for the Renault 11 and Renault 9), and worldwide image-building. Similarly, *economic factors* are pushing the automotive industry toward globalization. For example, economies of scale, particularly on engines and transmissions, are very important, and few country markets provide enough volume to get full benefits of these econo-

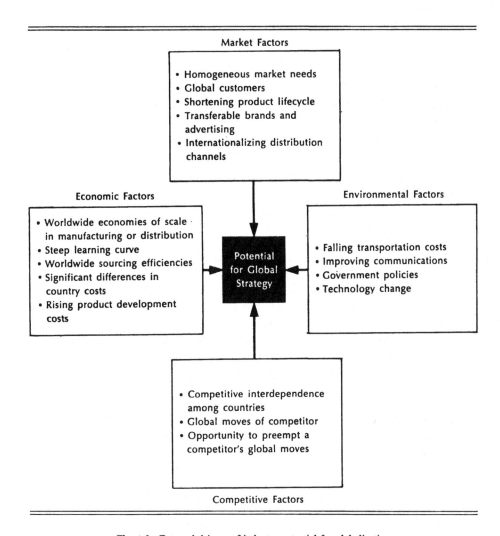

Chart 1 External drivers of industry potential for globalization.

mies of scale. Similarly, many car manufacturers have now moved to worldwide sourcing. In the *environmental* area, converging regulations (safety, emissions) and rapid technological evolution (new materials, electronics, robotics), all requiring heavy investment in R&D and plant and equipment, also are moving the industry inexorably toward globalization. Finally, *competitive* factors are contributing to globalization. Witness the increasing number of cooperative ventures among manufacturers—Toyota-GM, Toyo Kogyo-Ford, Chrysler-Mitsubishi. These ventures are putting pressure on all automotive manufacturers to go global.

In summary, managers wrestling with globalization issues should first analyze the four sets of industry forces to determine whether they compete in an industry that is global or globalizing. Next, they need to assess how global their companies are, and how global their competitors are, along the five dimensions defined previously. This step—which is illustrated in the Appendix— helps define the broad direction of the strategic moves needed to change their company's global competitive posture. A very difficult part remains: assessing whether the organization has the capacity to go global.

ORGANIZATIONAL FACTORS IN GLOBALIZATION

Organizational factors can support or undercut a business's attempt to globalize.[3] Therefore, taking a close look at how the organization will affect the relative difficulty of globalization is essential. Four factors affect the ability of an organization to develop and implement global strategy: organization structure, management processes, people and culture (see Chart 2). Each of these aspects of organization operates powerfully in different ways. A common mistake, in implementing *any* strategy, is to ignore one or more of them, particularly the less tangible ones such as culture.

Organization Structure

- *Centralization of global authority.* One of the most effective ways to develop and implement a global strategy is to centralize authority, so all units of the business around the world report to a common sector head. Surprisingly few companies do this. Instead, they are tied for historical reasons to a strong country-based organization where the main line of authority runs by country rather than by business. In a company pursuing a global strategy, the business focus should dominate the country focus. It's difficult, but necessary.
- *Domestic/international split.* A common structural barrier to global strategy is an organizational split between domestic and international divisions. The international division oversees a group of highly autonomous country subsidiaries, each of which manages several distinct businesses. A global strategy for any one of these businesses can then be coordinated only at the CEO level. This split is very common among US firms, partly for historical reasons and partly because of the enormous size of the US market. Ironically, some European multinationals with small domestic markets have separated out not their home market but the US market. As a result they find it difficult to get their US subsidiaries to cooperate in the development and implementation of global strategy. In one European company we know the heads of worldwide business sectors go hat in hand to New York to solicit support for their worldwide strategies.

Management Processes

While organization structure has a very direct effect on management behavior, it is management processes that power the system. The appropriate processes can even substitute to some extent for the appropriate structure.

- *Cross-country coordination.* Providing cross-country coordination is a common way to make up for the lack of a direct reporting structure. Some consumer packaged goods companies are beginning to appoint European brand managers to coordinate strategy across countries.
- *Global planning.* Too often strategic plans are developed separately for each country and are not aggregated globally for each business across all countries. This makes it difficult to understand the business's competitive position worldwide and to develop an integrated strategy against competitors who plan on a global basis.

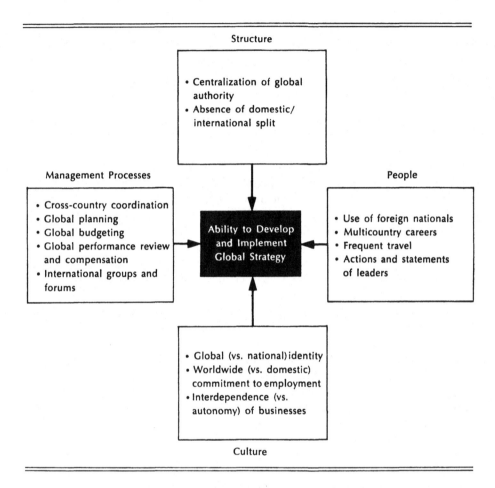

Chart 2 Internal factors that facilitate a global strategy.

- *Global budgeting.* Similarly, country budgets need to be consolidated into a global total for each product line to aid the allocation of resources across product lines. Surprisingly few companies do this.
- *Global performance review and compensation.* Rewards, especially bonuses, need to be set in a way that reinforces the company's global objectives. An electronics manufacturer, for example, decided to start penetrating the international market by introducing a new product through its strongest division. The division head's bonus was based on current year's world-wide sales, with no distinction between domestic and international sales. Because increasing his domestic sales was easier—and had a much quicker pay off—than trying to open new international markets, the division head didn't worry much about his international sales. Predictably, the firm's market penetration strategy failed.
- *International groups and forums.* Holding international forums allows exchange of information and building of relationships across countries. This in turn makes it easier for country nationals to gain an understanding of whether the differences they perceive between their home country and others are real or imagined. It also facilitates the development of common

products and the coordination of marketing approaches. For example, a French manufacturer of security devices uses councils of country managers, with different countries taking the lead on different products. While this approach is time-consuming, the company has found that this reliance on line managers makes it easier for various countries to accept the input of other countries, and thus for global approaches to be pursued by all.

People

Being truly global also involves using people in a different way from that of a multinational firm.

- *Use foreign nationals.* High-potential foreign nationals need to gain experience not only in their home country, but also at headquarters and in other countries. This practice has three benefits: broadening the pool of talent available for executive positions; demonstrating the commitment of top management to internationalization; and giving talented individuals an irreplaceable development opportunity. US companies have been slow to do this, particularly at the most senior ranks.

   Promoting foreigners, and using staff from various countries, has often paid off. In the 1970s, an ailing NCR vaulted William S. Anderson, the British head of their Asian business, to the top job. Anderson is widely credited with turning around NCR. A French packaged goods manufacturer undertook seven years ago to move its European staff from country to country. Today, of fifteen staff members working at headquarters, seven are French, three are English, three are German and two are Italian. The company credits this practice—among others—for its remarkable turnaround.
- *Require multicountry careers.* Making work experience in different countries necessary for progression, rather than a hindrance, is another step that helps a company become truly global. One electronics manufacturer decided to make a major push into Japan, but an executive offered a transfer there was loath to take it. He was unsure a job would remain for him when he came back. As he put it, "The road to the executive suite lies through Chicago, not Osaka."
- *Travel frequently.* Senior managers must spend a large amount of time in foreign countries. The CEO of a large grocery products company we have worked with spends half his time outside the United States—a visible demonstration of the importance and commitment of the company to its international operations.
- *State global intentions.* The senior management of a company that wants to go global needs to constantly restate that intention and to act accordingly. Otherwise, the rank and file won't believe that the globalization strategy is real. One test among many is the prominence given to international operations in formal communications such as the chairman's letter in the annual report and statements to stock analysts.

Culture

Culture is the most subtle aspect of organization, but, as shown below, it can play a formidable role in helping or hindering a global strategy.

- *Global (vs national) identity.* Does the company have a strong national identity? This can hinder the willingness and ability to design global products and programs. It can also create a "them and us" split among employees. One firm was making a strong global push, and yet many of its corporate executives wore national flag pins! European companies are generally well in advance of both American and Japanese firms in adopting a global identity.

- *Worldwide (vs. domestic) commitment to employment.* Many American companies view their domestic employees as more important than their overseas employees and are much more committed to preserving domestic employment than to developing employment regardless of location. This often leads them to decide to keep expensive manufacturing operations in the United States, rather than relocate them to lower-cost countries. This puts them at a competitive cost disadvantage and threatens their overall competitive position.
- *Interdependence (vs. autonomy) of businesses.* A high level of autonomy for local business can also be a barrier to globalization.

In sum, the four internal factors of organization structure, management processes, people and culture play a key role in a company's move toward globalization.

For example, a company with a strong structural split between domestic and international activities, management processes that are country—rather than business—driven, people who work primarily in their home countries, and a parochial culture is likely to have difficulty implementing integrated competitive strategies. If the analysis of external drivers has shown that such strategies are necessary for market, competitive, environmental, or economic reasons, top management needs to either adapt the internal environment to the strategic moves the company needs to make—or decide that the profound organizational changes needed are too risky. In the latter case, the company should avoid globalization and compete based on its existing organizational strengths.

CONCLUSION

There are many ways to pursue a global strategy. Industry forces play a major role in determining whether going global makes sense. An analysis of a company's competitive position against the five dimensions of globalization—major market participation, product standardization, activity specialization, uniform market positioning and integrated competitive strategy—helps define the appropriate approach for a globalization strategy. Finally, and very importantly, the ability of the organization to implement the different elements of global strategy needs to be considered.

Matching the external and internal imperatives is critical. For example, we have worked with a company whose culture included the following characteristics:

- A high degree of responsiveness to customers' requests for product tailoring.
- A strong emphasis on letting every business and every country be highly autonomous.
- A desire for 100% control over foreign operations.
- A commitment to preserving domestic employment.

The difficulty the company found in pursuing a globalization strategy is illustrated in the strategy/culture fit matrix in Exhibit 3. The matrix helped management articulate the pros and cons of the three major options they could pursue: a pure global strategy with an organizational revolution; a series of incremental changes in both strategy and organization, leading to a mixed strategy of globalization/national responsiveness; and an explicit rejection of globalization, accompanied with a conscious decision to build on the company's existing organizational and cultural characteristics to develop a pure national responsiveness strategy. This enabled them to make fundamental and realistic choices rather than assuming the unavoidable dominance of strategy over organization and of globalization over national responsiveness.

Competing globally is tough. It requires a clear vision of the firm as a global competitor, a long-term time horizon, a concerted effort to match strategy and organization changes, a cosmo-

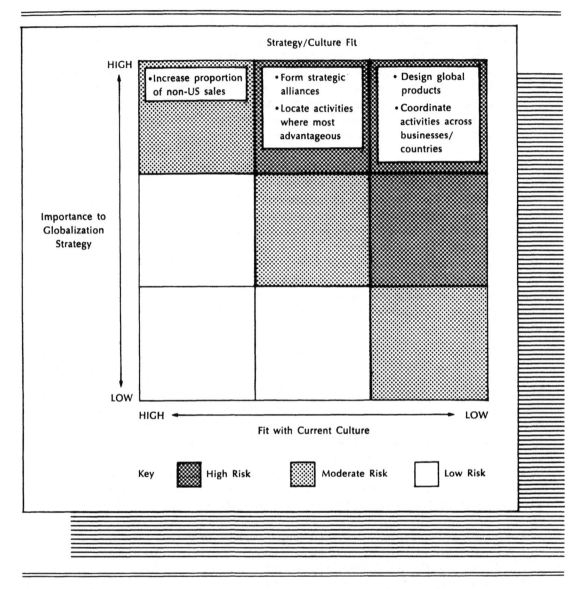

Chart 3 Identification of high-risk areas in implementing a global strategy.

politan view and a substantial commitment from the top. But the result can be the opportunity to gain significant competitive advantage through cost, focus, and concentration, and improved response to customers' needs and preferences.

APPENDIX

To illustrate use of the global strategy framework, or global strategy audit, we summarize here the experiences of two companies, both of them multibillion-dollar multinationals. One company, disguised as "TransElectronics," is a US-based concern operating in many aspects of electronics. The other company, disguised as "Persona," is a European-based manufacturer and marketer of consumer packaged goods. The two companies provide different views of the challenge of global strategy. TransElectronics is still developing as a fully multinational company and faces the challenge of accelerating that process to become a global competitor. Persona, on the other hand, has long been thoroughly multinational, with many highly autonomous companies operating around the world. Its challenge is to temper some aspects of that multinational autonomy to compete more effectively on a global basis.

TransElectronics

Step 1—Identify business unit
All six TransElectronics business sectors faced pressing issues of global competition. The Communications Sector had one division, Electron, based in the United States, that sold what we will call "transcramblers" against fierce European and Japanese competition. A major market, Japan, closed until recently to foreign competition, was beginning to open through a combination of TransElectronics' efforts and US government pressure on Japanese trade barriers. So developing a global strategy for transcramblers was a high priority for TransElectronics. A complication was that Electron was not a stand-alone business unit—other units had related responsibilities. As we will describe, this split of responsibilities was one of the major barriers to Electron's implementation of a global strategy.

Step 2—Evaluate industry potential for globalization
Market factors pushed for globalization: there were few differences among countries in what they wanted from transcramblers. On the other hand, few global customers existed because of strong national boundaries between public sector customers (PTTs), who accounted for a large share of the market.

Economic factors strongly pushed for globalization. There were substantial scale economies and learning effects, sourcing efficiencies could be gained by consolidating manufacturing, and Electron's labor costs—a significant part of the product's total cost—were much lower in Puerto Rico and Taiwan than they were in the United States.

Environmental factors also pushed for globalization. The privatization of some national PTTs was opening up previously closed markets, and products were becoming more standardized in Europe around a common format. An offsetting factor was local content requirements in many countries.

Competitive forces were also in line. Electron's major competitors (European and Japanese) took a global product approach with fewer price levels and minimum product customization. They also had largely centralized their manufacturing activities in just one or two countries each.

In conclusion, strong external forces pushed the transcrambler industry toward globalization. Not only was globalization already high, it was likely to continue increasing.

Step 3—Evaluate current extent of globalization
Market participation. Electron was quite global in its market participation. Its sale split among countries closely matched that of the industry.

Product standardization. Electron's product line was highly standardized—in fact, more so than its executives realized. They initially thought that their product was not standard across countries because 40% of the product cost was in a decoder that was different in each country. But digging deeper, however, they discovered that within the decoder only the software was unique. Furthermore, the software was embodied in purchased parts (masked ROMs). Therefore, there was no difference in the manufacturing process, only in the inventory to be kept. Also, the cost of developing the unique software was amortized over a large sales base. As a result, what initially appeared to be 40% nonstandard turned out to be 3% nonstandard.

Activity concentration. Electron's R&D and purchasing activities were specialized in the US, but much of their manufacturing was dispersed across the US, Puerto Rico, Taiwan, and Europe. Marketing was primarily done in the US. Selling, distribution and service were by necessity done locally but were not coordinated across countries. Electron's competitors were all much more centralized and coordinated.

Marketing uniformity. The product positioning of transcramblers was consistent across countries, as was that of Electron's competitors. If anything, TransElectronics' marketing policies were too uniform, given a rigid pricing policy that did not allow Electron to adapt to the wide variations in price across countries. As a result, Electron did not use price as a strategic weapon.

Integration of competitive moves. Electron did not integrate its competitive moves across countries, nor did its competitors.

Step 4—Identify strategic need for change in the extent of globalization

From the previous analyses, Electron concluded that its extent of globalization was significantly lower than the industry potential, and lower than its competitors' globalization. Furthermore, the industry potential for globalization was steadily increasing. It was clear that Electron had a strong need to develop a more global strategy. The next issue was whether Electron would be able to implement such a strategy.

Step 5—Evaluate organizational factors

Structure. TransElectronics' structure worked in two major ways against a global strategy. First, TransElectronics operated with a strong domestic/international split within each sector. Second, worldwide responsibilities for Electron's business were scattered throughout the organization. The Electron division itself had responsibility for some product development, some manufacturing and some marketing. Other divisions in the US and overseas shared these responsibilities. Selling was the responsibility of both local non-US countries, and in the US, of a totally separate distribution group for the entire communications sector. In effect, there was no one manager below the sector head who had global authority over transcramblers.

Management processes. The budget process worked against a global approach. The Electron division budgeted only a total number for overseas sales, without country targets. The International Group in the Communications Sector set country quotas for the entire sector, without product quotas or product-by-country quotas. The strategic planning process did not help either. The Electron division and the International Group developed separate plans simultaneously. There were no international components in the bonus for domestic managers.

People. TransElectronics' employee practices worked against a global approach. There were few foreign nationals in the US at either corporate or divisional levels. There were many foreign nationals overseas, but these were mostly in their home countries, and there was little movement between international and domestic jobs. In particular, the US divisions were reluctant to give up people, and overseas assignments were not seen as being part of a desirable career track.

Culture. TransElectronics' corporate culture worked against a global view in both obvious and subtle ways. At the obvious level, TransElectronics was very much an American company with a "them-us" mentality. Indeed, the chairman had made speeches calling for increased trade barriers against Japanese firms. More subtly, TransElectronics had a very strong culture of being responsible to customer requests for product tailoring, born of a heritage of selling exclusively to a very small number of automotive customers. This culture worked strongly against attempts to standardize globally.

Step 6—Identify organizational ability to implement globalization

TransElectronics clearly had a very low organizational ability to develop a global strategy for transcramblers. They had certainly experienced many difficulties in their fitful attempts at doing so.

Step 7—Diagnose scope and direction of required changes

In summary, the most important business changes that Electron had to make were to exploit more opportunities for product standardization and to specialize somewhat more where different activities (particularly manufacturing) were conducted.

More widespread changes were needed in terms of management and organization. While many aspects of these needed to change, the most implementable change was in terms of management process. TransElectronics adopted for the transcrambler business a global strategic planning process and globally based evaluation and compensation. These relatively modest changes would pave the way for future acceptance of the more radical changes needed in organization structure, people and culture.

Persona

Step 1—Identify business unit

As in the case of Electron, there were difficulties in defining the relevant business unit. Persona had operating companies around the world that sold many kinds of personal-care as well as other household products. The global strategy audit was conducted for one particular product, "hairfloss," that was sold around the world.

Step 2—Evaluate industry potential for globalization

Market factors pushed strongly for globalization: market needs were very much the same around the world within income categories—higher-income countries were earlier users of the new variants and ingredients that were introduced every few years. Brand names and advertising were also widely transferable—some competitors used just one major brand name and essentially the same advertising campaign around the world.

Economic factors were less important, given that product costs were only about 25% of total costs, economies of scale were low and price was not a major basis of competition. Also the low value-to-weight ratio of hairfloss made it uneconomical to ship far. Nonetheless, there was some centralized manufacturing on a multicountry regional basis, e.g., parts of Western Europe, Southeast Asia and Africa.

Environmental factors did not particularly favor globalization. In Western Europe, however, the increasing importance of multicountry media, particularly satellite television with wide reception, and of the European Economic Community, pushed for regional, if not global, approaches.

Competitive behavior was the major force pushing the industry to globalization. Persona faced three major worldwide competitors, multinationals like itself. Two of these competitors took a much more standardized approach than Persona—they concentrated their resources behind the same one or two brands of hairfloss in each country. In contrast, Persona tended to market three or four brands in each country, and these brands were different among major countries. Persona's competitors also were quick to transfer successful innovations from one country to the next, while Persona's brand fragmentation hindered its efforts. This global fragmentation seemed to be a major reason behind Persona's slipping market share and profitability.

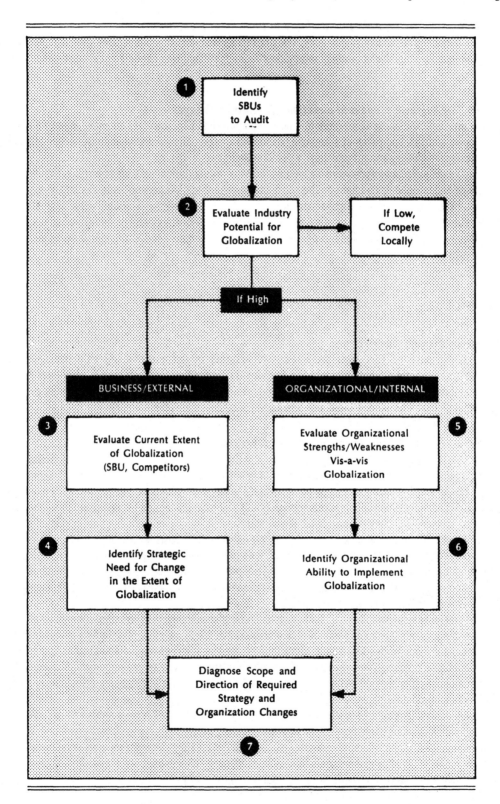

Chart 4 The steps of the global strategy audit.

Persona concluded that there were strong external forces pushing the hairfloss industry toward globalization—at least to the extent of coordinated regional operations—and this push toward globalization was likely to increase in the future.

Step 3—Evaluate current extent of globalization

Market participation. Persona participated in markets that accounted for almost 90% of worldwide (excluding communist countries) hairfloss volume. The largest competitor, not Persona, participated in almost 100%.

Product standardization. Persona's hairfloss product line was quite highly standardized around half a dozen variants. Persona generally marketed a large number of variants in wealthier countries, but the variants were still basically the same across countries.

Activity concentration. Like most consumer packaged goods multinationals, Persona practiced very little specialization by country. Persona fielded a full business operation in most countries.

Marketing uniformity. On this dimension of globalization Persona was severely lacking because of its multiple brands, multiple product positionings and multiple advertising campaigns.

Integration of competitive moves. Persona did not do much to integrate its competitive moves across countries, although it had begun recently to experiment with such attempts.

Overall, Persona's actual extent of globalization was somewhat lower than that of its competitors.

Step 4—Identify strategic need for change in the extent of globalization

In conclusion, while Persona's worldwide hairfloss strategy was quite global in some respects, the lack of marketing uniformity was the biggest problem. The key variables that Persona could manipulate were brand name and positioning. First, to increase local marketing muscle, Persona needed to reduce the number of brands in each country to two. Second, to achieve the benefits of global market uniformity, they had three broad alternatives:

1. A different brand but common positioning for each product variant in each country.
2. A common regional brand and positioning.
3. A common global brand and positioning.

Because Persona already had strong brand names around the world that it did not want to abandon, and because a common positioning would achieve most of the benefits of uniformity, the company concluded that the second alternative was best. The next issue was whether Persona would be able to implement such a strategy.

Step 5—Evaluate organizational factors

Structure. Persona's structure made it difficult to develop and implement a global strategy. Persona operated with a strong geographic structure that was overlaid with a worldwide product direction function at corporate. This function, however, had advisory rather than direct authority over the individual country businesses. Furthermore, the direction function did not include the US.

Management processes. The budget and compensation systems worked against global strategy. These were done on a strictly local basis, although aggregated geographically. But there was no mechanism to encourage local participation in a worldwide effort. A strategic plan was developed globally, but local acceptance was voluntary.

People. On this score, Persona was very capable of implementing a global strategy. Its managers were drawn from all over the world, and transfer both among countries and to and from corporate were common.

Culture. Culture was the biggest barrier. Persona had a very strong culture of giving autonomy to its local managers. Although corporate leaders increasingly wanted to give direct orders on strategy, they were loath to risk the possible loss of local accountability and commitment.

Step 6—Identify organizational ability to implement globalization

Like TransElectronics, Persona also had a low organizational capacity for global strategy but for somewhat different reasons.

Step 7—Diagnose scope and direction of required changes

In summary, the most important business changes that Persona had to make in hairfloss were to reduce its number of brands in each country and to develop a common brand by region and common positioning for each major product variant.

Organizationally, changing the structure would create too much disruption. What was needed was a greater willingness by corporate to push countries to adopt a global approach. A first step was a directive that all countries should launch the new "high-gloss" variant within a six-month period. Persona hoped that a successful experience of common action would start moving the culture toward greater acceptance of global strategies.

Further Steps

A global strategy audit provides four concrete outputs:

- An assessment of how global the industry is today and is likely to become in the future.
- An understanding of how global the firm's approach is today and how it compares to its competitors and to the industry potential for further globalization.
- An identification of the organizational factors that will facilitate or hinder a move toward globalization.
- A broad action plan, specifying strategic and organizational change priorities.

The audit, in and of itself, does not provide the details of a competitive strategy. If its output has shown that adopting some form of global strategy is indeed desirable, the audit needs to be followed by another effort aimed at developing a detailed global strategy. Among the decisions that will need to be made are the definition of a competitive posture in various countries (i.e., in what part of the world should we compete on our own, and in what part should we form alliances?); the articulation of specific functional strategies (manufacturing, marketing, financial, etc.) and, for each function, of the appropriate balance between global and local approaches (for example, all elements of manufacturing could be global, while some elements of marketing, such as sales promotion, might remain local); and the adoption of organizational mechanisms aimed at reinforcing the strategic objectives sought.

However, the audit provides a relatively simple and quick way to get answers to some of the most complicated questions facing corporate management today. It also greatly facilitates the undertaking of the strategy development phase that follows, because it has identified the major thrusts that are needed. Furthermore, it has the potential for avoiding major errors—such as a move toward globalization when none is warranted. Finally, it sensitizes the organization to the issues and to the commitments needed if it really decides to compete globally.

NOTES

1. See Theodore Levitt's arguments in "The Globalization of Markets," *Harvard Business Review,* May-June 1983, pp. 92-102. For a counterargument, see Susan P. Douglas and Yoram Wind, "The Myth of Globalization," *Columbia Journal of World Business,* Winter 1987, pp. 19-29.

2. For related frameworks on the role of industry forces in global strategy, see Thomas Hout, Michael E. Porter, and Eileen Rudden, "How Global Companies Win Out," *Harvard Business Review,* September-October 1982, pp. 98-109. Also Porter, "Changing the Patterns of International Competition," *California Management Review,* Winter 1986, pp. 9-40; and Porter, editor, *Competition in Global Industries,* Boston, MA: Harvard Business School Press, 1986. Bruce Kogut takes a somewhat different view in "Designing Global Strategies," *Sloan Management Review,* Summer 1985, pp. 15-28, and Fall 1985, pp. 27-38.

3. For a discussion of organizational issues in global strategy, see Christopher A. Bartlett, "MNCs: Get Off the Reorganization Merry-Go-Round," *Harvard Business Review,* March-April 1983, pp. 138-146; Christopher A. Bartlett and Sumantra Goshal, "Tap Your Subsidiaries for Global Reach," *Harvard Business Review,* November-December 1986, pp. 87-94. Also Gary Hamel and C. K. Prahalad, "Do You Really Have a Global Strategy?" *Harvard Business Review,* July-August 1985, pp. 139-148; and C. K. Prahalad and Yves L. Doz, *The Multinational Mission: Balancing Local Demands and Global Vision,* New York: The Free Press, 1987.

4. For global marketing strategy, see John A. Quelch and Edward J. Hoff, "Customizing Global Marketing," *Harvard Business Review,* May-June 1986, pp. 59-68.

5. For a discussion of different types of global strategic planning, see Balaji S. Chakravarthy and Howard V. Perlmutter, "Strategic Planning for a Global Business," *Columbia Journal of World Business,* Summer 1985, pp. 3-10; and David C. Shanks, "Strategic Planning for Global Competition," *Journal of Business Strategy,* Winter 1985, pp. 80-89.

6. See John J. Dyment's discussion of global budgeting in "Strategies and Management Controls for Global Corporations," *Journal of Business Strategy,* Spring 1987, pp. 20-26.

Part Two

Review and Questions

Review

Must *all* companies adopt global strategies to compete in a global marketplace? This question and related issues are addressed by the three papers in Part Two.

At the start of his paper, Porter asks, "What are the distinctive questions for competitive strategy that are raised by international as opposed to domestic competition?" In responding, he asserts that the appropriate unit of analysis is the *industry* because that is where competitive advantage is won or lost. Also, the pattern of international competition differs markedly from one industry to another. These differences range from multidomestic industries, where competition in one country is independent of competition in other countries, to global industries, where a firm's position in one country is significantly affected by its position in other countries. In a multidomestic industry, a firm may choose whether to compete internationally, but in a global industry, a firm must integrate its activities on a worldwide scale to ensure linkages among countries. Even in a global industry, however, the firm must maintain some country perspective. Indeed, a key question in global strategy is how to balance country and global perspectives.

To help formulate global strategies, Porter offers a model based on the concept of a "value chain." He asserts that competitive advantage can be understood only at the level of discrete activities rather than from the firm as a whole. The distinctive issues in international strategy are expressed in two dimensions: the *configuration* of its value chain or the answer to the question, Where in the world is the activity performed?, and (2) the *coordination* of its value chain, or the answer to the question, How are like activities performed in different countries coordinated with each other? Configuration runs from concentration in one country to dispersal over all countries; coordination runs from low to high. Global strategy is defined as a strategy in which a firm seeks to gain competitive advantage from its international presence through concentrating activities, coordinating dispersed activities, or both. Porter believes that the imperatives of global strategy are shifting in ways that will require international firms to rebalance configuration and coordination.

In drawing a distinction between global strategy and comparative advantage, Porter introduces the concept of *global platform*. Global platform explains how a country's comparative advantage and demand characteristics can create an environment that gives an advantage to firms domiciled in that country in terms of competing *globally* in a particular industry.

Morrison, Ricks, and Roth assert that two fundamental assumptions drive the thinking about global strategies: (1) a large number of competitors use global strategies, and (2) global strategies can improve performance. A research project involving 115 medium and large MNCs and 103 affiliated subsidiaries in North America, Japan, and Europe was undertaken to examine these twin assumptions.

According to the authors, U.S. managers in the past held that the U.S. market was paramount and that business practices successful at home would be successful abroad. Many U.S. companies thus entered the foreign market either by exporting or by establishing foreign subsidiaries as "miniature replicas" of the U.S. parent. But this home-country orientation began to unravel in the late 1970s with the decline in U.S. economic dominance. By the mid-1980s, several academic articles argued the merits of global strategies. This notion appealed to corporate managers, largely because global strategies are best managed through tight central control. However, the authors' research failed to uncover widespread support for global strategies. U.S. firms and, to a lesser extent, Japanese and European firms, continued to regard the home market as preeminent in investment, production, and other ways. Managers viewed the advantages of globalization as more theoretical than real.

In the last half of the 1980s, the rise of *regional* blocs led many companies to reassess their international strategies. Regionalization is viewed by managers as a stepping stone to more effective global competition. To the majority of companies studied, regionalization is a compromise between global strategies and traditional strategies adopted by miniature replica subsidiaries. From their research results, the authors argue that even companies in so-called global industries should determine their competitive strategies on a region-by-region basis although those strategies may also call for transregional "facilitation."

In sum, Morrison, Ricks, and Roth assert that international competition remains more regional than global. What is missing from their paper, however, is an indication of how regionalization varies by industry. From the perspective of Porter's model, different industries or businesses would have different value chains, and different activities in the *same* value chain of a firm's business could be local, regional, or global, depending on the balance of configuration/coordination advantages and disadvantages.

Yip, Loewe, and Yoshino offer a systematic approach to developing and implementing a global strategy. Each company first decides whether it must become a worldwide competitor to survive. This difficult decision depends on managers understanding global strategy, knowing what to do, and getting their organization to make it happen.

To define global strategy, the authors identify five different dimensions of being global. Managers need to assess how global their company is and how global their competitors are along the five dimensions of being global.

Should a company globalize a particular business? To answer this question, the authors introduce a model of "external drivers" that would enable the globalization of an industry: market, economic, environmental, and competitive factors. Managers analyze these factors to determine the globalization potential of their particular industry. After defining the moves necessary to change their company's global competitive posture, managers need to assess whether their company's organization has the capability to go global. This ability to develop and implement a global strategy depends on the organization structure, management processes, people, and culture.

Matching the external imperative and "industry drivers" with the internal imperatives of organizational capability is critical in deciding on a global strategy. In an appendix, the authors apply this *global strategy audit* to two disguised MNCs.

The main contribution of Yip, Loewe, and Yoshino is the specification of a decision process that leads to the development and implementation of a global strategy when the industry drivers of globalization are strong. Although not discussed in the paper, this decision process applies to nonglobal (multidomestic or regional) strategies if the industry drivers are weak. Hence, this process is consistent with the value chain and regionalization approaches of the other two papers in Part Two.

Questions

1. How does Porter define a *multidomestic* industry? A *global* industry?
2. Why, according to Porter, does a firm in a multidomestic industry have a choice to compete internationally? Why is this choice denied a firm in a global industry?
3. What is Porter's value chain?
4. How is global strategy defined by the configuration or coordination of a firm's value chain?
5. What factors favor concentration of a value-chain activity?
6. What factors favor coordination of a value-chain activity?
7. What is Morrison, Ricks, and Roth's "miniature replica" approach to international markets?
8. What caused an upsurge in regional competitive pressures in the last half of the 1980s?
9. What is the argument for regional strategies as opposed to global strategies?
10. According to Yip, Loewe, and Yoshino, what are the five dimensions of being global?
11. What are the external drivers of industry potential for globalization?
12. What steps are involved in a global strategy audit?

Part Three
Designing Organizations to Carry Out International Strategies

Chapter 8

Strategy and Structure in Multinational Corporations: A Revision of the Stopford and Wells Model

William G. Egelhoff
New York University

Abstract *The Stopford and Wells study of strategy and structure in multinational corporations produced a now familiar model relating certain types of structure to certain elements of a firm's international strategy. This paper re-examines the important relationships expressed by the model, using data from a recent study of 34 large U.S. and European multinationals. While some of the relationships are supported, others are not. A new element of strategy, the relative size of foreign manufacturing, is introduced, and found to be an important predictor of structure. Based on the findings, a revised model for relating strategy and structure in MNCs is proposed.*

INTRODUCTION

As the international strategies of firms evolve, and become more complex, it is increasingly difficult to know which types of organizational structure facilitate implementing them. While models linking strategy and structure exist, there is a pressing need for further development. The first empirical work which sought to relate structure to the strategy of an organization was Chandler's (1962) study of 70 large U.S. corporations. It tended to show that as a company's product/market strategy changed it was important that the organization's structure also change to support implementation of the new strategy. Additional studies by Pavan (1972), Channon (1973), Rumelt (1974), and Dyas and Thanheiser (1976) further demonstrated that certain strategies need to be supported by certain structures. A number of empirical studies have also attempted to describe the relationship between strategy and structure for multinational corporations (MNCs) (Brooke and Remmers, 1970; Daniels, Pitts and Tretter, 1984, 1985; Fouraker and Stopford, 1968; Franko, 1976; Stopford and Wells, 1972). Of these, the Stopford and Wells study was the largest and most comprehensive, and it also developed the most explicit theory linking strategy and structure in MNCs.

Reproduced by permission of John Wiley and Sons Limited from *Strategic Management Journal*, Vo. 9, pp. 1–14, 1988.

THE STOPFORD AND WELLS MODEL OF INTERNATIONAL STRATEGY AND STRUCTURE

In their book on strategy implementation, Galbraith and Nathanson (1978) credit Stopford and Wells with having extended the earlier strategy-structure models of Chandler (1962) and Scott (1971) to include international strategy and structure. Figure 1 shows the critical variables and relationships of the Stopford and Wells model, which was empirically derived from data collected on 187 large U.S. MNCs.

Below the international division boundary in Figure 1, foreign product diversity and foreign sales are both relatively low. MNCs employing this strategy tended to support it with an international division structure. As foreign product diversity increased, companies in the sample tended to use product division structures. Similarly, companies pursuing strategies leading to a relatively high percentage of foreign sales tended to use area division structures. When a company's strategy contained both high foreign product diversity and a high percentage of foreign sales. Stopford and Wells hypothesized that MNCs will tend to employ matrix or mixed structures, but the question mark (placed there by Galbraith and Nathanson) indicates there was only weak support for this in Stopford and Wells' data. Although the Stopford and Wells study took place in U.S. MNCs, subsequent research by Franko (1976) in European MNCs tended to confirm the relationships shown in Figure 1.

Recent Concerns About International Strategy and Structure

While recent research has raised some questions about the validity of the international division boundary of the Stopford and Wells Model (Bartlett, 1979, 1983; Daniels et al., 1984; Davidson, 1980; Davidson and Haspeslagh, 1982), the other relationships have essentially gone unchallenged and remain intact. In fact, with the exception of a study by Daniels et al. (1985), the upper and right-hand sides of the model (those portions associated with relatively high levels of foreign

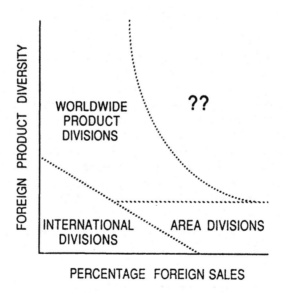

Figure 1 The Stopford and Wells model showing the relationship between strategy and structure in multinational corporations (Reprinted by permission from *Strategy Formulation: The Role of Structure and Process*, by Galbraith and Nathanson. Copyright © 1978 by West Publishing Company. All rights reserved.)

sales and/or foreign product diversity) have remained largely untested since the original research by Stopford and Wells and Franko. These portions of the model (and especially the portion represented as a question mark) are of growing significance, however, since the strategies of more and more MNCs are moving in this direction.

In fact, recent literature has raised a number of specific questions about strategy-structure relationships in the more strategically complex portions of the Model. First, Galbraith and Na- thanson (1978) ask what international strategy fits the matrix structure, since both they and Davis and Lawrence (1977) noted a probable trend toward matrix structures in MNCs. Stopford and Wells suggested that matrix (and mixed) structures might be appropriate for firms in the upper right-hand corner of the model (where both foreign sales and foreign product diversity are high), but their data provided only weak support for this relationship. Since the widespread move to matrix structures expected by Davis and Lawrence has not occurred, despite the fact that many MNC strategies today contain relatively high levels of foreign sales and foreign product diversity, the question about what international strategy fits a matrix structure would still seem to be an open one.

A second issue with strategy-structure implications seems to be raised by Hout, Porter and Rudden (1982). They believe that the increasing growth in global interdependency can best be exploited by global strategies, where the appropriate unit of analysis for strategic planning and management is the global market for a product instead of multiple domestic markets. They point out that global strategies require new, more centralized forms of structure, that can integrate managerial decision-making across many domestic markets that were previously dealt with in a decentralized manner.

A third issue that seems to be influencing international strategy is increasing host government pressure for more national responsiveness in the strategies of MNCs (Doz, 1980; Doz and Prahalad, 1980). This pressure is generally reflected in calls for more local manufacture and R&D, a balance between exports and imports, and sometimes products and technologies that are consistent with national interests. This trend obviously runs counter to the previous trend for global strategies.

These new trends toward global strategies and more national responsiveness have largely come to prominence since the Stopford and Wells study, and subsequent research has not really attempted to integrate these developments into the existing set of strategy-structure relationships for MNCs. This is perhaps not surprising, since the new issues in international strategy seem to be still in the exploratory research phase, while research done under the strategy-structure paradigm has evolved to the point where it requires clearly defined concepts and operational measures. Yet it is important that attempts start to be made to integrate some understanding of the new issues and trends in international strategy into the established set of strategy-structure relationships (as represented by the Stopford and Wells model). Otherwise our understanding of strategy will increasingly outstrip our understanding of how to organize to implement such strategy. In contrast to the decade-long lags between changes in strategy and changes in structure observed by Chandler's study (1962), it is increasingly important for MNC managements to understand strategy-structure relationships and anticipate changes in order to minimize periods of misfit.

The purpose of the present study is to reexamine the key strategy-structure relationships of the Stopford and Wells study and to introduce a new element of international strategy— foreign manufacturing—which Stopford and Wells and other researchers have not considered. The new element is especially important because it seems to capture some of the more recent changes and trends that are altering and complicating the international strategies of MNCs.

STRUCTURES FOR CONDUCTING INTERNATIONAL BUSINESS

This section describes the five types of structure that appeared in the Stopford and Wells study, and are presently used to manage international operations: international divisions, worldwide product divisions, area divisions, matrix structures, and mixed structures. With an international division structure, all foreign subsidiaries report to an international division that is separate from the domestic operations. Communications between the international division and the company's domestic operations are usually poor (Brooke and Remmers, 1970), but there is generally considerable flexibility for foreign subsidiaries to develop strategies that vary according to local conditions. Thus an international division structure facilitates implementing strategies that are responsive to local or national concerns, while it hinders carrying out global product/market strategies.

A worldwide product division structure extends the responsibilities of the domestic product divisions to cover their product lines on a worldwide basis. It tends to centralize and integrate strategic decision-making for a product line, since a single subunit (the product division) has global responsibility for the performance of a product line. This structure is especially suited for realizing global specialization and economies of scale in R&D, manufacturing, and even marketing. At the same time this structure will be less sensitive to local political and economic conditions, since it emphasizes optimizing strategic performance on a global basis.

An area division structure divides the world into geographical areas, each with its own HQ. Each HQ is responsible for all of the company's products and business within its geographical area. Consequently this structure tends to coordinate around, and optimize, performance within a geographical area. Coordination between areas is usually poor (Williams, 1967). To the extent that political and economic conditions within an area are more similar than they are between areas, this structure should lead to strategies that are more responsive to local conditions than those of a worldwide product division structure, but less so than those of an international division structure.

A matrix structure is an overlaying of two of the structures already discussed. Foreign operations report in along two different channels to two different kinds of HQs. For example, in a product division × area division matrix structure, a plastics business in Germany would report in to both the worldwide plastics division HQ (the product channel) and the European area HQ (the geographical area channel). Such a structure can simultaneously develop and implement strategy along two different dimensions. The product division hierarchies will each tend to optimize their product line's performance by coordinating R&D, manufacturing, and perhaps certain aspects of marketing on a global basis. The area division hierarchies, on the other hand, will be largely concerned with exports into and out of a region, achieving economies of scale and market share within a region, and conforming to local government, union, and societal conditions within the region. This added flexibility to simultaneously develop and implement strategy along two different dimensions is not without cost (Davis and Lawrence, 1977; Goggin, 1974). Dual hierarchies involve more managers and staffs, and since the goals and strategic concerns of the two often concern the same resources, considerable managerial effort has to be put into constructive conflict resolution.

Mixed structures involve some foreign operations reporting in to one kind of HQ and other foreign operations reporting in to a different kind of HQ. For example, in a product division and area division mixed structure, the German plastics operations may report in to the worldwide plastics division HQ, while the German cosmetics operations report in to the European HQ. Mixed structures are appropriate when one product line requires a global strategy while another needs to be largely responsive to regional or national conditions.

HYPOTHESES TO BE TESTED

The Stopford and Wells Model can be represented by the following three hypotheses, which the present study will empirically test:

> *Hypothesis 1: Companies with worldwide product division structures will tend to have higher levels of foreign product diversity than companies with international division or area division structures.*

> *Hypothesis 2: Companies with area division structures will tend to have a greater percentage of foreign sales than companies with international division or product division structures.*

> *Hypothesis 3: Companies with matrix and mixed structures will tend to have relatively high levels of both foreign product diversity and foreign sales.*

Not included in these hypotheses is the influence of a new element of strategy on structure, which was included in the present study after preliminary interviews with MNC executives revealed that they thought it significantly affected the parent-foreign subsidiary relationship. This element was what a number of executives saw as a growing shift from exports (from the parent country) to foreign manufacture and the trans-shipment of products within regions. Pressures for more local manufacture and fewer exports from the parent have been discussed by others (Doz and Prahalad, 1980). While there appear to be various reasons for this increase in foreign manufacturing (e.g. host government pressures for local manufacturing, the emergence of tariff-free trading areas such as the Common Market, lower manufacturing costs), they were not *per se* the subject of this study. Instead, it was the influence that this factor seemed to have on the structuring of the parent-subsidiary relationship that argued for its inclusion in the study.

Not only does foreign manufacturing reduce the operating interdependency between the parent's domestic operations and a foreign subsidiary, it seems to frequently increase interdependency among subsidiaries within a region. Since many foreign markets are too small to justify world-class production facilities, there has been a tendency to concentrate production of a product at one point in a region and then trans-ship such products between countries within a region. This kind of regional interdependency appeared to be most strong in Europe (where it is obviously facilitated by the Common Market), but was also apparent in the Far East and to a lesser extent in parts of Latin America. Managers indicated that growth in foreign manufacturing and regional interdependency required regional plans, staffs, and sometimes regional headquarters.

METHOD

Sample

The sample contained 24 U.S. and 26 European headquartered MNCs and was spread across the following industry groups: auto/truck, electrical/telecommunications equipment, industrial equipment, chemicals, pharmaceuticals, consumer-packaged goods, and tires. From the *Fortune Directories of the 500 Largest U.S. Industrial Corporations* and the *500 Largest Industrial Corporations Outside the U.S.*, the 50 largest companies in these industries (including three not in these industries) were selected. Companies with less than 15 percent foreign sales, or with only minimal foreign manufacturing, were excluded for not being sufficiently multinational. Several companies were also excluded because it was common knowledge they were experiencing major international operating problems. Thus the sample should be representative of the population of large, successful MNCs. This approach is generally similar to that used in the Stopford and Wells study, which also confined itself to firms in the *Fortune 500*.

Data for the present study were collected through structured interviews conducted at each company's headquarters and from published company documents. Type of structure was first discovered during the interviews. Thirty-four companies had one of the structures covered by the Stopford and Wells Model (see Table 1). Of the remaining 16 MNCs, five had a worldwide functional division structure, one a direct reporting structure, one a structure based on size of foreign subsidiary, and nine some form of matrix or mixed structure that was not based on area divisions and product divisions. Since the purpose of this paper is to deal with those structures represented in the Stopford and Wells Model, only the 34 MNCs with similar structures are used in the subsequent analyses.

Table 1 shows considerable relationship between nationality and the type of structure used by a company. MNCs with an international division or area division structure tend to be U.S. companies, while those with worldwide product division structures tend to be European. As a result of differences in goals and environments, European MNCs may consistently possess different international strategies than U.S. MNCs, and, as a consequence, they may frequently require different structures than U.S. companies. Chandler (1962), Stopford and Wells (1972), and other strategy-structure researchers have argued that all organizations much achieve a satisfactory fit or congruence between their strategies and structures if they are to be successful. The present study takes the view that the nature of this fit between strategy and structure should not differ with the nationality of the parent company, even though strategies and their elements (such as the percentage of foreign sales) will clearly vary with nationality.

Studies of U.K. companies (Channon, 1973); French and German companies (Dyas and Thanheiser, 1976); and Italian companies (Pavan, 1972) have tended to find the same relationships between specific elements of strategy (e.g. product diversity) and structure as Chandler and Stopford and Wells found in U.S. companies. Egelhoff (1982) has advanced a conceptual argument for the invariance of critical strategy-structure relationships across cultures. He argues that the information-processing capacities of a structure are essentially the same whether the structure is populated with Germans or Americans, and, consequently, the capacity of a structure to cope with or fit a given strategy can be generalized across nationalities.

Measures

The classification of organizational structure was done by either obtaining, or in some cases constructing with the help of organizational members, organization charts for each company. At least 1/2 hour was spent with organization members directly discussing the structure and how it worked. The total interview time spent in each company varied from 5 to 8 hours, and a great

Table 1
Structure and Nationality of Companies

	U.S.	Europe	Total
International divisions	6	1	7
Area divisions	8	2	10
Product divisions	2	10	12
PD × AD matrix		2	2
PD & AD mixed	2	1	3
	18	16	34

Note. PD × AD — Product divisions × Area divisions matrix structures;
PD & AD — Product divisions & Area divisions mixed structures.

deal of additional data, not used in the present study, was also collected. The collection of this additional data generally provided an opportunity to validate the initial classification of structure.

Foreign product diversity was measured by the number of broad product lines a company offered for sale in two designated foreign countries. In all but a few cases, one was the company's largest European subsidiary and the other was Brazil. Since both tended to be large, actively developed markets for most companies in the sample, the product offerings in these two markets were considered representative of the company's total foreign product offering. Correlation between these two measures was high ($R = 0.87$), and the highest of these two measures was used to represent the company's foreign product diversity.

The number of broad product lines in a subsidiary was measured during interviews with knowledgeable company executives. In order to be considered a separate broad product line, products had to have either a different manufacturing technology (i.e. cannot be made with the same manufacturing facility) or different customers and end uses, or both. For example, in a pharmaceutical company, pharmaceuticals, veterinary supplies and cosmetics are considered separate broad product lines. This approach led to eight categories of foreign product diversity, where the final category was 'eight or more' broad product lines (four companies fell into this final category).

The concept of product diversity as an important contingency variable for organizational structure was first defined and operationalized by Chandler (1962). Although he did not develop a quantitative measure of product diversity, he identified its impact on organizational structure in terms of the different kinds of technical knowledge and customer characteristics with which the organization had to cope. The present study's attempt to measure product diversity in terms of technological and market differences is consistent with Chandler's original notion about why product diversity creates pressures for new organizational structures.

The Stopford and Wells study used a different operational measure of foreign product diversity. It measured the number of two-digit SIC codes which were represented by a company's foreign manufacturing. Using this method, Stopford and Wells identified three levels of foreign product diversity, ranging from none (all products in one SIC code) to high (products in three or more SIC codes). Generally, it appears the SIC codes reflect technology and market differences, although the linkage has not been made as explicit as with the broad product line measure used in the present study.

The percentage of foreign sales was measured by the percentage of a company's sales occurring outside the parent country. In instances where a U.S. company's Canadian operations were organizationally treated as a part of U.S. operations and management for the two was integrated, Canadian sales were considered to be domestic rather than foreign. The Stopford and Wells study treated all Canadian sales as domestic sales for U.S. firms.

Some have also wondered whether the European countries should not be treated as a part of the domestic market for European MNCs. This is a debatable issue, but at the present time we think European managers tend not to view Europe as a single national market. While European MNCs often treat neighboring countries as markets they understand very well and can depend upon, both strategically and organizationally they tend to respect and distinguish between the national differences more than U.S. or Canadian firms generally do with the North American market. Among the sample companies, the only exception was the way some German MNCs tended to treat the Austrian market.

The size or percentage of foreign manufacturing was operationalized as the percentage of foreign sales accounted for by foreign manufacturing rather than exports from the parent country. This was measured by dividing the value of foreign manufacturing (adjusted by the gross profit margin to make it equivalent to sales volume rather than cost of goods sold) by foreign sales. In a few instances where this information was not available, it was calculated by using foreign manufacturing assets to estimate the percentage of total company manufacturing occurring outside of the parent country, which was then divided by the percentage of foreign sales. This concept has not been previously measured and, of course, was not included in the Stopford and Wells Model.

It is important to notice how the concept of a firm's strategy has been operationally measured in the study. Mintzberg has defined strategy as 'consistent patterns in streams of organizational decisions' (1979: 25). If various decisions made in a firm have led it to diversify into many different product areas (as measured by the number of broad product groups or SIC codes in its product line), we say it is pursuing a diversified product strategy. Similarly, if decisions in a firm have led it to develop many foreign manufacturing facilities (as measured by the percentage of foreign manufacturing), we say it pursues a strategy of sourcing foreign sales from local manufacturing rather than from parent country exports. Thus we tend to operationally measure a strategy with its trail of outcomes, because it is too difficult to directly measure the 'streams of organizational decisions' in order to discern the 'patterns', which actually comprise the strategy. Other research studies that have attempted to quantitatively measure strategy have also tended to measure outcomes rather than decisions (Daniels et al., 1984; Franko, 1976; Stopford and Wells, 1972).

Table 2 shows the correlation among the three contingency variables. As might be expected in relatively mature, successful MNCs, there is a significant positive correlation between foreign product diversity and the percentage of foreign sales, but they are still sufficiently independent elements of a company's strategy to be considered separately.

RESULTS

Several types of analyses were performed on the data. First, one-way ANOVA was used to directly test the first two hypotheses developed from the Stopford and Wells Model. The third hypothesis had to be examined visually, since there are not enough firms with matrix and mixed structures in the sample to support statistical analysis. Finally, a multivariate discriminant analysis was used to simultaneously examine the relationship between structure and all three of the contingency variables (elements of strategy).

Testing the Stopford and Wells Hypotheses

Table 3 shows the mean levels of the three elements of strategy by type of structure. One-way ANOVA contrasts were used to determine the significance of the differences between international division, area division, and product division structures. Since there are only two firms with matrix structures and three with mixed structures in the sample, significance of difference involving these types of structure could not be measured. Hypothesis 1 stated that MNCs with worldwide product division structures will tend to have more foreign product diversity than firms with

Table 2
Correlation Among the Contingency Variables ($N = 28$–33)

		1	2
1	Foreign product diversity		
2	Percentage foreign sales	0.49*	
3	Percentage foreign manufacturing	−0.16	−0.25

*$p < 0.01$.

Table 3
Mean Values of Elements of Strategy by Type of Structure

	International divisions	Area divisions	Product divisions	PD × AD matrix	PD & AD mixed
Foreign product diversity	1.7	3.4	5.8[a]	6.0	4.3
Percentage foreign sales	34[a]	47	61	92	52
Percentage foreign manufacturing	76	91[c]	61	86	82

[a]Different from area divisions at $p < 0.01$ and international divisions at $p < 0.001$.
[b]Different from area divisions at $p < 0.05$ and product divisions at $p < 0.01$.
[c]Different from product divisions at $p < 0.001$.

either an international division or area division structure. The sample data clearly support this hypothesis.

Hypothesis 2 stated that MNCs with area division structures will tend to have a greater percentage of foreign sales than firms with either international division or product division structures. This hypothesis is only partially supported by the data. Companies with area division structures do have a significantly greater percentage of foreign sales than companies with international division structures, but less than companies with worldwide product division structures. The Stopford and Wells study found that companies with area division structures tended to have a greater percentage of foreign sales than companies with product division structures. This was reflected in the model, which further implied that if companies possess both high product diversity and a high percentage of foreign sales, they should tend to have matrix or mixed structures. In the present study, however, the group of MNCs operating with worldwide product division structures tend to possess both high foreign product diversity and a high percentage of foreign sales.

Hypothesis 3 stated that MNCs with matrix and mixed structures will tend to have relatively high levels of both foreign product diversity and foreign sales. While this cannot be tested with any statistical measure, we can examine whether the few matrix and mixed structures in the sample tend to support or contradict this hypothesis. Clearly the two MNCs with matrix structures tend to support it. Their mean foreign product diversity is 6 (ranging from 5 to 7) and their mean percentage of foreign sales is 92 (ranging from 88 to 96).

The three MNCs with mixed product and area division structures provide a somewhat different picture. Their mean foreign product diversity is 4.3 (ranging from 2 to 7). Their mean percentage of foreign sales is 52 (ranging from 36 to 71). The high variances would seem to indicate that it is impossible to generalize about the levels of foreign product diversity and foreign sales that are or should be associated with mixed structures. Actually, mixed structures are some weighted average of product division and area division structures (i.e. some percentage of an MNCs foreign operations are organized under worldwide product divisions and the remaining percentage is organized under area divisions). Since the weighting will vary from company to company, there is no conceptual basis for specifying a unique set of contingency conditions for mixed structures.

Thus the results support some parts of the Stopford and Wells Model, but raise questions about other parts of the model. Hypothesis 1 is fully supported, while hypotheses 2 and 3 are partially supported. Where the present study primarily differs from the Stopford and Wells study is in how to distinguish between the strategic domains in MNCs with product division structures and those with area division structures. Stopford and Wells concluded that high levels of foreign product diversity lead to product division structures while high levels of foreign sales lead to area division structures. The present study finds that both structures tend to be associated with relatively high percentages of foreign sales, and that only foreign product diversity distinguishes in a significant way between the strategic domains of the two.

Stopford and Wells also suggested that strategies involving high levels of both foreign product diversity and foreign sales could best be addressed with matrix and mixed structures. The present study finds that this particular strategic domain seems to be occupied by MNCs with product division and matrix structures. The present findings also suggest that mixed structure companies can vary widely in their strategic domains (as measured by foreign product diversity and foreign sales) and that they should be excluded from the kind of contingency model Stopford and Wells have attempted to construct.

The Influence of Size of Foreign Manufacturing

Table 3 shows how the third element of strategy, percentage of foreign manufacturing, varies across the five structures in the sample. MNCs with area division structures tend to be associated with significantly higher levels of foreign manufacturing than MNCs with worldwide product division structures. As previously discussed, strategies which provide for a high level of foreign manufacturing create high interdependencies between foreign subsidiaries within a region and reduce interdependency between foreign subsidiaries and the parent's domestic operations. The area division structure fits this kind of interdependency. It provides a high level of coordination and information processing between subsidiaries within a region. A lower percentage of foreign manufacturing and more exports means there is less opportunity for economies of scale through regional coordination and integration. Following this strategy implies less interdependency among subsidiaries within a region, and more interdependency between a subsidiary and the parent. The worldwide product division structure provides the kind of coordination and information processing which fits this kind of interdependency. Thus, foreign manufacturing, the third element of strategy, seems to provide a meaningful way of distinguishing between the strategic domains of MNCs with area division structures and those with worldwide product division structures.

A Multivariate Analysis

In order to examine the fit between structure and the three elements of strategy simultaneously, a multiple discriminant analysis was run using the four types of structure as the groups and the three elements of strategy as the independent variable. Mixed structures were excluded from the analysis, since their high variance along the dimensions of strategy makes them indistinguishable as a separate group or category. The results of the discriminant analysis appear in Table 4. The standardized discriminant coefficients indicate the relative contributions of the independent variables to the discriminant function. Both foreign product diversity and the percentage of foreign sales load heavily on the first function.

The second discriminant function can largely be associated with the percentage of foreign manufacturing. It is statistically significant at the $p = 0.11$ level. The third discriminant function is neither meaningful nor statistically significant.

Table 5 shows how successful the discriminant model is in predicting the structure of each company, given knowledge of the three elements of strategy. The discriminant model could predict the actual structure of a company in 74 percent of the cases, which is significantly better than the chance probability of predicting only 31 percent of the cases correctly.

Table 6 shows the centroids of each of the four groups (types of structure) measured along the three discriminant functions. The first discriminant function, which most heavily reflects foreign

Table 4

Multiple Discriminant Analysis of the Three Elements of Strategy on Type of Structure

Dependent variable: Type of structure

| Independent variable | Discriminant function | | | F-value |
	1	2	3	
Foreign product diversity	0.72	0.08	0.70	8.76***
Percentage foreign sales	0.59	0.38	−0.71	7.18**
Percentage foreign manufacturing	−0.35	0.93	0.14	3.76*
Canonical correlation	0.84	0.50	0.27	
Wilks lambda	0.21***	0.69†	0.93	

†$p = 0.11$; *$p < 0.05$; **$p < 0.01$; ***$p < 0.001$.

Note: All values under the three discriminant functions are standardized discriminant coefficients.

product diversity, clearly separates product division and product division × area division matrix structures from international division and area division structures. This can be viewed as another test of hypothesis 1. The second discriminant function, which largely reflects the percentage of foreign manufacturing, separates area division and product division × area division matrix structures from international division and product division structures. While the second discriminant function is only significant at the $p = 0.11$ level, it is consistent with the previous significant finding in Table 3, that level of foreign manufacturing (and not level of foreign sales, as hypothesized by Stopford and Wells) best distinguishes between the strategic domains of area division and

Table 5

Predicted Type of Structure from Coefficients of Discriminant Functions

| Actual group membership | Predicted group membership | | | |
	International divisions	Area divisions	Product divisions	PD × AD matrix
International divisions	6	1	0	0
Area divisions	2	7	1	0
Product divisions	1	1	8	2
PD × AD matrix	0	0	0	2

Note: Structures of MNCs correctly classified = 74 percent.

Table 6

Centroids of the Four Structural Groups Measured Along the Discriminant Functions

| Group | Discriminant function | | |
	1	2	3
International divisions	−1.90	−0.55	−0.13
Area divisions	−0.63	0.68	0.13
Product divisions	1.47	−0.29	0.09
PD × AD matrix	1.82	0.79	−1.16

worldwide product division structures. It is also clear from the analysis of centroids that the strategic domain of the product division × area division matrix structure resembles that of the product division structure when it comes to foreign product diversity (discriminant function 1), and resembles that of the area division structure when it comes to percentage of foreign manufacturing (discriminant function 2). Thus the multivariate discriminant analysis tends to support and extend the conclusions which were drawn from the earlier bivariate analysis.

DISCUSSION AND REVISION OF THE STOPFORD AND WELLS MODEL

The sample data of the present study have supported some of the hypotheses underlying the Stopford and Wells Model, but failed to support others. Stopford and Wells observed that the strategic domain of international division companies can be characterized by relatively low levels of foreign product diversity and foreign sales. This is confirmed by the present study.

Product Divisions Versus Area Divisions

Stopford and Wells further hypothesized that the strategic domains of area division and product division MNCs differed by level of foreign product diversity and level of foreign sales, since these differences occurred in their sample. The present study confirms the hypothesized difference in foreign product diversity, but fails to find a significant difference in terms of percentage of foreign sales. Both area division and product division structures seem to fit strategies that involve relatively high percentages of foreign sales (the mean being 47 percent for area structures and 61 percent for product division structures). This is a highly significant deviation from the Stopford and Wells findings and Model.

The reason why MNCs in the present study with product division structures possess such a high percentage of foreign sales undoubtedly lies in the fact that the majority are European-headquartered, while those in the Stopford and Wells study were all U.S.-headquartered. It is difficult for European companies to become large, prominent MNCs without having a high percentage of foreign sales, due to the limited size of most home country markets. While this explains the relatively higher percentage of foreign sales in European MNCs, it does not explain why these companies operate with worldwide product division structures instead of matrixing or mixing product divisions with area divisions as the Stopford and Wells Model would predict. It would appear that Stopford and Wells have found part of the answer, but not all of it. Clearly, worldwide product division structures can and do support international strategies containing high percentages of foreign sales.

The reason this was not apparent in the Stopford and Wells study is because it was confined to U.S. MNCs and did not measure the percentage of foreign manufacturing (a third important element for defining the strategic domain of MNCs). The MNCs with area division structures in both the Stopford and Wells study and the present study tend to have high percentages of foreign sales. The present study, however, found that while this strategic condition is necessary, it is not sufficient to specify an area division structure. Large European MNCs with worldwide product divisions also tend to have a high percentage of foreign sales. It is possible that the Stopford and Wells companies with area division structures also had a high percentage of foreign manufacturing—and that it was this strategic condition along with a high percentage of foreign sales that led to the selection of an area division structure. It is also possible that the Stopford and Wells companies with product division structures possessed relatively lower levels of foreign manufacturing, insufficient to require the kind of coordination and information processing necessary to realize area synergies and economies of scale. Thus the empirical findings of both the

Stopford and Wells study and the present study might be consistent and reconcilable, if all of the data were available.

When MNCs support foreign sales with exports from the parent, the primary interdependency is between a foreign subsidiary and the parent's domestic operations. The worldwide product division structure provides the kind of information processing and integration required to coordinate this kind of interdependency. When the strategy is to support foreign sales with extensive foreign manufacturing, important interdependencies usually develop between foreign subsidiaries within a region or area, as the company now attempts to realize area economies of scale to replace the economies of scale which were formerly provided by centralizing production of the product in the parent. The area division structure provides the kind of information processing and integration required to coordinate this kind of interdependency.

Matrix Structures

A second major area where the present study differs from the Stopford and Wells Model deals with matrix structures. Here the difference is not so much contradiction as extension of the model. Both the Stopford and Wells study and the present study observed very few product division × area division matrix structure companies (three and two respectively). This part of the Model must therefore rely more on the logic underlying it, and the consistency of the limited empirical data with that logic, than upon any significant empirical testing. Davis and Lawrence (1977) have argued that matrix structures tend to fit situations requiring a dual focus (e.g. equal pressures to organize around products and areas) and high information processing within the organization. The present study found that product division × area division matrix structures tend to occur when there is both high foreign product diversity and a high percentage of foreign manufacturing. These two elements of strategy require a dual focus and different kinds of information processing. They require the kind of information processing and integration that can only be provided by the simultaneous existence of product divisions and area divisions.

The product division × area division matrix companies in the sample also tend to have a high percentage of foreign sales, as hypothesized by Stopford and Wells. Unlike the Stopford and Wells Model, however, the present study found a high percentage of foreign sales and high foreign product diversity to be necessary but not sufficient conditions for a product division × area division matrix structure. A high percentage of foreign manufacturing is also required. It is, again, quite possible that the three Stopford and Wells matrix companies had a high percentage of foreign manufacturing, but this was not measured. Thus the present study extends the Stopford and Wells Model to include a third precondition for product division × area division matrix structures.

A Revised Model

Based on the above findings, Figure 2 shows a revised model linking strategy and structure in MNCs. International strategies which involve a relatively low percentage of foreign sales and low foreign product diversity tend to fit international division structures. Such strategies and structures facilitate responsiveness to national interests. Both the Stopford and Wells and the present study supported this relationship.

Strategies involving high foreign product diversity and a low percentage of foreign sales probably tend to be transitional strategies for successful companies, as they attempt to increase their percentage of foreign sales by introducing more product lines. The Stopford and Wells study found these strategies to be associated with worldwide product division structures. The present study, which observed only the largest MNCs, found no companies in this strategic domain and, therefore, could not test this relationship.

When international strategies involve relatively high percentages of foreign sales, supporting structures tend to be those which provide higher levels of coordination and information processing between a foreign subsidiary and other sectors of the company. It is in this area that the revised model based on the present study alters and extends the Stopford and Wells Model. Worldwide product division structures provide a high level of coordination and information processing between a company's foreign operations and its domestic product operations. This tends to fit strategies involving high foreign product diversity and substantial exports from the parent to the foreign subsidiaries. This is a global strategy that requires a global structure with less potential for national or even regional responsiveness.

When the strategy involves manufacturing a high percentage of the goods needed to support foreign sales abroad, foreign subsidiaries become relatively more interdependent with each other, and interdependency between the foreign and domestic operations of the company decreases for operational matters. The revised model shows that area division structures provide the type of coordination and information processing needed to handle the interdependency associated with this strategy. Such strategies and structures are not global, but regional, and therefore more responsive to regional and national interests than global product strategies and structures.

When the international strategy involves both high levels of foreign product diversity and foreign manufacturing, foreign subsidiaries will tend to be highly dependent on the parent for product and technical knowledge, and highly interdependent with neighboring subsidiaries in the area for operating synergies and economies of scale. This requires the dual coordination and information processing provided by worldwide product divisions and area divisions. The model shows that matrix structures containing both product divisions and area divisions fit such strategies.

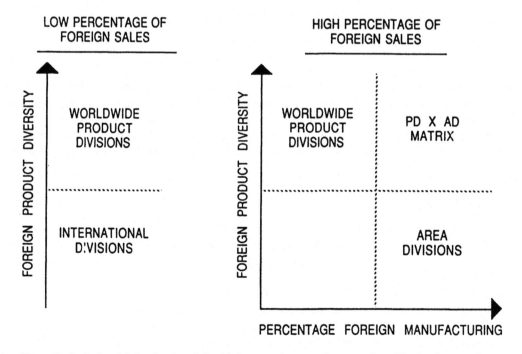

Figure 2 Revised model showing the relationship between strategy and structure in multinational corporations.

Managerial Implications

There are a number of managerial implications which follow from this revision of the Stopford and Wells Model. The first is that MNCs do not have to abandon worldwide product division structures when the size of foreign operations becomes large, as Stopford and Wells suggest. There are numerous successful European MNCs with worldwide product division structures. A second implication is that MNCs should not adopt an area division structure if they still rely largely on exports from the parent country to supply foreign operations. Most large U.S. MNCs have developed large foreign manufacturing operations to support their foreign sales, but many European MNCs still rely heavily on exports from the parent country. If these European MNCs move to supply more of their foreign sales with foreign manufacturing, one would expect that ultimately they will also change their structures to either area division or product division × area division matrix structures, to restore good fit between strategy and structure.

Research Implications

The primary implication for researchers of strategy and structure in MNCs is the importance of foreign manufacturing as an element of international strategy. This variable appears to significantly modify the impact of the size of foreign operations on structure, and in the present study was the most important discriminator between area division and product division structures. It is possible that foreign manufacturing is operationally measuring some of the difference between global product strategies and more regionally and nationally responsive strategies. Doz (1980), Doz and Prahalad (1980), and Hamel and Prahalad (1983) have generally defined the forces favoring such responsiveness in terms of political and cultural factors. While this is undoubtedly true, the potential for area synergies and economies of scale, as selected in the size of foreign manufacturing, probably combines with political and cultural factors to encourage regional strategies and structures.

By revising and extending the original Stopford and Wells model, the present study has sought to advance our understanding of critical relationships between strategy and structure in MNCs. The revised model is unfortunately more complex than the original model. It uses a three-dimensional instead of a two-dimensional framework to partition the strategic domains of MNCs. Yet this complexity seems warranted, since it allows the model to identify and take into account increasingly important trends toward globalism and regionalism in international strategies.

Both the recent Daniels et al. (1985) study and the present study reveal a strong need for additional research on the more strategically complex portions of the strategy-structure relationship. The present study has suggested that foreign manufacturing is an important aspect of the recent trends toward global strategies and more national and regional responsiveness. Other contingency variables need to be identified and operationalized that will tap other dimensions of these trends. Examples would include the role of international versus domestic R&D in a firm's strategy, and the need to globally transfer technology within and between firms. As mentioned earlier, exploratory research seems to be uncovering increasingly complex forms of international strategy, and extending the strategy-structure paradigm and model to address it is a major challenge facing those who seek to better understand the multinational corporation.

Our bias is to study strategy-structure fit in multinational samples of MNCs. As was the case in the present study, this tends to widen both the range of available international strategies and the number of structural alternatives employed. Both of these encourage the development of more comprehensive strategy-structure models. As international competition has become increasingly multinational (i.e. involving MNCs from different countries) there is an accompanying need to understand both strategy and strategy-structure relationships from a more comprehensive or multinational perspective.

REFERENCES

Bartlett, C. A. 'Multinational structural evolution: The changing decision environment in international divisions'. Doctoral dissertation, Harvard Business School, Boston, MA. 1979.

Bartlett, C. A. 'MNCs: get off the reorganization merry-go-round'. *Harvard Business Review*, 61(2). 1983, pp. 138–146.

Brooke, M. Z. and H. L. Remmers. *The Strategy of Multinational Enterprise*. American Elsevier, New York, 1970.

Chandler, A. D. *Strategy and Structure: Chapters in the History of Industrial Enterprise*. MIT Press, Cambridge, MA, 1962.

Channon, D. F. *The Strategy and Structure of British Enterprise*, Division of Research, Graduate School of Business Administration, Harvard University, Boston, MA, 1973.

Daniels, J. D., R. A. Pitts and M. J. Tretter. 'Strategy and structure of U.S. multinationals: An exploratory study', *Academy of Management Journal*, 27(2), 1984, pp. 292–307.

Daniels, J. D., R. A. Pitts and M. J. Tretter. 'Organizing for dual strategies of product diversity and international expansion', *Strategic Management Journal*, 6, 1985, pp. 223–237.

Davidson, W. H. *Experience Effects in International Investment and Technology Transfer*, UMI Research Press, Ann Arbor, MI, 1980.

Davidson, W. H. and P. Haspeslagh. 'Shaping a global product organization', *Harvard Business Review*, 60(4), 1982, pp. 125–132.

Davis, S. M. and P. R. Lawrence. *Matrix*, Addison-Wesley, Reading, MA, 1977.

Doz, Y. L. 'Strategic management in multinational companies', *Sloan Management Review*, Winter 1980, pp. 27–46.

Doz, Y. L. and C. K. Prahalad. 'How MNCs cope with host government intervention', *Harvard Business Review*, March-April 1980, pp. 149–157.

Dyas, G. P. and H. T. Thanheiser. *The Emerging European Enterprise: Strategy and Structure in French and German Industry*, Macmillan, London, 1976.

Egelhoff, W. G. 'Strategy and structure in multinational corporations: An information-processing approach', *Administrative Science Quarterly*, 27, 1982, pp. 435–458.

Fouraker, L. E. and J. M. Stopford. 'Organizational structure and multinational strategy', *Administrative Science Quarterly*, 13, 1968, pp. 47–64.

Franko, L. G. *The European Multinationals: A Renewed Challenge to American and British Big Business*, Greylock Publishing, Stamford, CT, 1976.

Galbraith, J. R. and D. A. Nathanson. *Strategy Implementation: The Role of Structure and Process*, West Publishing, St. Paul, MN, 1978.

Goggin, W. C. 'How the multidimensional structure works at Dow Corning', *Harvard Business Review*, January-February 1974, pp. 54–65.

Hamel, G. and C. K. Prahalad. 'Managing strategic responsibility in the MNC', *Strategic Management Journal*, 4, 1983, pp. 341–351.

Hout, T., M. E. Porter and E. Rudden, 'How global companies win out', *Harvard Business Review*, September-October 1982, pp. 98–108.

Mintzberg, H. *The Structure of Organizations: A Synthesis of the Research*. Prentice-Hall, Englewood Cliffs, NJ, 1979.

Pavan, F. D. J. 'The strategy and structure of Italian enterprise', Doctoral dissertation, Harvard Business School, Boston, MA, 1972.

Rumelt, R. P. *Strategy, Structure, and Economic Performance*, Division of Research, Graduate School of Business Administration, Harvard University, Boston, MA, 1974.

Scott, B. R. Stages of corporate development, 9-371-294, BP, 988, Intercollegiate Case Clearinghouse, Harvard Business School, Boston, MA, 1971.

Stopford, J. M. and L. T. Wells, Jr. *Managing the Multinational Enterprise,* Basic Books, New York, 1972.

Williams, C. R. 'Regional management overseas', *Harvard Business Review,* 45, 1967, pp. 87–91.

Chapter 9

Organizational Environments and the Multinational Enterprise

Philip M. Rosenzweig
Harvard University

Jitendra V. Singh
University of Pennsylvania

Abstract *Multinational enterprises (MNEs) serve as catalysts for reconceptualizing organization-environment relations because they operate simultaneously in multiple nations. We argue that subsidiaries of MNEs face dual pressures: They are pulled to achieve isomorphism with the local institutional environment, and they also face an imperative for consistency within the organization. We develop hypotheses regarding the factors that influence the structures and processes of MNEs. Based on an examination of the pressures imposed on MNEs, we offer a refined concept of organizational environments as complex and fluid, and we suggest implications for future research in organization theory.*

With the growing interdependence of the world economy, the organizational landscape is increasingly populated by firms that own and control activities in more than one country. Such multinational enterprises (MNEs) have received considerable attention in the fields of economics (e.g., Caves, 1982a) and strategic management (e.g., Bartlett & Ghoshal, 1989; Prahalad & Doz, 1987), but have less frequently been the focus of study in organization theory. The MNE, nevertheless, poses several interesting issues for organization theorists. On one hand, a multinational enterprise is a single organization that operates in a global environment, with a need to coordinate its far-flung operations. On the other hand, an MNE is comprised of a set of organizations that operate in distinct national environments. These subsidiaries face not only a local environment, but also the context of the whole enterprise, which they draw upon for resources and administrative practices.

Recognition of the need to incorporate an international perspective into organizational theory is not new. Scott (1983: 172) asserted that consideration of the international dimension of organizational environments "is likely to form an important part of the research agenda during the next decade." Eight years later, however, the nature of this research agenda remains relatively unexamined.

Reprinted from the *Academy of Management Review*, Vol. 16, No. 2 (1991). By permission of the Academy of Management.

The objectives of this paper are twofold. First, we seek to understand the multinational enterprise using concepts from the field of organization theory. We use existing theory to produce a distinct understanding of the organizational structures and processes in MNEs. Second, we draw on the experience of multinational enterprises to offer a refined concept of organization-environment relations. Based on this reconceptualization, we offer specific suggestions for further research.

ORGANIZATIONAL ENVIRONMENTS AND NATIONAL BOUNDARIES

Since the advent of open-systems models of organization, theorists have been interested in the relationship between organizations and their environments. The maintenance of an organization is recognized as being dependent upon an exchange with outside parties (Child, 1972; Hannan & Freeman, 1989; Pfeffer & Salancik, 1978; Thompson, 1967). Environmental forces also influence organizational structures and decision making (Aldrich & Pfeffer, 1976; Lawrence & Lorsch, 1967).

Much effort has been devoted to the description of organizational environments. Some researchers have typed environments as stable or uncertain (Lawrence & Lorsch, 1967); placid, disturbed, or turbulent (Emery & Trist, 1965); and simple-complex or static-dynamic (Duncan, 1972). Others have enumerated the domains of the environment, which include industry structure, technology, government regulations, and culture (Daft, 1989; Scott, 1981).

A concept of the environment is an important feature in a number of leading theories, including ecological theory, resource dependence theory, and institutionalization theory. Rarely, however, have these avenues of research considered explicitly the relation between national boundaries and the boundaries of organizational environments. Some prominent works, notably by Pfeffer and Salancik (1978), provide extensive discussions of organizational environments without giving any consideration to national boundaries. Others (e.g., Daft, 1989) identity the *international domain* as something in addition to, and therefore separate from, other environmental domains, implying that these other domains are essentially national in scope.

Ecological models of organization, for example, emphasize the importance of environmental selection in determining patterns of organizational founding, mortality, and change (Singh & Lumsden, 1990). According to one view, organizations are relatively inert and either die or are absorbed by other organizations as environmental conditions change (Hannan & Freeman, 1977). Although organizations may at times make radical changes to their structure, environmental selection processes favor organizations whose structures are inert (Hannan & Freeman, 1984). Other empirical studies have suggested that although an organization's core characteristics are subject to selection forces, peripheral characteristics may be subject to adaptation, thereby improving the chances of survival (Singh, House, & Tucker, 1986).

Ecological theory does not, ex ante, include national boundaries in its concept of the environment. Empirical studies have tended, however, to examine populations that exist entirely within national boundaries. Examples include newspapers in Argentina and Ireland (Carroll & Delacroix, 1982) and voluntary social service organizations in metropolitan Toronto (Singh, Tucker, & House, 1986). In part, the choice to study organizations within a given nation reflects the need to examine organizations sufficiently similar and abundant to constitute a well-bounded population. Such organizations are often small and are unlikely to span national lines. As a consequence, researchers of organizational ecology have not had to consider variations in environment across nations. Thus, the question as to whether characteristics of environments differ across nations, and therefore impose uneven selection pressures on multinational enterprises, has not been posed at all.

Resource dependence theorists view organizations as actively engaged in exchanges with the environment in order to improve performance and increase the chances of survival (Pfeffer & Salancik, 1978). In contrast with ecological models, organizations are thought to possess greater adaptability and to be able to alter their environments.

Similar to the ecological concept of the environment, however, resource dependence theory gives little explicit consideration to the ways that national boundaries affect an organization's ability to command resources. For example, an organization may need inputs of capital, skilled labor, managerial expertise, and advanced technology. Some of these resources (e.g., skilled labor) may be relatively immobile, making the organization dependent on resources in a relatively small geographic area, whereas other resources may be more easily obtained from a great distance (e.g., capital). Furthermore, some resources may move relatively freely between nations (e.g., transfers of executives), whereas others may be subject to governmental restrictions (e.g., technology). If we accept the premise that organizations are dependent on resources from their environment, national boundaries would appear to be important factors that influence the scope of resources available to them.

Institutionalization theory asserts that organizations are affected by "common understandings of what is appropriate and, fundamentally, meaningful behavior" (Zucker, 1983: 105). Structural change is therefore only partly driven by competitive pressures (DiMaggio & Powell, 1983; Meyer & Rowan, 1977). Quite apart from seeking maximum efficiency, organizations may seek to adopt structures or processes that reflect the institutional environment, defined as a "set of highly established and culturally sanctioned action patterns and expectations" (Lincoln, Hanada, & McBride, 1986: 340). Such environmental isomorphism may come about through coercive, mimetic, or normative pressures (DiMaggio & Powell, 1983).

Institutionalization theory gives prominence to the legal and cultural factors that organizations face (Scott, 1983). Because legal and cultural factors are often specific to a nation, the concept of institutional environments is implicitly congruent with national boundaries. Organizations studied in empirical research on institutionalization, not surprisingly, often operate entirely in one nation: Topics of study have included institutionalization of civil service reforms in major American cities (Tolbert & Zucker, 1983) and administration of public schools (Rowan, 1982; Tolbert, 1985). The national environment implied in these studies is that of the United States. Similarly, structural characteristics of Hungarian agricultural collectives bear the marks of specific institutional requirements of that centralized national economy (Carroll, Goodstein, & Gyenes, 1988). Because the legal and social institutions of a nation are critical components of institutional environments, national boundaries implicitly constitute their lines of demarcation.

The importance of national boundaries in organization-environment relations has been noted on occasions. Toward the end of their classic study, Lawrence and Lorsch (1967: 230) observed that the multinational firm faces special challenges of differentiation and integration because it "has attempted not only to span the necessary differences among functional and product specialists, but also to bridge unavoidable differences among cultures." Among the issues that managers in MNEs must consider include "the necessary interdependence among units employing members with different cultural origins" (Lawrence & Lorsch, 1967: 230) and the degree of cultural differences between such units. Lawrence and Lorsch thus recognized the importance of national boundaries in organizational environments, but did not address the matter fully. Meyer and Rowan (1977) recognized that institutional environments may differ by nation, but they were interested in differences between national environments primarily as a way to test hypotheses about institutionalization theory. They did not address the complexities facing organizations that exist simultaneously in multiple environments.

ENVIRONMENTS OF MULTINATIONAL ENTERPRISES

The neglect of national boundaries in treatments of organizational environments is probably not a serious oversight for studies of small firms whose scope is entirely domestic or for public agencies specific to one nation. However, such a concept is clearly inadequate for multinational enterprises because these operate simultaneously in multiple countries.

If multinational enterprises, like all organizations, are thought of as open systems that exchange resources with their environments, a fundamental question must be addressed: What is the nature of the organizational environment faced by a multinational enterprise?

One approach would be to think of an MNE as a single entity that faces a global environment. The domains of such a global environment would include industry structure, technology, and so forth, but these would be global rather than national in scope. Thus, the MNE would face a global competitive domain, a global political domain, a global social domain, and a global technological domain.

Such a view may at first seem appealing, but it introduces an unrealistic assumption of a homogeneous and monolithic environment. An MNE does not exist within a seamless global environment; rather, the many subsidiaries of an MNE often face the demands of specific local environments. The MNE simultaneously confronts differing national environments.

According to a second view, a polar opposite approach, MNEs would be conceived of as a set of subunits, and each subunit would operate entirely within a single nation, unaffected by goings on elsewhere in the world. These subsidiaries would be dependent only on resources within national boundaries, and they would be indistinguishable from other organizations in the domestic population. Such a view makes allowances for variations in local environments faced by foreign subsidiaries, but it runs the risk of exaggerating the importance of national boundaries and differences between nations. It does not consider precisely what binds these subsidiaries together—shared management, the strategic roles of each subsidiary in furthering overall organizational objectives, and the ability to shift resources within the organization. Such a concept, if taken to the extreme, imagines the MNE to be little more than a portfolio of unrelated and independent domestic organizations.

A third view avoids both of these extreme positions: The MNE is regarded as a set of differentiated structures and processes, and each of these structures and processes exists in the many subunits of the organization. These structures and processes, in turn, are affected by a variety of environmental forces, some of which are specific to the host country and some of which are global in nature. They face, at the same time, a pressure for conformity to conditions in the local environment and an imperative for consistency within the multinational enterprise.

This view, which emphasizes the tension between forces for global integration and national responsiveness, has been developed explicitly by Porter (1986) and Bartlett (1986). It has served as the basis for subsequent works in international business strategy (Bartlett & Ghoshal, 1989; Doz, 1980; Doz, Bartlett, & Prahalad, 1981; Doz & Prahalad, 1984), and it is embraced in this article.

CONFLICTING PRESSURES FOR CONFORMITY IN MULTINATIONAL ENTERPRISES

Adaptation of MNEs to National Environments

Much attention has been paid to the similarities and differences in organizational structure and managerial practices across countries. Early studies of comparative labor economics suggested that the ongoing global industrialization was producing a convergence of managerial practices

(Kerr, Dunlop, Harbison, & Myers, 1960). It was suggested that organizational structures were becoming more similar across nations, partly because of the diffusion of technology. More recently, however, notions about a convergence of industrial practices have given way to a recognition that *persistent cultural traits* contribute to lasting national variations. As Dunlop, Harbison, Kerr, and Myers (1975: 35) concluded: "There will never be total convergence because of the clash between the 'uniformities' growing out of the logic of industrialism and the 'diversities' springing from political, social, and cultural differences."

Organizational theorists, too, have studied similarities and variations in organizational structure across nations. Taking a structural contingency perspective, members of the Aston group tested the hypothesis that relations between organizational structure and the task environment are stable across countries. Data from American, British, and Canadian firms support the claim that organizational structure is insensitive to national culture and that there is a "culture free context of organizational structure" (Hickson, Hinings, McMillan, & Schwitter, 1974: 59).

Other studies, however, have revealed differences in organizational forms across countries. Horvath, McMillan, Azumi, and Hickson (1981) found differences in the formal structure and control systems among Swedish, British, and Japanese organizations. Comparing the organizational structures of Japanese and American manufacturing firms, Lincoln and his colleagues (1986: 338) found significant country differences in centralization and formalization after controlling for technology, size, and other variables. They concluded that "Japanese organizations are embedded in a tighter institutional environment than U.S. organizations," and that differences in institutional environments are associated with differences in organizational structure.

Such variations are in keeping with an institutional view of organizations. To survive and prosper, subsidiaries of MNEs tend to take on the characteristics of other organizations in the local environment.[1] Such isomorphism may be mandated by local regulation, in which case it would be an example of coercive isomorphism, or it may reflect the economic pressures of firms adapting their products to local preferences. Yet, if we conceive of organizations as social entities as well as technical entities, we must recognize how local subsidiaries of MNEs come to reflect the values, norms, and "locally accepted practices" of the societies in which they operate (Westney, 1989: 12).

Consistency Between Subsidiaries in MNEs

If subsidiaries of MNEs face pressures to adapt to the institutional demands of host countries, and therefore tend to become isomorphic with other local organizations, they also face pressures for consistency with other subunits of the MNE. The tendency for subsidiaries to resemble each other is due to two factors: organizational replication and the imperative of control.

Replication of organizational structure. The establishment of foreign subsidiaries often follows the process of replication (Nelson & Winter, 1982), as organizations enact existing routines and standard operating procedures when setting up new operations. The tendency to replicate existing organizational features may be especially great in multinational enterprises because doing business in a foreign country poses relatively high ambiguity and uncertainty (DiMaggio & Powell, 1983; March & Olsen, 1976). Furthermore, as foreign subsidiaries employ technologies

---

[1]Here, "organizations in the local environment" refer to local domestic organizations, but they can also include the subsidiaries of other MNEs. If the local competitors are comprised primarily of the subsidiaries of other MNEs, there may be, in aggregate, a diminished need to conform to the local institutional environment, but such distinctions are beyond the scope of this article.

similar to other subunits in the MNE, it is expected that their organizational structures and processes would be similar.

The resulting similarity between headquarters and foreign subsidiary has been called the *mirror effect* (Brooke & Remmers, 1970). As an example, Procter & Gamble explicitly sought to design each new foreign subsidiary as an "exact replica of the United States Procter & Gamble organization" in the belief that using "exactly the same policies and procedures which have given our company success in the United States will be equally successful overseas" (cited in Bartlett & Ghoshal, 1989: 38).

The tendency for such replication is at times pursued to an excessive degree; in setting up a foreign subsidiary, Robock and Simmonds (1989: 581) noted that "the new manager is likely to impose management patterns on the subsidiary that worked well in other environments but that do not suit the local situation." Although the foreign subsidiary's structure and processes may be modified later, such modification may only be a moderate adjustment from the initial anchor created by replication rather than an adjustment sufficient to meet local conditions.

The imperative of control of foreign operations. The need to control foreign activities is not only a precondition for foreign direct investment (Caves, 1971; Hymer, 1976), but it also remains an ongoing concern of the MNE. In order to achieve and maintain control of their operations, multinational enterprises face several complexities not encountered by domestic firms: communication is more difficult due to geographic distance and language barriers, evaluation of performance is complicated by shifts in currency exchange rates, and interactions between headquarters and subsidiaries may be affected by cultural differences (Mascarenhas, 1982).

Given the challenges of establishing and maintaining control in international operations, it is not surprising that mechanisms of control and coordination have become important topics in the study of MNEs. Among the means of coordination and control that have been studied are accounting-based mechanisms (Shapiro, 1978), human resource management (Edstrom & Galbraith, 1977), corporate culture (Jaeger, 1983), delegation of decision making (Egelhoff, 1988), and "fit" governance structures (Ghoshal & Nohria, 1989). Each mechanism is designed to regulate activities of the foreign subsidiary in order to meet organizational objectives. (An extensive review of this research is provided by Martinez and Jarillo, 1989).

The crux of our discussion comes into focus when we juxtapose pressures for isomorphism with the local environment and pressures for consistency within the multinational enterprise. As shown in Figure 1, any given element of organizational structure or process can be depicted in terms of pressures for isomorphism with the local environment on the y axis and pressures for consistency within the organization on the x axis.

For example, consider a foreign subsidiary that has been required by local law to adopt specific hiring practices and labor policies. Such coercive isomorphism would be represented as high pressure for adaptation to the local environment. As another example, the firm's internal financial reporting system might be specified by headquarters in order to achieve consistent evaluation of subsidiary performance and efficient allocation of resources. The need for standardized financial reporting and budgeting would be represented by a relatively high degree of pressure for internal consistency within the MNE.

The elements of structure or process in a foreign subsidiary can be represented in terms of the dual pressures in Figure 1. If we represent foreign subsidiaries in different countries on a third dimension—the z axis—we can depict a given element of structure or process as it is found in different foreign subsidiaries of the MNE. Pressures for conformity to local conditions and for internal consistency may vary from subsidiary to subsidiary, resulting in a varied pattern of

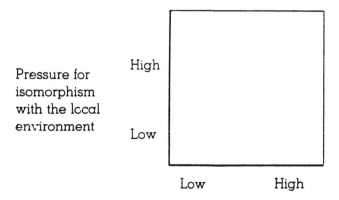

Pressure for isomorphism with the local environment

High

Low

Low   High

Pressure for consistency within the multinational enterprise

Figure 1   Conflicting pressures on a subsidiary of a multinational enterprise.

structures and processes in the enterprise as a whole. When the imperative for internal consistency is high, such variation may be relatively low; when internal consistency is not critical, subsidiaries may, to a greater extent, adapt to local conditions.

Because Figure 2 depicts a single element of structure or process as it is manifested across the many national subunits of the organization, depicting all elements requires a fourth dimension. Thus, the entire MNE can be conceived as a vector of coordinates along four axes: the element of organizational structure or process, country location of the subsidiary, pressure for local conformity in the host country, and pressure for consistency within the MNE. The complex pattern that emerges, with elements of foreign subsidiaries showing varying degrees of conformity to local demands, and with subsidiaries in different countries resembling other subunits of the MNE to

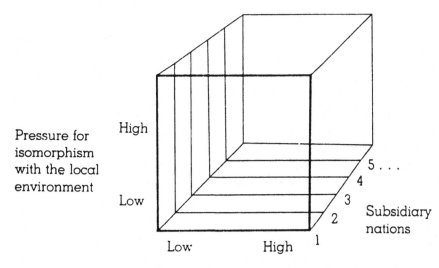

Pressure for isomorphism with the local environment

High

Low

Low   High

5 . . .
4
3
2
1

Subsidiary nations

Pressure for consistency within the multinational enterprise

Figure 2   Variations in structure or process across subsidiaries of a multinational enterprise.

greater or lesser degrees, captures the complex organizational pattern of multinational enterprises. Each vector of coordinates represents one solution to the complex task of organizing and managing a multinational enterprise.

VARIABLES THAT MAY AFFECT SUBSIDIARY STRUCTURE AND PROCESS

Figures 1 and 2 allow us to depict the pattern of organizational structure and process within the MNE, but they do not identify the specific factors that produce this pattern. A number of these independent variables are presented here in a series of hypotheses. Some of these hypotheses are new, whereas others have been tested in empirical studies. We offer them as a collection dealing with the theme of organization theory and the multinational enterprise.

Legal and Regulatory Constraints

The host country's legal regulations represent a strong environmental pressure faced by subsidiaries of MNEs. Doz and his colleagues (1981) enumerated a number of political pressures imposed by national governments on multinational enterprises. To the extent that the state imposes specific regulations regarding pricing policy, labor practices, or other aspects of management, the subsidiary may have little choice but to conform. An MNE may choose not to locate a subsidiary in a given country, or it may seek special dispensation, but otherwise it faces compelling environmental pressures. Described as coercive pressures for isomorphism (DiMaggio & Powell, 1983), these may be among the strongest environmental pressures faced by foreign subsidiaries of MNEs.

> *Hypothesis 1: The similarity of an MNE subsidiary to other firms in the host country will be positively related to the presence of legal imperatives.*

Multidomestic and Global Industries

In his discussion of international competition, Porter (1986) distinguished global industries, in which a firm's competitive position in one country is affected by competition in other countries, from multidomestic industries, in which competition in each country is independent of competition in other countries. Examples of global industries include automobiles and electronic equipment. Multidomestic industries include retailing and consumer goods, although even these industries are showing signs of becoming increasingly global.

Foreign subsidiaries of MNEs in multidomestic industries are relatively self-sufficient organizations. They rely primarily on inputs from the local environment, set prices based on local competition, and otherwise compete with different firms—including subsidiaries of other MNEs—in the country. By contrast, foreign subsidiaries in global industries exhibit a higher degree of interdependence with other subsidiaries within the MNE. Such subsidiaries may be specialized operations that perform only a single step in a global value-added chain (Kogut, 1985), such as assembly or sales.

Foreign subsidiaries in multidomestic and global industries have sharply different relations to the national environments in which they operate. Because they are usually more dependent on local resources, foreign subsidiaries in multidomestic industries have a relatively greater need to gain legitimacy locally and are reliant on income from sales in local markets. Therefore, they may manifest more completely the features of other host-country organizations. By contrast, foreign subsidiaries in global industries may depend on the other units in the MNE to provide managerial know-how, technology, capital, and key personnel. These subsidiaries also may depend on intracorporate sales if they transfer output elsewhere in the organization instead of selling a finished product on the local market. Consequently, these subsidiaries are less dependent on the local environment, are under less pressure to conform to institutional norms, and, otherwise, are less sensitive to selection pressures faced by firms in the same country. Thus, their organizational structure and managerial practices may resemble more fully those found elsewhere in the MNE.

Hypothesis 2: The similarity of an MNE subsidiary to other firms in the host country will be greater in multidomestic industries than in global industries.

Shared Technology

Internalization, particularly as a means to capture the full benefits of proprietary technology, is a leading theoretical explanation of the multinational enterprise (Caves, 1982b; Hill & Kim, 1988; Rugman, 1981). MNEs often transfer technology to foreign subsidiaries because distinctive technology frequently constitutes the firm-specific advantage that allows the MNE to compete successfully against local firms. Such transfers not only diffuse specific technology, they also may serve to transfer technology-related patterns of organizational structure. The use of similar technology by subsidiaries of an MNE can lead to similarities in organizational structures and processes.

Hypothesis 3: The similarity of an MNE subsidiary to other subunits of the MNE will be positively related to the degree of similarity of their technologies.

Parent Country Culture

It was noted previously that pressures for consistency within the MNE are related to concerns about uncertainty. Because tolerance for uncertainty, operationalized as *uncertainty avoidance* by Hofstede (1980), varies between nations, we may hypothesize that mechanisms of subsidiary control, and by extension the responsiveness of subsidiaries to the local environment, may vary between MNEs of differing parent nationalities.

As an example, Japanese firms, which rate high on *uncertainty avoidance*, tend to insist on greater similarity within the organization than American firms and therefore exert relatively strong internal control (Yoshino, 1976). Bartlett and Ghoshal (1989) also found that Japanese MNEs rely on centralization of decision making to a greater degree than U.S. or European MNEs. American MNEs, by contrast, may accept relatively greater diversity within the firm, and thus allow foreign subsidiaries to achieve greater similarity to local organizations.

Hypothesis 4: The similarity of an MNE subsidiary to other firms in the host country will be positively related to the tolerance for uncertainty in the parent country culture.

Cultural Distance

Hofstede (1980) found that national cultures vary significantly along four indices of work-related values. By depicting nations on the basis of their scores on these dimensions, we can characterize them as relatively similar to, or distant from, each other. The United States, Canada, and the United Kingdom, for example, are relatively close in cultural distance, but they are relatively more distant from many Asian and Latin American countries.

The cultural distance between nations of the parent and subsidiary may affect the choice of control mechanisms. If the parent and subsidiary are from similar cultures, there may be less of a need to impose formal controls because a high degree of understanding already exists. Thus, the choice of control system may not only reflect the parent culture (as in the case of Japan, noted above), but it also may be related to the relative similarity or difference in cultures between parent and subsidiary.

Hypothesis 5: Reliance on formal mechanisms of control will be positively related to the cultural distance between the MNE headquarters and the MNE subsidiary.

Composition of the Work Force

Multinational enterprises differ in the extent to which they staff foreign affiliates with employees from the home country. Some MNEs may fill important positions in foreign subsidiaries with expatriate home-country nationals, whereas others rely increasingly on host-country nationals (Tung, 1984).

One key reason for the importance of movement of personnel from the headquarters of the MNE to the foreign subsidiary is that organizational practices are frequently transferred in this manner. Thus, the structural designs of emerging semiconductor manufacturers were influenced by the earlier expertise of the founders, which they carried to the new organization (Brittain & Freeman, 1980). Structural variations and decision-making processes often diffuse in this manner, according to personnel flows (Baty, Evan, & Rothermel, 1971; Pfeffer & Leblebici, 1973).

The prominence of expatriates can be measured either in terms of their number compared to local nationals or in terms of the influence of positions they hold. Whatever way it is operationalized, we would expect that a major presence of expatriates would be associated with the subsidiary's similarity to the parent. In an empirical study that tested this hypothesis, Lincoln, Olson, and Hanada (1978) found that the similarity in functional specialization between California-based subsidiaries of Japanese MNEs and the parent firm was positively related to the presence of "carriers" of Japanese culture, who included primarily Japanese-Americans.

Hypothesis 6: The similarity of an MNE subsidiary to the MNE headquarters will be positively related to the prominence of parent-country expatriates in the subsidiary.

Whereas this hypothesis treats the prominence of expatriates in a subsidiary as an independent variable affecting organizational structure, the degree to which an MNE relies on expatriates may itself be the result of cultural characteristics. Japanese firms, for example, often rely on expatriates to a greater extent than firms from many other countries (Tung, 1984; Yoshino, 1976). Furthermore, it is important to note that use of expatriates may not simply reflect the preference of the MNE, but it may reflect compliance with the laws of the host country. Thus, Hypothesis 1, regarding the coercive pressures of such laws, may affect the presence of expatriates.

Acquired Versus Greenfield Subsidiaries

To this point, our discussion of foreign subsidiaries has assumed they are founded de novo, with subsidiary structure often replicating that of the parent. In many cases, however, MNEs acquire existing operations, and acquired operations have organizational structures in place. In these instances, the parent may be more likely to leave most existing structures intact, demanding conformity only on a few elements of organizational structure or process. We would therefore expect to find greater similarity between the parent and greenfield subsidiaries than between the parent and acquired subsidiaries.

Hypothesis 7: The similarity of an MNE subsidiary to other firms in the host country will be higher for acquired subsidiaries than for greenfield subsidiaries.

The choice of entry strategy may be linked, of course, to the national culture of the parent. As demonstrated by Kogut and Singh (1988), MNE parents with high cultural distance to the subsidiary country may be more likely to choose greenfield ventures rather than to acquire existing operations. This choice may be partly based on the desire to maintain closer control and predictability of operations.

Dependence of the Host Country on the MNE

The tendency of a foreign subsidiary to resemble organizations in the local environment reflects its dependence on resources and institutions in the host country. Such an imperative for isomorphism may be moderated, however, when the subsidiary is part of an MNE on which the host country's economy is highly dependent. If the subsidiary contributes an important economic activity to the host country, the host country may become more dependent on the subsidiary than vice versa. Such a situation may be more common in some less developed countries, where a single MNE may have a relatively more powerful presence, than in some industrialized countries.

> *Hypothesis 8: The similarity of an MNE subsidiary to other firms in the host country will be negatively related to the dependence of the host country on the subsidiary.*

This set of hypotheses, although by no means exhaustive, illustrates how a variety of concerns within organization theory can be used to illuminate the particular issues that characterize the MNE.

REFINING CONCEPTS OF THE ORGANIZATIONAL ENVIRONMENT

The dual pressures on foreign subsidiaries of intrafirm consistency and isomorphism with local environmental conditions have been the subject of much discussion in the literature of international business strategy (e.g., Bartlett & Ghoshal, 1989; Doz, 1980; Doz, Bartlett, & Prahalad, 1981; Doz & Prahalad, 1984). Managers in multinational enterprises must achieve "the strategic integration of their operations in various countries in the presence of strong forces for national responsiveness and fragmentation" (Doz & Prahalad, 1984: 55). They may seek the advantages of the transnational company, which develops its strategy globally and acts locally (Bartlett, 1986; Bartlett & Ghoshal, 1989). The major task of this section, however, is not to contribute to the discussion of multinational strategic management, but to draw on this examination of multinational enterprises to refine current concepts of the organizational environment. The important implications of this discussion for organizational theory are enumerated as follows:

1. **National boundaries are an important force in defining organizational environments.** Existing concepts of the organizational environment have either neglected the issue of national boundaries or conceived of an *international domain* that is separate from other, implicitly national, environmental domains. For many elements of organizational structure and process, however, national boundaries are critical features that define organizational environments, and these should be considered explicitly in all theories that examine organizations in relation to their environments.

2. **National boundaries are of varying importance for different elements of organizational structure and process.** National boundaries do not affect all elements of organizational structure and process equally. Specific elements of an organization may be greatly affected by the distinct institutional, legal, or cultural features of the nation in which it resides. Other elements, including technology and economic competition may instead by affected by global or regional factors that

are not particular to a given nation Although national boundaries are important in composing organizational environments, they do not have equal effects on all elements of an organization.

3. The subsidiary of an MNE faces an environment that includes other subunits within the MNE. In addition to its reliance on the local environment, subsidiaries of MNEs look to each other, as well as to headquarters, for needed resources. A subsidiary's environment therefore includes both elements external to the firm in the local environment and elements internal to the firm elsewhere in the world. The ability to draw on resources from other parts of the MNE, and the imperative for consistency within the MNE, act as counterweights to pressures for adaptation to the local environment.

4. Subsidiaries of MNEs can act as conduits that introduce changes into the host country's environment. To this point, we have sought to identify the forces that affect structure and managerial processes in subsidiaries of MNEs. Our hypotheses suggest the variables that affect organizational structure and processes at a given time, but we have not described how the dual pressures imposed on foreign subsidiaries may lead to changes over time. To be specific, the pressures for consistency within the MNE, due both to initial replication and the ongoing imperative for control, can result in the introduction of new structural forms and managerial practices in a given nation. As stated by Buckley and Casson (1976: 44), "Foreign investment itself is a mechanism for the transfer of social attitudes and social structures, so that similarities between nations not only influence, but are influenced by, foreign investment."

As an example, Westney (1989) noted that high levels of R&D spending by subsidiaries of MNEs have been imitated by local firms in Canada and Australia, leading to higher levels of R&D spending in those economies. As local firms have changed their practices to imitate the practices of successful MNE subsidiaries, the local environment has been changed.

A further example is provided by the Marriott Corporation's experience in opening a luxury hotel in Hong Kong (Basler, 1989). Following company-wide practices, Marriott hired employees to work a five-day work week, thus challenging the local norm of a six-day work week. According to a Marriott spokesman, the corporation was following the labor practices it uses everywhere in the world, except in Saudi Arabia, where the five-day work week is prohibited by law.

Competitors in Hong Kong reacted angrily to Marriott's initiative. "We believe when in Rome, do as the Romans," said the general manager of a rival luxury hotel. "Marriott should follow the general rules and practices we have here" (Basler, 1989: D10). In an effort to punish Marriott, other hotels refused to include Marriott in their listings guide and barred its limousines from special airport waiting areas.

Despite these punitive efforts, Marriott maintained its labor policies and speculated that "within 18 months, there will be some other major cracks in Hong Kong's six-day work week" (Basler, 1989: D10). Hong Kong's prevailing management practices, and perceptions of appropriate human resource management, were likely to be changed by the introduction of practices from an American company's foreign subsidiary. Rather than seeking a fit with the existing national environment, Marriott sought to maintain consistency across its many subsidiaries. Thus, practices introduced by the tendency for intraorganizational consistency may bring about changes in the local institutional environment.[2]

5. Subsidiaries of MNEs can act as conduits by which features of the host country's environment are introduced throughout the organization. Foreign subsidiaries also may act as

---

[2]Marriott's actions in Hong Kong also can be thought of as a competitive tactic to attract capable employees from other hotels, which does not, of course, invalidate the institutional argument. Marriott may have found that maintaining intraorganizational consistency of employment practices gave it a welcome competitive advantage.

conduits for change in the reverse direction: from the host country to other subunits in the MNE. Managerial practices extant in a national environment may be adopted by a foreign subsidiary and may, in turn, be transmitted throughout the MNE.

For example, Unilever, the Anglo-Dutch consumer products giant, facilitates this diffusion of management practices through a method called "Best Proven Practice."[3] Its headquarters identifies innovations and superior practices in subsidiaries and acts as an agent in diffusing these practices to other subunits within the organization.

Therefore, MNEs can act as conduits for the transfer of organizational features from the local environment to other parts of the organization as well as from the MNE to the host country's environment. The result is a force for the homogenization of managerial practices across nations, although, as noted by Dunlop and his colleagues (1975), there are strong limits to such convergence.

6. National environments are increasingly linked, and they affect each other through a variety of mechanisms. In addition to depicting the MNE as one mechanism by which distinct national environments may come to affect each other, there are a variety of other such mechanisms, which include multinational clients and regulatory bodies (Nohria & Ghoshal, 1990) as well as the electronic and print media, educational institutions, professional accreditation, and international consulting firms.[4] As the effects of these linkages continue to grow, MNEs will find themselves operating in national environments that increasingly resemble each other, due not to the economic imperative of industrialization, but to the institutionalization of patterns of accepted behavior. On one hand, the MNE is an agent of change, linking diverse national environments; on the other hand, the MNE must respond to national environments whose accepted patterns of behavior continually shift as they influence each other through a variety of linkages.

Overall, these six observations produce a concept of organizational environments as both complex and fluid. This concept not only emphasizes the importance of national boundaries in demarcating distinct organizational environments, but it also argues that national boundaries are of varying importance for different elements of the MNE. This concept gives explicit attention to the pressures imposed by national environments on subsidiaries of MNEs, yet it shows how intraorganizational consistency allows subsidiaries to resist such pressures. It stresses that national environments differ in culture and law, but at the same time it suggests that MNEs act as conduits that can diffuse administrative practices between nations and can lead to similarities between national environments. Finally, it acknowledges that other institutional forces create linkages between national environments, so that the MNE must respond to changes in a complex set of environments.

RESEARCH IMPLICATIONS FOR ORGANIZATION THEORY

The refinements to the concept of organizational environments that we have advanced, and the relation of multinational enterprises to their environments that we have proposed, provide the

---

[3]Unilever's "Best Proven Practice" technique was described to the first author in an interview with an executive in a French subsidiary of Unilever, Astra-Calvé.

[4]The authors are grateful to Nitin Nohria for suggesting this point.

basis for some new lines of inquiry in organization theory. In particular, they refocus attention on two central questions: How do environments affect organizations? and How do organizations affect their environments?

Many studies have conceived of environments as exogenous to organizations and as imposing undifferentiated pressures on them. The multinational enterprise, comprised of interdependent subunits located in several countries, suggests that the pressures imposed by environments on organizations are not uniform. The ways in which these pressures vary constitute an important area of research.

Resource dependence theory suggests that an organization's structure reflects the need to manage uncertainty and dependence related to importing resources from the environment. If we conceive of MNE subsidiaries as facing an environment composed of MNE subunits elsewhere in the world, in addition to the local environment, we may suggest that organizations have some ability to resist dependence on the local environment. By drawing on resources from elsewhere in the MNE, dependence on the local environment is reduced. The relative multidomestic or global emphasis of the MNE's industry may be an important element in establishing the degree of dependence on the local environment: Subsidiaries of MNEs in multidomestic industries may strongly resemble other host-country firms in their dependence on local resources, whereas MNE subsidiaries in global industries may be less dependent on the local environment but more dependent on the MNE parent and on other subsidiaries. Survival of subsidiaries in global industries may be linked less to resources in the local environment and more to resources from elsewhere in the MNE.

Examining the effect of environments on organizations can also help elaborate the research regarding institutionalization theory. A central feature of studies in institutionalization theory emphasizes the pressures on organizations to take on the structural forms sanctioned by their environments (DiMaggio & Powell, 1983; Meyer & Rowan, 1977). The ideas advanced in this article suggest that subsidiaries of MNEs face environments that include not only the local institutional environment but also, in a very real sense, other parts of the MNE. Because these subsidiaries may experience pressure to maintain structural similarity with that of the parent, they may experience a resistance to isomorphism with their local institutional environment. Institutionalization theory, applied to organizations that span national lines, must consider not only the pressures for environmental isomorphism, but also the resistance to such isomorphism (Westney, 1989).

A consideration of the unique nature of MNEs and the roles they play in organizational populations suggests ways that some questions may be rethought in organizational ecological research. Until now, most of the populations studied have been bounded by national environments. For example, Hannan and Freeman (1989) reported results on the dynamics of competition in the population of semiconductor manufacturers in the United States. Whereas the empirical results are appropriate for the early history of the semiconductor industry, they may not adequately capture the ecological forces at work in the semiconductor industry in more recent times. The survival of U.S. manufacturers of semiconductors is now strongly influenced by Japanese manufacturers such as Fujitsu, Toshiba, and Hitachi. If the semiconductor industry is conceived of as spanning national environments, it may be found that firms within this population face varying environmental conditions. By extension, relatively generous conditions in one country, such as Japan, may make it more difficult for competing organizations in other nations to survive. A more accurate characterization of the population of semiconductor manufacturers would account for both the environmental conditions in multiple countries and the effects of such conditions in one country on survival of firms in another country. Our conjecture is that the lessons of this example apply to other industries as well.

The view of organizational environments as fluid also has implications for research into ways that organizations affect their environments. Institutionalization theory has been concerned with the ways in which organizational forms and practices are diffused, often within the boundaries of a particular country. If we accept the view that subsidiaries of MNEs may act as conduits by which one national environment may influence another, new avenues of inquiry become evident.

Just as MNEs may be able to resist pressures for isomorphism with institutional environments, so too may national environments vary in their acceptance of or resistance to newly introduced structures and processes. Practices introduced by the subsidiaries of MNEs will vary in the extent of adoption, the speed of adoption, and the degree to which they are modified in the new country. These, in turn, are influenced by competitive pressure, cultural distance, relative importance of the subsidiary, and so forth. The examples of Marriott in Hong Kong and R&D spending in Australia and Canada suggest that competitive pressure is positively related to institutionalization of managerial practices from abroad. By contrast, other variables, including the relative distance between cultures, may be associated with the relative difficulty of institutionalization. Research regarding the conditions that moderate the transnational diffusion of organizational structures and processes, especially as facilitated by intrafirm transfers by MNEs, builds on prevailing concepts of the institutional environment.

CONCLUSION

Much research in organization theory has examined organization-environment relations without explicit regard for national boundaries. Historically, this may have been an acceptable approach, and it may be appropriate for studies of institutionalization in public sector organizations or for ecological studies of smaller organizations.

However, for research on organizations that face competitive pressures from overseas, or whose operations span national lines, such a simple concept of the environment is inadequate. Multinational enterprises are comprised of subunits that face pressures for isomorphism with the local environment as well as pressures for internal consistency. We have reexamined the nature of organization-environment relations by drawing on the particular experience of multinational enterprises. Based on this analysis, we have set forth a number of hypotheses regarding the relative impact of these dual pressures and have offered a refined concept of organizational environments.

Providing an improved concept of organizational environments is especially important for the advancement of organization theory in light of the increasing activity of multinational enterprises. The pace of foreign direct investment—both greenfield investments and cross-national acquisitions—continues to increase. The impending integration of the European Economic Community has triggered a new round of international acquisitions, as MNEs search for larger productive capacities and seek a presence in new markets. Changes in the economies of eastern Europe have led to joint ventures that were unimaginable a few years ago.[5] Japanese firms, which until now have favored greenfield investments as a strategy of foreign entry, are becoming more active in the acquisition of foreign firms and thus increasingly face the challenge of adapting organizational structures in foreign countries.

These trends highlight the growing importance of organizations that span national lines.

---

[5] International joint ventures, an increasingly common organizational form, introduce additional complexities: Not only do they face local environmental pressures, but they also draw on the resources and administrative practices of different nationalities. Although beyond the scope of this article, international joint ventures represent an additional avenue of inquiry in organization theory.

Indeed, organizations that neither operate in multiple countries nor are directly affected by competitors and practices in other countries are rapidly becoming the exception rather than the rule. If organization theory is to provide a way of understanding these increasingly prevalent and important organizations, a more comprehensive yet flexible concept of the environment than that found in prevailing theories must be advanced. Recognition of differences between local national environments, which are distinct yet able to influence each other and which are spanned by firms that simultaneously face multiple environments, is a step toward that goal.

REFERENCES

Aldrich, H. E., & Pfeffer, J. 1976. Environments of organizations. *Annual Review of Sociology*, 2: 79–105.

Bartlett, C. A. 1986. Building and managing the transnational: The new organizational challenge. In M. E. Porter (Ed.), *Competition in global industries*: 367–401. Boston: Harvard Business School Press.

Bartlett, C. A., & Ghoshal, S. 1989. *Managing across borders: The transnational solution*. Boston: Harvard Business School Press.

Basler, B. 1989. Marriott defies a Hong Kong custom. *The New York Times*, February 6: D10.

Baty, G., Evan, W., & Rothermel, T. 1971. Personnel flows in interorganizational relations. *Administrative Science Quarterly*, 16: 430–443.

Brittain, J. W., & Freeman, J. 1980. Organizational proliferation and density dependent selection. In J. R. Kimberly & R. Miles (Eds.), *The organizational life cycle*: 291–338. San Francisco: Jossey-Bass.

Brooke, M. Z., & Remmers, H. L. 1970. *The strategy of multinational enterprise: Organization and finance*. London: Longman.

Buckley, P. J., & Casson, M. 1976. *The future of the multinational enterprise*. New York: Holmes & Meier.

Carroll, G. R., & Delacroix, J. 1982. Organizational mortality in the newspaper industries of Argentina and Ireland: An ecological approach. *Administrative Science Quarterly*, 27: 169–198.

Carroll, G. R., Goodstein, J., & Gyenes, A. 1988. Organizations and the state: Effects of the institutional environment on agricultural cooperatives in Hungary. *Administrative Science Quarterly*, 33: 233–256.

Caves, R. E. 1971. International corporations: The industrial economics of foreign investment. *Economica*, 38: 1–27.

Caves, R. E. 1982a. *Multinational enterprise and economic analysis*. Cambridge: Cambridge University Press.

Caves, R. E. 1982b. Multinational enterprises and technology transfer. In A. M. Rugman (Ed.), *New theories of the multinational enterprise*. New York: St. Martin's Press.

Child, J. 1972. Organization structure, environment, and performance: The role of strategic choice. *Sociology* 6(1): 1–22.

Daft, R. L. 1989. *Organization theory and design* (3rd ed.). St. Paul: West.

DiMaggio, P. J., & Powell, W. W. 1983. The iron cage revisited: Institutional isomorphism and collective rationality in organizational fields. *American Sociological Review*, 48: 147–160.

Doz, Y. L. 1980. Strategic management in multinational companies. *Sloan Management Review*, 21(2): 27–46.

Doz, Y. L., Bartlett, C. A., & Prahalad, C. K. 1981. Global competitive pressures and host country demands: Managing tensions in MNCs. *California Management Review*, 23(3): 63–73.

Doz, Y. L., & Prahalad, C. K. 1984. Patterns of strategic control within multinational corporations. *Journal of International Business Studies*, 15(2): 55–72.

Duncan, R. B. 1972. Characteristics of organizational environments and perceived environmental uncertainty. *Administrative Science Quarterly*, 17: 313–327.

Dunlop, J. T., Harbison, H. H., Kerr, C., & Myers, C. A. 1975. *Industrialism and industrial man reconsidered*. Princeton: The Inter-University Study of Labor Problems in Economic Development.

Edstrom, A., & Galbraith, J. 1977. Transfer of managers as a coordination and control strategy in multinational corporations. *Administrative Science Quarterly*, 22: 248–263.

Egelhoff, W. G. 1988. *Organizing the multinational enterprise: An information processing approach.* Cambridge, MA: Ballinger.

Emery, F. E., & Trist, E. L. 1965. The causal texture of organizational environments. *Human Relations,* 18: 21–32.

Ghoshal, S., & Nohria, N. 1989. Internal differentiation within multinational corporations. *Strategic Management Journal,* 10: 323–337.

Hannan, M. T., & Freeman, J. 1977. The population ecology of organizations. *American Journal of Sociology,* 82: 929–964.

Hannan, M. T., & Freeman, J. 1984. Structural inertia and organizational change. *American Sociological Review,* 49: 149–164.

Hannan, M. T., & Freeman, J. 1989. *Organizational ecology.* Cambridge, MA: Harvard University Press.

Hickson, D. J., Hinings, C. R., McMillan, C. J., & Schwitter, J. P. 1974. The culture-free context of organizational structure: A tri-national comparison. *Sociology,* 8: 59–80.

Hill, C. W. L., & Kim, W. C. 1988. Searching for a dynamic theory of the multinational enterprise: A transaction cost model. *Strategic Management Journal,* 9: 93–104.

Hofstede, G. 1980. *Culture's consequences: International differences in work-related values.* Beverly Hills, CA: Sage.

Horvath, D., McMillan, C. J., Azumi, K., & Hickson, D. J. 1981. The cultural context of organizational control: An international comparison. In D. J. Hickson & C. J. McMillan (Eds.), *Organization and nation: The Aston programme IV.* London: Gower.

Hymer, S. H. 1976. *The international operations of national firms: A study of direct foreign investment.* Cambridge, MA: MIT Press.

Jaeger, A. M. 1983. Transfer of organizational culture overseas. *Journal of International Business Studies,* 14(2): 91–114.

Kerr, C., Dunlop, J. T., Harbison, H. H., & Myers, C. A. 1960. *Industrialism and industrial man.* Cambridge, MA: Harvard University Press.

Kogut, B. 1985. Designing global strategies: Comparative and competitive value-added chains. *Sloan Management Review,* 26(4): 15–28.

Kogut, B., & Singh, H. 1988. The effect of national culture on choice of entry mode. *Journal of International Business Studies,* 49: 411–432.

Lawrence, P. R., & Lorsch, J. W. 1967. *Organization and environment.* Boston: Harvard University Press.

Lincoln, J. R., Olson, J., & Hanada, M. 1978. Cultural effects on organizational structure: The case of Japanese firms in the United States. *American Sociological Review,* 43: 829–847.

Lincoln, J. R., Hanada, M., & McBride, K. 1986. Organizational structures in Japanese and U.S. manufacturing. *Administrative Science Quarterly,* 31: 338–364.

March, J. G., & Olsen, J. P. 1976. *Ambiguity and choice in organizations.* Bergen: Universitetesforlaget.

Martinez, J. I., & Jarillo, J. C. 1989. The evolution of coordination mechanisms in multinational corporations. *Journal of International Business Studies,* 52: 489–514.

Mascarenhas, B. 1982. Coping with uncertainty in international business. *Journal of International Business Studies,* 12(2): 87–98.

Meyer, J. W., & Rowan, B. 1977. Institutionalized organizations: Formal structure as myth and ceremony. *American Journal of Sociology,* 83: 340–363.

Nelson, R. R., & Winter, S. G. 1982. *An evolutionary theory of economic change.* Cambridge, MA: Belknap Press.

Nohria, N., & Ghoshal, S. 1990. *Requisite complexity: Organizing headquarters-subsidiary relations in MNCs.* Working Paper 91-109, Harvard University, Division of Research, Graduate School of Business Administration, Boston.

Pfeffer, J., & Leblibici, H. 1973. Executive recruitment and the development of interfirm organizations. *Administrative Science Quarterly,* 18: 449–461.

Pfeffer, J., & Salancik, G. 1978. *The external control of organizations.* New York: Harper & Row.

Porter, M. E. 1986. Changing patterns of international competition. *California Management Review,* 28(2): 9–40.

Prahalad, C. K., & Doz, Y. L. 1987. *The multinational mission: Balancing local demands and global vision.* New York: Free Press.

Robock, S. H., & Simmonds, K. 1989. *International business and multinational enterprise* (4th ed.). Homewood, IL: Irwin.

Rowan, J. 1982. Organizational structure and the institutional environment: The case of public schools. *Administrative Science Quarterly,* 27: 259–279.

Rugman, A. M. 1981. *Inside the multinationals: The economics of internal markets.* New York: Columbia University Press.

Scott, W. R. 1981. *Organizations: Rational, natural, and open systems.* Englewood Cliffs, NJ: Prentice-Hall.

Scott, W. R. 1983. The organization of environments: Network, cultural, and historical elements. In J. W. Meyer & W. R. Scott (Eds.), *Organizational environments:* 155–175. Beverly Hills, CA: Sage.

Shapiro, A. C. 1978. Evaluation and control of foreign operations. *International Journal of Accounting Education and Research,* 14: 83–104.

Singh, J. V., & Lumsden, C. J. 1990. Theory and research in organizational ecology. *American Review of Sociology,* 16: 161–195.

Singh, J. V., House, R. J., & Tucker, D. J. 1986. Organizational change and organizational mortality. *Administrative Science Quarterly,* 31: 587–611.

Singh, J. V., Tucker, D. J., & House, R. J. 1986. Organizational legitimacy and the liability of newness. *Administrative Science Quarterly,* 31: 171–193.

Thompson, J. D. 1967. *Organizations in action.* New York: McGraw-Hill.

Tolbert, P. 1985. Resource dependence and institutional environments: Sources of administrative structure in institutions of higher education. *Administrative Science Quarterly,* 30: 1–13.

Tolbert, P., & Zucker, L. 1983. Institutional sources of change in organizational structure: The diffusion of civil service reform, 1880–1930. *Administrative Science Quarterly,* 23: 22–39.

Tung, R. L. 1984. Human resource planning in Japanese multinationals: A model for U.S. firms? *Journal of International Business Studies,* 15(2): 139–149.

Westney, D. E. 1989. *Institutionalization theory and the multinational enterprise.* Paper prepared for Workshop on Organizational Theory and the MNC, INSEAD, September 1989.

Yoshino, M. Y. 1976. *Japan's multinational enterprises.* Cambridge, MA: Harvard University Press.

Part Three

Review and Questions

Review

According to Stopford and Wells, a systematic relationship exists between a company's international strategy and its organization structure. An international division is adopted when international strategy involves a low degree of foreign-product diversity and a low percentage of foreign sales. Conversely, a mixed or matrix structure is used when there is a high degree of foreign-product diversity and a high percentage of foreign sales. Between these two extremes, worldwide product divisions are associated with a high degree of product diversity but a low percentage of foreign sales, while area divisions are associated with a low degree of product diversity but a high percentage of foreign sales.

In the light of new trends in company strategy and recent changes in the international environment, Egelhoff reexamines the relationships between strategy and structure. He finds that both product and area division structures are associated with high percentages of foreign sales and that only foreign-product diversity distinguishes between the strategic domains of the two structures. A third element of strategy, namely, percentage of foreign manufacturing, influences the choice of organization structure. By creating high interdependence among foreign subsidiaries within the same region, a high percentage of foreign manufacturing combined with a high percentage of foreign sales favors an area division. A high degree of product diversity combined with a high percentage of foreign sales and a high percentage of foreign manufacturing favors a matrix structure.

Rosenzweig and Singh examine relationships between an MNC's structure and processes and its environment by using foreign subsidiaries as the unit of analysis. These subsidiaries face dual pressures to adapt to the local institutional environment and to maintain consistency within the organization. The authors assert that individual subsidiaries perform boundary-spanning roles through which the MNC transacts and negotiates with its differentiated, complex, fluid environment. Specific variables affecting the structure and processes of country subsidiaries include legal and regulatory constraints, the multidomestic or global nature of the industry, shared technology, parent-country culture, the work force, acquired versus greenfield subsidiaries, and dependence of the host country on the subsidiary.

Both papers in Part Three ground their analysis in organization theory. Egelhoff uses strategy as an independent variable in examining specific types of organization structure. Strategy, in this case, represents a view from the headquarters or parent country. In contrast, Rosenzweig and Singh see the environment as the primary determinant of organization structure, emphasizing *elements* of structure and processes. Thus an MNC's structure is a convex of coordinates, each coordinate representing an individual foreign subsidiary.

Because they differ in approach and orientation, much can be gained by combining the two articles. The environment-strategy-structure framework offers a comprehensive conceptualization of their mutual relationships. The inclusion of foreign subsidiaries opens avenues for contributions from other disciplines. The challenge, nevertheless, remains in one's ability to operationalize in the international environment and to include different types of strategy in the analysis.

Questions

1. What are the environment-strategy-structure relationships?
2. At which level of the analysis, i.e., corporate, business, country, or region, should one study environment, strategy, and structure?
3. To what extent is increasing global interdependence bringing about a convergence of country environments?
4. How would a convergence of country environments affect the structure and processes of MNCs?
5. How, if at all, can the strategic importance of its foreign subsidiaries affect the MNC's organization?
6. What effects might an increase in regional economic integration have on an MNC's structure and organizational processes?
7. How do managers conceptualize their organizational environment?

Part Four
Managing Technological Innovation on a Global Scale

Chapter 10

Technology Development in the Multinational Firm: A Framework for Planning and Strategy

Farok J. Contractor and V. K. Narayanan
Rutgers University

Abstract *The authors' purpose is to improve the coupling between technology development and corporate strategic planning in multinational firms by providing a much needed technology planning framework.*

The framework, which is developed in some detail, divides the planning process into three stages: technology scanning, strategy development (product level) and implementation (country level). In the first stage an answer is sought to the question, "What technologies (as distinct from businesses) are we, or should we be in?"; in the second, the aim is to develop a strategy for each of the products from the chosen technologies; in the third, details of implementation on a country-by-country basis are worked out. Although presented as a sequence of three stages, the framework is to be applied iteratively.

The authors argue that technology for all its vital importance to a global company, cannot be treated as a profit centre. This is part of the difficulty in implementing the technology management function, especially in multidivisional and global firms. They believe that use of this framework will make it easier to integrate technology development into the strategic planning process. In addition it will serve to integrate managers from different parts of the company into a formalized technology planning exercise.

INTRODUCTION

The need to incorporate the technological dimension in the strategic planning function of the firm has long been recognized as crucial in a globally competitive environment. But company practice and the scholarly literature have lacked a standard paradigm. Many companies feel that there is a poor coupling between technology development and strategic planning, possibly due to a lack of adequate planning frameworks for technology.

According to a Booz-Allen and Hamilton survey of 800 U.S. executives, two-thirds felt their companies were making inadequate use of their technologies in the strategic development of the firm (Ford, 1988). Among the reasons was the divisionalization of companies which tends to compartmentalize and fragment technology strategy. Some product divisions may not be aware of valuable technologies available from other divisions; the problem is often acute when units of a

Reprinted by permission of Basil Blackwell Ltd. from *R&D Management, 20, 4, 1990.*

transnational firm are geographically and administratively scattered in distinct regional or national profit centres. The management of technology—that is to say, its development, transfer and optimal utilization in the multinational firm—is a function that cuts across the product as well as the geographic dimensions of the company. Increasingly, technology needs to be developed and used by more than one product group or nation for maximum efficiency and exploitation. Moreover, a typical technology cycle from research to commercialization takes about ten years whereas a normal corporate planning cycle is three to five years; finally, the R&D function may be overly centralized.

A planning framework should address the following concerns. First, the Research and Development process can no longer be considered sequential, but rather synchronous with global manufacturing and global marketing decisions (Takeuchi and Nonaka, 1986). This calls for an enlarged role for the R&D manager. But most firms are organized with regions or global product divisions as profit centres (Chandler, 1986; Porter, 1986). How to harness the apparently different technology strategies and capabilities of various divisions into an overall global strategy direction for the firm is a key issue tackled by this paper. Second, the environment in many industries has undergone such a rapid transformation that technology acquisition from other firms sometimes has as great a strategic importance as internal development or the sale of technology beyond the firm's boundaries. Third, multi-product and multinational companies have begun to focus on the critical issue of inter-divisional transfer of technology and coordination between different R&D facilities (De-Meyer and Mizushima, 1989). Finally, the effective utilization of the company's technical assets across the many country markets the firm may operate in, is an issue growing in importance.

MANAGING TECHNOLOGY IN THE MULTINATIONAL AND MULTI-PRODUCT COMPANY

Managements used to product divisions or countries as profit centres often neglect the development of a technology strategy. It is difficult to think in terms of a technology as a profit centre or as a unit of measure since its boundaries are often fuzzy and spill over into several product areas. A company that has developed a technology has to know whether to use it in-house and/or how to transfer it to other industries, and in several nations for a full return on its investment. In doing so it must decide which end-applications it will exploit internally, by itself manufacturing and marketing products, and which industries it will serve by contractual transfers such as licensing or joint ventures. When the end-applications are very diverse such as the use of information systems, no computer firm these days can claim to have fully exploited its commercial opportunities without partners and licensees internationally (Wiseman, 1988).

The second reason it is difficult to think of technology as a profit centre is because the lifecycle of a technology may be longer or shorter than that of a product depending on how narrowly we define each.

Third, ordinary capital budgeting and manager evaluation methods break down when a technology is the unit of measurement (Leonard-Barton and Kraus, 1985). Ordinary ROI criteria may not correctly measure the true strategic benefits and costs of a technology program because its externalities are not well measured (Morone, 1989). For instance, investments in Computer-Aided Manufacturing and Robotics often appear to generate a poor ROI because their benefits (external to the manufacturing division) such as superior service and delivery to customers are not incorporated into the analysis (Goldhar and Jelinek, 1982). Using another example, the ROI from a transfer of technology under licensing or joint venture may appear to be superior to that from a fully-owned subsidiary—until, that is, the negative externality of subsequent competition from the licensee or partner is factored in (Contractor, 1985). This is especially true when transferring technology to capable partners in Japan.

On the input side, technology transcends the product and country dimensions since research, development and manufacturing involve numerous techniques, all of which may not be possessed by the firm. This requires a worldwide search followed by an internal development versus external acquisition decision.

Globalization presents the manager with two additional strategy decisions at the manufacturing level. First, the configuration of pieces of the manufacturing and distribution chain must be optimized geographically. The cost of internal technology transfer and coordination of foreign affiliates are two determining variables (Bartlett and Ghoshal, 1987). Second, the costs of internal development and manufacture are weighed against the alternative of an intermediate product simply being bought in. There can be strikingly different strategy solutions in the same industry. Toyota and Nissan for instance, have 18 employees per thousand vehicles produced, compared to over 100 employees for General Motors (Eckard, 1984). The bulk of the difference is not productivity but the vastly greater level of sub-contracted parts and component purchases in the Japanese firms.

Such differences are not just technological, but cultural and organizational. A useful planning framework would link these issues and provide criteria for evaluating questions such as the optimal degree of integration with suppliers, the optimal level of global standardization, and the degree to which the firm will utilize its technical assets by establishing fully-owned foreign subsidiaries versus sharing its technologies with corporate partners and licensees.

This paper proposes that such decisions need to be made at the same time as the R&D function and feed back into it. In today's environment, technology development and international strategy can no longer be separate or sequential decisions. They have to be synchronous (Takeuchi and Nonaka, 1986).

The analytical framework presented in this paper is intended to initiate a common thinking process in a company, between the technologists and business managers who frequently have very different assumptions, approaches to risk, time values and "rules of evidence" (Gold, 1988). This framework is an important first step in initiating a systematic analysis of technology policy by different personnel in a global company. However there is an equally important set of process, behavioural and organizational learning issues, relating to the interaction of diverse personnel from various parts of the firm (Maidique and Zirger, 1985). For want of space these are not covered in this paper and may be the subject of a future article. Here we present the framework.

THE OBJECTIVE OF THIS PAPER: A TECHNOLOGY PLANNING FRAMEWORK

This paper presents a three stage planning process, 1. Technology Scanning and Audit (Firm level), 2. Development Strategy (Technology/Product level) and, 3. Implementation and Utilization (Country level).

The *first* stage is a company-wide inventory, categorization and selection of technologies and an assessment of the firm's overall competitive position. It asks questions such as 'What technologies are, or ought we to be in?'

The *second* stage occurs at the technology-specific or product level. For those technologies chosen to be developed, the second level treats questions such as the allocation of costs over various aspects of the development process, the optimal configuration of global suppliers and co-development partners, speed/cost tradeoffs, the optimal level of global standardization and the degree of vertical integration. Here the focus is on formulating a development and commercialization strategy for a particular product type.

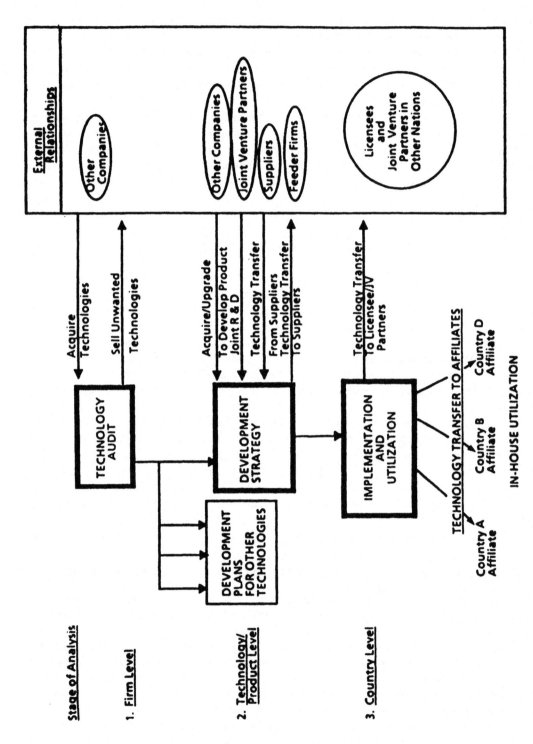

Figure 1 A technology planning methodology for the multinational firm.

The *third* stage called Implementation and Utilization treats the optimum utilization of a developed technology at the country level, incorporating criteria such as the characteristics of the technology, its codifiability, transferability to other nations, the appropriability of profits from the fully-owned subsidiary mode versus a joint venture or a licensing arrangement, and other external factors such as diffusion of technology to potential competitors.

We now describe each stage in some detail.

STAGE 1: TECHNOLOGY AUDIT

During the first stage the firm strives to answer the question 'What technologies should we be in?' Operationally, this means identifying actual and potential technologies inside and outside the firm, assessing the product applications that might emerge, categorizing technologies that define the distinctive competence of the company and deciding how to fill the gaps in the technology portfolio by either internal development, joint research with another firm or external acquisition. As part of planning stage 1 two subordinate issues are also tackled, namely technology progression and an intellectual property strategy in a global arena.

Technology Inventory

Technology inventory refers to the process of identifying all technologies strewn throughout the multinational and multidivisional firm. It may appear surprising, but many companies do not know what is in their technology portfolio. To be meaningful, identification should be specific, not general. For example, a general identification as 'biotechnology' is valueless since biotechnology is a cluster of widely differing technologies from genetic engineering to bio-gas.

Entirely new strategic directions are sometimes revealed by changing the unit of measurement or analysis from a product or nation to a technology. For instance, Martin Marietta's portfolio of *businesses* or divisions includes aerospace, as well as construction aggregates obtained from quarrying operations (Westwood, 1984). Quarrying cost and efficiency depend on the proper placement of explosive charges so as to produce fragments of optimal size, detonated and placed optimally for easy collection. For defence applications the aerospace division had developed ultra-high-speed imaging techniques to track missiles and projectiles. By defining the *technology* rather than the business as the unit of analysis the company spotted the applicability of this new technique to the construction aggregates division. The new technology which can record images of a millionth of a second or less in (literally) explosive environments, was put to use in improving rock fragmentation efficiency through an optimum distribution and timing of charges in a quarry face, improving productivity in quarries by '15–30 percent' (Westwood, 1984). The technology can also be sold or licensed externally.

Levitt's famous question "What Business Are We Really In?" may thus be restated to read 'What Technologies Are We Really In?' (Levitt, 1960). Otherwise, opportunities are missed for want of asking the right question.

A technology inventory process thus identifies and enables the application of a proprietary technology to other divisions of the firm. It also identifies external technology transfer opportunities (whose competitive impact may first be assessed by members of the planning team called 'Gatekeepers,' [Goldstein, 1987]).

Technology Scanning

This is the process of identifying technologies external to the firm that may affect its technology profile. A considerable literature on scanning the technological environment is currently avail-

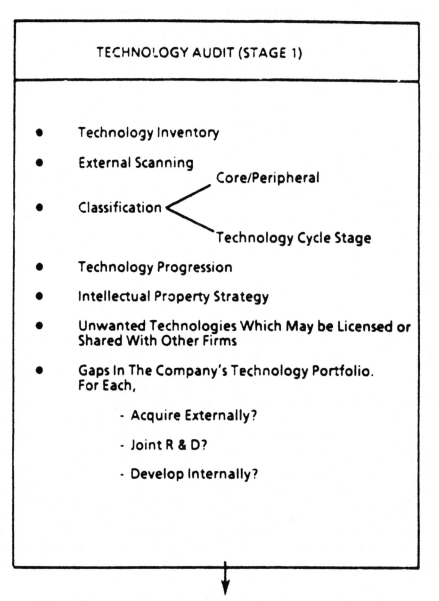

TECHNOLOGY AUDIT (STAGE 1)

- Technology Inventory
- External Scanning
- Classification
  - Core/Peripheral
  - Technology Cycle Stage
- Technology Progression
- Intellectual Property Strategy
- Unwanted Technologies Which May be Licensed or Shared With Other Firms
- Gaps In The Company's Technology Portfolio. For Each,
  - Acquire Externally?
  - Joint R & D?
  - Develop Internally?

Go To Stage 2
Development Plan

Figure 2   Steps in the technology audit process.

able (see Fahey and Narayanan, 1986). Scanning complements the inventory process to determine the firm's desired technology portfolio and because critical 'make or buy' decisions hinge on an awareness of external developments.

Besides an investigative element, scanning requires maintaining interpersonal and organizational linkages with relevant actors. For example, W. R. Grace's laboratory in Japan is partly motivated to serve as a window on developments in Japan. Similarly, Rockwell established an office of external technology development to ensure a continuing exchange of information, in their case from Europe.

Classification of Company Technologies

The next step would be to classify each technology as Base, Core or Peripheral. Since base technologies are known to most competitors, transferring these to other firms outside the industry need not have competitive implications. An example would be ovens and furnaces which are basic to the steel industry but find applications in several others. Core technologies, on which competitive advantage is based may not be easily shared outside the firm even in the mature stage. An example of a peripheral technology is the rather complex art of galvanizing a car body which requires precise application of currents and control over bath chemistry. This kind of technology is peripheral to a large auto company, but it is a very desirable technology to other industries. Some firms have established 'Technology Marketing Groups' to fully exploit the potential of peripheral but valuable technical assets.

Each technology may also be classified according to its stage in its technology cycle. This forces focus on the time element, on how the firm is doing *vis-à-vis* competitors, and on the technology progression issue.

Technology Progression

Technology Progression refers to managing a technology portfolio so that it contains products and technologies at various stages of development and maturity. This is important for balanced long term growth and strategic direction, as well as to ensure that the 'cash cows' will finance new developments—and conversely that the company will in fact have new developments to be financed in the future. Technology progression is an especially crucial aspect for start-up firms to manage. Smith and Fleck (1988) report that new high-technology firms exhibit a high dependence on technology transfer to and from external companies in the early years. Technology acquisitions are for rapid starts. Technology sales are to raise crucially-needed cash. In a later stage there is a greater use of in-house development and commercialization. The firm's business may make a corresponding progression. A biotechnology firm may move from contract research and testing for others, to manufacture of diagnostic kits, and finally to the mass marketing of drugs. In pharmaceuticals and computers the marketing function increasingly presents a formidable, capital-consuming obstacle to be tackled last. Technology progression is therefore a joint technology and financial planning exercise. The entire technology planning exercise has to be multidisciplinary, drawing personnel from several parts of the company.

Intellectual Property Strategy

As part of the overall Technology Audit procedure a firm should formulate a patent and intellectual property strategy. The environment now is quite different from a decade ago.

For the majority of industries in the past, patents were seen as having symbolic value, applied for on defensive grounds, rather than as valuable cash-generating assets in their own right. The company's technology was judged to reside in unpatented 'know-how' rather than in the patent, *per se*, in most industries. Worse, in the 1970s two-thirds of judgments in U.S. courts were made against the patent holder (Kerr, 1988). And a vastly greater number of patents were, and to a considerable extent continue to be, 'worked around' by competitors without legal challenge. Worst of all, the very act of filing in some nations could reveal proprietary secrets, while an underdeveloped legal system provided no effective protection there.

In the 1980s the environment has changed considerably for the computer, semiconductor, pharmaceutical, chemical, and other industries that depend on patents. For these industries, intellectual property protection has become an important strategy and marketing consideration. As the number of technologically proficient firms has increased globally, as competitors are better able to assimilate and reproduce technology, the importance of patent protection is more keenly felt. At the same time, in the U.S. under the Reagan administration, executive and judicial attitudes towards patent rights and anti-trust issues underwent a change. A special federal court for patent appeals was set up in 1982. Appeals heard there have doubled from the 1983 total of 172 (Kerr, 1988), and the rights of patent holders are upheld more frequently than in the 1970s. Enforcement and recourse are also tighter overseas. In 1987, Texas Instruments was said to have collected $191 million in settlements from Asian chip makers. Suits, such as Polaroid's multi-billion dollar claim on Kodak, pepper the headlines.

Today patents have a far more important competitive strategy implication than cash settlements. They are used to stake out a market, to negotiate cross-licensing arrangements, and for technology and territorial swaps rather than for cash value. The strategy lesson has not been lost on foreign firms which, since the mid-1980s, have registered half the patents in the U.S. In 1986 Hitachi topped the list for patents awarded in the U.S.

Outcome of the Technology Audit

The Technology Audit process results in identification and categorization of technologies to be abandoned, developed further and those which may be exchanged, licensed or shared with joint venture partners. The latter may be handed over to a Technology Marketing department for external exploitation. The rest are intended for internal development, and a Development Plan is drawn up for each (in Stage 2 of the Technology Planning Methodology). At the same time, gaps in the company's technology portfolio are identified, with a recommendation to fill the gap by either external acquisition, joint R&D, or via internal development.

STAGE 2: THE DEVELOPMENT STRATEGY FOR EACH TECHNOLOGY IMPACT OF INTERNATIONAL FACTORS

Stage 2 of the planning process is concerned with the development of *one* technology at a time. This may lead to one, or a multiplicity of products, applications and manufacturing processes. Nevertheless, it is important, during the development stage, to keep the manufacturing and tooling aspects in mind from the very start for the most important expected products. In Japanese firms there are often two teams set up simultaneously. While the development venture team is working on the technical aspects, a manufacturing process team is already formulating design and manufacturing specifications. For many industries, we are no longer in Utterback and Abernathy's (1975) comfortable, sequential world where production and manufacturing innovation became crucial only in the later stages of the technology cycle (as they themselves later recognized).

At the technology development stage itself, the firm has to plan for

- Development time vs. cost tradeoffs
- The anticipated level of integration (or quasi-integration with joint venture partners, suppliers, etc.). This affects development costs and time, as well as later manufacturing decisions.
- Allocation of total development costs over various sub-activities such as tooling, pilot plant, startup, and market studies.
- Anticipated speed of imitators and the expected dominant design standards in the industry
- Optimal degree of globalization

DEVELOPMENT STRATEGY FOR A TECHNOLOGY (STAGE 2)

● Company's Position Relative to Competitors
- Development Times
- Level of Integration

● Distribution of Costs in Development Stage

● Acquisition of Technology
- From Licensing
- Joint Venture R & D
- From Suppliers

● Globalization issues
- Standardization of Design/Manufacturing
- Minimum Economic Scale
- Degree of Vertical Integration
- Tariff/Transport/Other Barriers
- International Product Cycle
- Variations Across Nations in
  · Consumer Behaviour
  · Distribution
  · Advertising Practices

Go To Stage 3
Utilization Audit

Figure 3 Considerations in formulating the development plan.

Development Costs and Time

Recently, there has been a burgeoning of ideas about the value of speed as a competitive tool, not only in production (Schmenner, 1988) but also in development of new products (Takeuchi and Nonaka, 1986). We discuss here the development cost vs. time tradeoff. In general, development costs are spread over the sub-categories of (a) Product or process specifications, (b) Pilot plant, (c) Tooling and equipment, (d) Startup including training of personnel and, (e) Market studies.

Two planning decisions are needed:

1. Overall level of expenditure versus development.
2. Allocation of budgeted expenditures over the above sub-categories.

In a world of accelerating product cycles the company that can develop an item faster has a survival edge. Recent work suggests that the Japanese outperform some U.S. industries in terms of shorter development times and/or development costs. Mansfield's (1988) work with 30 matched pairs of American and Japanese firms showed that, in part, Japanese companies have a faster development and commercialization time because of their greater expenditures to consciously shorten the development stage. For all industries Mansfield found the Japanese operating on the time-cost tradeoff function at a point where their costs would show a nine percentage points increase in order to reduce time by one percent; by comparison the U.S. all-industry mean elasticity was about four. That is to say, Japanese firms appear willing to expend on average twice the funds to achieve equivalent reductions in development and commercialization time. Why? Apparently, some of them place a far higher premium on being first (or early) to market as a strategic imperative.

Many Japanese firms on the other hand have lower development costs than comparable American firms in the same industry. There are two explanations. The first has to do with the allocation of development costs within the sub-categories shown in Table 1. The Japanese allocate a far higher percentage of expenditures to tooling and equipment compared to U.S. firms which spend more than double the Japanese level on market studies. Second, the Japanese place a far greater reliance on external technical relationships with suppliers and sub-contractors. The value-added to sales ratio in Toyota or Nissan's factories was about 15 to 20 percent compared to 48 percent for GM in the first half of the 1980s (Eckard, 1984). But the term sub-contracting or outsourcing has a different connotation in Japan. The relationship is not merely contractual. Interlocking equity ownership, intense transfers of technology both ways, and non-adversarial, cooperative behaviour make for what is really a co-development and co-manufacturing relationship. Mansfield's (1988) all-industry comparison from a sample of 30 matched pairs of Japanese and American companies, concludes that the speed and lower cost of development in Japanese industry is partially explained by their external relationships.

Figure 4 depicts three alternative scenarios which the planning group should consider. Scenario A shows our firm having a shallower slope than competitors on the development cost-time tradeoff. If so, it may consider moving from a point such as X to point Y. Even if competitors matched the higher level of expenditures to point Z, our firm would still enjoy time advantage $T_Z - T_Y$. The increase in expenditure $C_Y - C_X$ is justified only if the consequent lead time over competitors $T_Y - T_X$ enables the firm to descend the experience and scale curve first and capture a larger market share—or by having the company's standards adopted as the industry norm. In scenario B our firm and competitors have fairly similar time-cost tradeoff curves. Increased development expenditures are not justified as they may set off negative-sum, oligopolistic countermoves. In Scenario C our firm is able to move to an entirely new, and lower, curve by using

Table 1

Percentage Distribution of Innovation Costs, 100 Firms, Japan and the United States, 1985

				Percent of innovation cost going for			
	Applied research	Preparation of product specifications	Prototype or pilot plant	Tooling and manufacturing equipment and facilities	Manufacturing startup	Marketing startup	Total
All industries combined							
Japan	14	7	16	44	10	8	100
United States	18	8	17	23	17	17	100

Source: Mansfield, E., 'The Speed and Cost of Industrial Innovation in Japan and the United States: External vs. Internal Technology,' *Management Science*, October 1988.

173

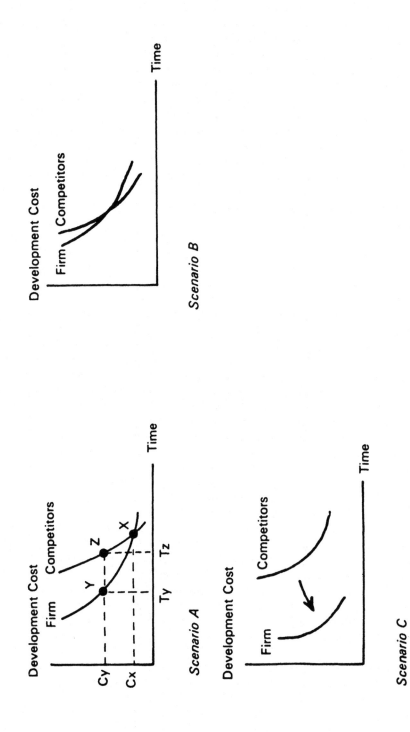

Figure 4 Alternative scenarios for development cost-time tradeoffs.

external relationships such as co-development joint ventures and help from suppliers as in the case of the Japanese auto industry.

The above diagrams are not entirely theoretical abstractions. Some firms calculate alternative budgets for the development expenditure on a particular technology and assess times for each. At the very least, the above figures provide the basis for an informed discussion within the planning group. The Japanese, as well as several American and European companies appear very conscious of the strategic value of such an exercise.

'With global competition, it is becoming imperative for a firm to examine each technology in the development stage for (a) The time-cost tradeoff (b) Competitors' time-cost functions (c) Determining at what point on the function the firm chooses to be—that is to say, what it will spend, and (d) Relationships with suppliers and partners which may lower development times and cost.

Acquisition of Technology

The alternative of acquiring the technology (or pieces of it) externally, should form part of the planning process at this stage. There are various arrangements such as R&D partnerships, development joint ventures, licensing, and contracted research. While we will not examine the benefits and costs of each, we can state some general criteria for evaluating them against each other and the in-house development alternative.

We begin with an overall criterion, useful not only during negotiations, but also useful in identifying acquisition targets. A technology sale between companies may occur when the value of a technology is perceived to be considerably higher by the purchaser than by the company that developed it—so much so, that the incremental profitability to the acquiring firm less the transaction and adaptation cost to the acquirer must be greater than the technology's perceived profitability to the developer, with the final purchase price lying somewhere in between. Otherwise there would be no sale.

Why would the buyer and seller place unequal values on a technology? The reasons are both structural and perceptual.

Among structural reasons are (i) Capital constraints in the developer firm, (ii) Diversification advantages to the acquiring firm, not enjoyed by the present technology owner. These could be geographical, as well as diversification in a product line sense, (iii) Incremental costs of commercialization and launch greater in the developer firm than in the acquiring company, (iv) Preemption of a third competitor from acquiring a significant technology, and (v) Other complementarities or externalities eventually accruing to the purchaser, which the seller cannot enjoy.

In regard to the last point, it is still worth reiterating an assertion made by several authors (Maidique and Zirger, 1985; Gold, 1988; Morone, 1989) that the long term strategy implications and complementarities are often far more important than the narrow calculations of capital budgeting and profit estimates can capture—especially if the time values and perceptions embedded in the calculation do not incorporate the viewpoints of the technology/R&D personnel, as well as executives in different parts of the global firm.

Among perceptual reasons (Why a technology's value is rated differently across companies, as well as across departments in the same firm) are (i) variations in perceptions of the speed vs. cost tradeoffs shown in Figure 4, (ii) sensitivity to the competitive ramifications of linking the firm to a technology developed by others, (iii) questions of whose designs will dominate the industry, (iv) the perceived maturity of the technology, and (v) the possible atrophying of internal technical capability. Stopford and Baden-Fuller (1987) report that it is not so much the economics of production, as perceptions of the 'strategic future' of the European appliance industry, that explains the variations in technology, scale and productivity between European companies. Italian firms were described as believing in European integration, and as having a longer-term orientation than their British counterparts who are said to pursue a policy of defending their 'national niche.'

Later in the paper, we discuss the third alternative of co-developing a technology via contracted or cooperative relationships. There are benefits and costs. For instance, joint ventures and co-development partnerships are often quicker and entail lower overall development costs; but the market has to be shared, and today's partners may become tomorrow's enemies.

'Globalization' and Its Link to Technology Planning

'Globalization' involves, in part, international plant location and product design decisions. These are determined by minimum economic scale, transport cost, protectionist barriers, after-sales service, flexible manufacturing and other design and production technology questions best considered at the development stage and not after manufacturing methods and specifications are finalized.

Consider two alternative strategies depicted in Figure 5. A 'global' approach strives to cut costs and realize efficiencies by reducing the differences in models of a product sold in different nations. In the development and engineering stages, economies of scale and rationalization are planned from a few large, low-cost plants to serve the world market.

A 'local responsiveness' strategy on the other hand tries to introduce variations, from one country to another, in product design, after-sales service and other technical parameters, in order to suit local customers and governments better. The scale of production is necessarily smaller and the number of plants worldwide is larger compared with a global strategy. The multinational firm can afford to be more decentralized, enabling local managers to be more responsive to local country conditions. Many designs of the product are needed, preferably with easy adaptability to different customer tastes or technical standards. (Also, the overall strategy of the firm can more

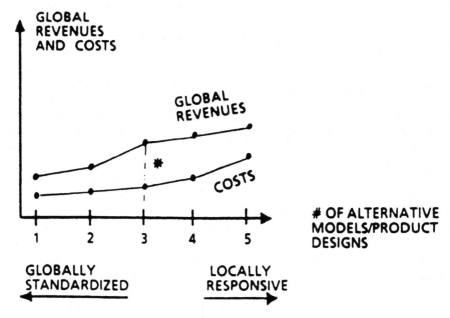

Figure 5 The optimum level of globalization.

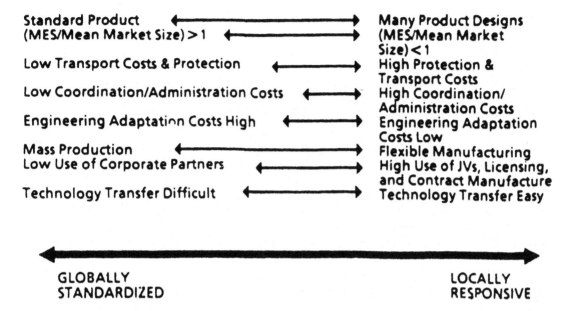

Figure 6 Variables affecting the optimal degree of globalization.

easily include joint venture and licensing arrangements in certain nations, a theme we will return to in Stage 3, the Utilization Audit).

Which of the two strategies is best? As Figure 5 suggests, 'neither' is the likely answer for the majority of industries. The optimum lies somewhere in between. A local responsiveness strategy is rewarded by worldwide total sales revenue increasing with a larger number of models adapted to conditions in each national market. But costs would then increase as well, with a larger number of smaller scale plants and duplication of facilities and staff. Hence the optimum level of local responsiveness versus globalization is likely to be found in an intermediate position.

At the development stage we need to consider technical as well as managerial variables which will affect the optimal degree of globalization of a product. Some are shown in Figure 6, such as Minimum Efficient Scale (MES) of manufacture. Consider the evolution of the television receiver industry. MES has gone from 50,000 receivers per year in the early 1960s, to 500,000 sets in the late 1970s, to 2.5 million in the 1980s (Bartlett and Ghoshal, 1987). This is more than one maker can hope to sell in many countries. Globalizing firms have therefore to assess the ratio of MES over the mean size of the market in the countries they serve. By comparison, pharmaceutical manufacture is amenable to very small scale of efficient manufacture, enabling formulations to be easily varied to suit local medical practice and regulations, without a large cost penalty.

Such strategy questions should be considered at the development stage and not after engineering and specifications are finalized. If considered early enough, it may be possible to develop manufacturing processes that are efficient at smaller scales of operation. This is especially true with computer-aided design and manufacturing, and with the flexible use of corporate partners overseas. An alternative approach is to design the product so as to build in easy, or relatively low cost adaptability to local tastes and conditions.

Consider the large appliance industry (refrigerators, washers, dryers, etc.). Baden-Fuller and Stopford (1988) report that "the market for domestic appliances in Europe is not united" because of persistent "cultural distinctions", brand loyalty and high national entry barriers in the distribution end of the business. Some companies, however, believe that globalization is setting in and that there is a convergence in buyer preferences. In these companies appliances are being redesigned with substantially fewer parts and flexible manufacturing systems which enable variations in output types despite production on a larger scale. In such a case the engineering adaptation costs for switching from one model to another are dramatically reduced. For the large appliance industry in general, Baden-Fuller and Stopford's empirical study presents a mixed picture, with entrenched national firms and considerable impediments to the further concentration of manufacture in fewer and larger plants.

Compared to one factory in each nation, a multinational firm which attempts to serve many markets from a few plants has significantly higher coordination and administrative costs, and risks arising from supply interruptions, currency and political fluctuations. These act counter to the tendency to entirely centralize global operations. These risks may also be perceived by customers who do not wish to be so dependent on a foreign supplier. In the telecommunications and other 'strategic' industries customers, who are often governments, mandate local value-added and joint ventures with local firms to reduce such perceived risks. Despite pouring billions into R&D on state-of-the-art switching equipment, the two leading firms of the early 1980s, AT&T and ITT, failed in their globalization drive; ITT sold off its business entirely.

Today alert companies make the search for the optimum number of models part of their development planning. While some industries such as large appliances move towards fewer variations; others such as automobiles and consumer electronics may be moving towards more choice. Between 1980 and 1985 Matsushita doubled their worldwide models of tape recorders and portable audio equipment (Bartlett and Ghoshal, 1987). In the context of Figure 5 above, Matsushita's incremental development and production costs of introducing an additional model was more than recouped by the incremental global revenue resulting from offering customers a larger choice responsive to local tastes.

Thus each firm hunts for its optimum between the extremes of complete global standardization and producing a different model for each country market—an engineering and strategy exercise that begins at the development stage.

STAGE 3: IMPLEMENTATION AND UTILIZATION AUDIT

The focus at this level of the technology planning exercise is on maximizing the international utilization of the developed product. One country at a time is examined to determine the optimal mode of business. In the broadest sense the firm needs to decide whether to extend its own organization into the foreign nation by means of a fully-owned subsidiary (S), or whether to go in for a contractual mode such as contract manufacture (C), or Licensing (L) the process and/or product design to an independent firm which learns the technology and manufactures the item in the country. In the middle of the spectrum are various quasi-contractual or quasi-integrated modes such as minority-owned joint ventures (JVM), and majority-owned joint ventures (JVS) which function like a subsidiary despite some shareholding by another firm.

Overall, the company ends up with a global pattern of business shown in Figure 8, a planning matrix of products versus countries. In the majority of product/country combinations the markets would simply be served by imports; or no business at all is feasible because of impediments to investment and trade such as protectionist barriers, transportation costs, restriction on foreign investment in certain sectors, and political or currency convertability risks.

For a newly developed product how does a firm decide on which mode is best for a country? Choosing between a firm's own controlled and integrated subsidiary, or a contractual transfer of technology, or quasi-integration with another partner firm is a complex exercise. For each option not only do market revenues and production costs vary, but with joint venture partners and

---

IMPLEMENTATION AND UTILIZATION AUDIT (STAGE 3)

- Create a Technology/Country Matrix
- Assess Market Potential for Each Cell of the Matrix
- For Surviving Combinations Choose Business Mode based on

  - Appropriability of Revenues

  - Global Strategy Fit

  - Cost/Ease of Technology Transfer

  - Reduction in Risk and Cost by accepting JV partners/licensees

  - Opportunity Costs

  - Danger of Creating Competitors

Figure 7 Steps in the utilization audit.

licensees the share of revenues and costs allocated to each firm is also subject to negotiation. Other strategic implications such as creating a potential competitor also need to be considered. Figures 9 and 10 provide some strategic guidance.

Figure 9 shows a decision tree of major options, and it plots them on a return versus 'degree of control' map. In general, a fully-owned subsidiary provides the highest potential return as well as control over strategy and operations. But as Figure 10 indicates it also carries the highest level of risk since the largest invested assets are at stake. Contracted modes carry the lowest degree of control in a long-run strategic sense, especially if a significant technology is transferred to an independent licensee who could eventually become a competitor. But such a risk can be contained by agreement provisions, a strong patent position, or most effectively, by remaining technologically one step ahead of licensees and joint venture partners. Moreover licensing bears the lowest level of commercial risk, most of which is borne by the licensee company.

A fully-owned foreign investment affords the firm the opportunity to appropriate the entire return on the investment and make its investment congruent with global strategy, unhindered by the possibly divergent and parochial objectives of partners. Fully-owned investments are preferred by firms which dominate the designs of products and have a strong patent position (Teece, 1988).

Figures 9 and 10 depict joint ventures as occupying the middle ground on the (1) Return (2) Risk (3) Control and (4) Competitor Risk dimensions. However we should remember that in recent years companies have found that joint ventures in some cases offer the best overall mix on these four dimensions—to the extent that firms often prefer them over the fully-owned subsidiary

Legend:

- C = CONTRACT EXPORT/PURCHASE
- L = LICENSING/TECHNOLOGY PARTNERSHIP
- JVM = MINORITY JOINT VENTURE
- JVS = MINORITY-OWNED JOINT VENTURE SUBSIDIARY
- S = FULLY-OWNED SUBSIDIARY
- ▨ = NO BUSINESS

	TELECOM DIVISION		IMAGING DIVISION		RESOURCES DIVISION		DEFENCE DIVISION	
	SWITCHES	FIBRE OPTICS	TV	STROBOSCOPY	EXPLOSIVES	QUARRYING	AIRCRAFT	MISSILES
COUNTRY A	▨	▨	S	L	▨	JVM	▨	▨
COUNTRY B	▨	L	C	▨	C	JVM	▨	▨
COUNTRY C	JVM	C	▨	S	▨	▨	▨	▨
COUNTRY D	▨	L	JVM	JVS	▨	▨	L	L
COUNTRY E	▨	▨	▨	▨	L	▨	▨	▨
COUNTRY Y	S	S	▨	JVM	L	▨	▨	JVS
COUNTRY Z	▨	C	JVM	JVM	C	▨	C	▨

Figure 8 Utilization audit matrix.

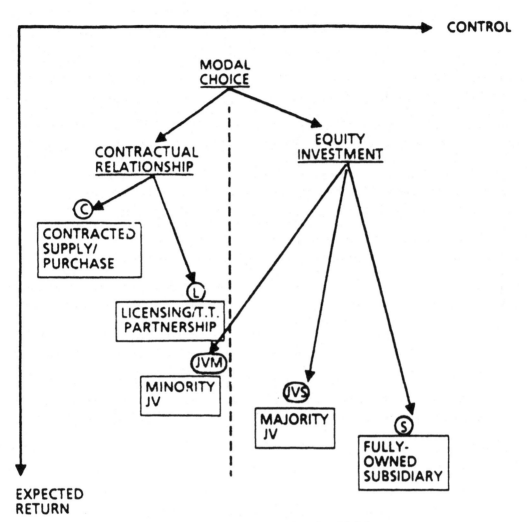

Figure 9 Control vs. return mapping of modal choices.

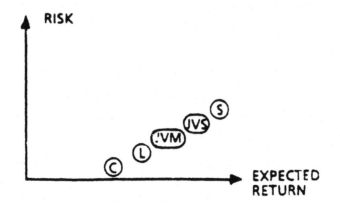

Figure 10 Risk vs. return map of alternatives.

alternative. For instance a company that enters a foreign market alone bears all the investment risk, and its unfamiliarity with the local market may carry a heavy penalty in reduced sales. This penalty can be mitigated by taking a local partner who also shares in the investment risk of a joint venture. Moreover, the local partner can significantly reduce investment costs if they have an existing manufacturing and distribution establishment in the nation. In such cases joint ventures are preferred over fully-owned investments.

In the case of a license, the risk is shifted even further away; the licensee makes the investment and bears the investment risk, allocating the technology supplying company a relatively safe, fixed percentage of revenues. This option is chosen when a company possesses a desirable technology but is unwilling to muster the managerial or financial investment, or face the perceived high risk in the nation, contenting itself with receiving a fixed royalty in return for very little or no incremental investment (over and above the sunk cost of development).

We should not make the mistake of assuming that licensing is undertaken mainly by small technology firms which lack the financial or management personnel resources to make their own investments. Larger, multidivisional and multinational companies have a much larger potential for a profitable licensing and joint venture program for their non-core technologies. The largest of companies such as a GM or a General Electric will typically have about a hundred or fewer majority or fully-controlled foreign investments for its core businesses. It is administratively and financially undesirable to have more. That still leaves hundreds or thousands of possible technology—country combinations unexploited on the matrix in Figure 8. Recall our earlier example of the auto company which had developed a new metal galvanizing technology with better rust protection of its cars in mind. Instead of neglecting the utilization of this technology with applications in other industries in virtually every nation, it can be licensed, or joint ventures set up to greatly increase the return on the R&D investment. And this may be done without the fear that there will be an adverse competitive impact on its main business of selling automobiles.

Medium and large companies have dozens to hundreds of such valuable but underutilized technologies strewn throughout the firm. It takes a technology inventory (Stage 1) plus a Utilization Audit (such as the one recommended in Stage 3) to maximize the return on a company's R&D investment.

SUMMARY

The paper has presented a methodology for technology planning in the multinational and multidivisional firm. Since a technology cannot be operationalized as a profit centre, nor easily regarded as a unit of administrative measurement, the role of technology in formulating strategy is often *ad hoc*, or neglected in many larger, multidivisional companies. This is not for lack of awareness. It is because corporate planning procedures have not fully integrated the technology management aspect.

This paper presents a three-stage technology planning framework. The first stage, called Technology Audit, is a company and world-wide identification of technologies within and outside the firm. At this stage of the planning exercise the planning group examines the technology progression issue and intellectual property strategy, and makes a broad assessment of technologies which may be shared with other firms and those to be reserved for the company's exclusive development. At the same time, gaps in the company's strategy are identified, with a recommendation for how they may be filled by internal development, external purchase of the technology, or by means of a joint venture partnership.

The second stage of the planning exercise called the Development Strategy focusses on one technology at a time. It treats issues such as development cost and time *vis-à-vis* competitors, time-cost tradeoffs in the development budget, allocation of the budget over sub-categories, acquisition of pieces of the technology from partners and suppliers, and the anticipated degree of globalization versus local responsiveness which in turn feeds back into product design and manufacturing technology decisions.

The third stage of the planning exercise is called the Implementation and Utilization Audit. A technology/country matrix is created; each cell is then assessed for market potential. For large, and even medium-sized firms, the matrix can have hundreds of cells. Many of these will be eliminated as having little potential. For a new technology or product the analysis next recommends the mode of business, ranging from fully-owned direct investments to arms-length licensing, with varieties of quasi-integrative or quasi-contractual options such as joint ventures, in between.

While the methodology is presented in three steps, in practice it is iterative. In essence, the exercise integrates the national and functional diversity of the firm into a formalized consideration of the most critical component of its long run strategic success—technology.

BIBLIOGRAPHY

Baden-Fuller, C. & Stopford, J. M. (1988) 'Why Global Manufacturing?', *Multinational Business*, Spring, pp. 15–25.

Bartlett, C. & Ghoshal, S. (1987) 'Managing Across Borders: New Strategic Requirements,' *Sloan Management Review*, pp. 7–17.

Chandler, A. (1986) 'The Evolution of Modern Global Enterprise,' in Porter, M., *Competition in Global Industries* (Boston: Harvard Business School Press).

Contractor, F. (1985) *Licensing in International Strategy: A Guide for Planning and Negotiations* (Westport, CT: Quorum Books).

De Meyer, A. & Mizushima, A. (1989) 'Global R&D Management,' *R&D Management*, Vol. 19, No. 2, pp. 135–145.

Eckard, E. (1984) 'Alternative Vertical Structures: The Case of the Japanese Auto Industry,' *Business Economics*, October, pp. 57–61.

Fahey, L. & Narayanan, V. (1986) *Macroenvironmental Analysis for Strategic Management* (St. Paul: West Publishing Co.).

Ford, D. (1988) 'Develop Your Technology Strategy,' *Long Range Planning*. Vol. 21, No. 5, pp. 85–95.

Gold, B. (1988) 'Charting a Course to Superior Technology Evaluation,' *Sloan Management Review*, pp. 19–27.

Goldhar, J. & Jelinek, M. (1982) 'CAM Sets New Rules for Production,' *Harvard Business Review*, pp. 85–91.

Goldstein, M. (1987) 'Gatekeepers Fit the Key into New Technology,' *Industry Week*, November 16, pp. 75–77.

Kennedy, C. (1988) 'Planning Global Strategies for 3M,' *Long Range Planning*, Vol. 21, No. 1, pp. 9–17.

Kerr, J. (1988) 'Management's New Cry: Fight for Your Technology Rights,' *Electronic Business*, August 15, pp. 44–48.

Lenz, R. & Engledow, J. (1986) 'Environmental Analysis Units And Strategic Decision Making: A Field Study of Selected Leading Edge Corporations,' *Strategic Management Journal*, Vol. 7, No. 1, pp. 69–83.

Leonard-Barton, D. & Kraus, W. (1985) 'Implementing New Technology,' *Harvard Business Review*, pp. 102–110.

Levitt, T. (1960) 'Marketing Myopia,' *Harvard Business Review*.

Maidique, M. & Zirger, B. (1985) 'The New Product Learning Cycle,' *Research Policy.* December.

Mansfield, E. (1988) 'The Speed and Cost of Industrial Innovation in Japan and the United States: External vs. Internal Technology,' *Management Science*, pp. 1157–1168.

Morone, J. (1989) 'Strategic Use of Technology,' *California Management Review*, Summer, pp. 91–112.

Porter, M. (1986) 'Competition in Global Industries: A Conceptual Framework,' in Porter, M., *Competition in Global Industries* (Boston: Harvard Business School Press).

Schon, D. (1967) 'Forecasting and Technological Change,' *Daedalus*, pp. 759–770.

Schmenner, R. (1988) 'The Merit of Making Things Fast,' *Sloan Management Review*, Fall, pp. 11–17.

Smith, J. & Fleck, V. (1988) 'Strategies of New Biotechnology Firms,' *Long Range Planning*, Vol. 21, No. 3, pp. 51–58.

Stopford, J. & Baden-Fuller, C. (1987) 'Regional-Level Competition in a Mature Industry: The Case of European Domestic Appliances,' *Journal of Common Market Studies*, December, pp. 173–192.

Takeuchi, H. & Nonaka, I. (1986) 'The New, New Product Development Game,' *Harvard Business Review*, Jan-Feb., pp. 137–146.

Teece, D. (1988) 'Capturing Value from Technological Innovation: Integration, Strategic Partnering and Licensing Decisions,' *Interfaces*, May-June, pp. 46–61.

Thomas, L. (1984) 'Technology and Business Strategy—The R&D Link,' *Research Management*, May-June, pp. 15–19.

Utterback, J. & Abernathy, W. (1975) 'A Dynamic Model of Process and Product Innovation,' *Omega*, Vol. 3, No. 6, pp. 639–656.

Westwood, A. (1984) 'R&D Linkages in a Multi-Industry Corporation,' *Research Management*, May-June, pp. 23–26.

Wiseman, C. (1988) 'Strategic Information Systems: Trends and Challenges over the Next Decade,' *Information Management Review*, Summer, pp. 9–16.

Chapter 11

Global R&D Management

Arnoud de Meyer
INSEAD

Atsuo Mizushima
Mitsubishi Research Institute Inc.

Abstract *Global R&D management, the management of company R&D effort distributed over different countries, a task that concerns multinational firms, has not been widely studied. The authors have therefore carried out in-depth studies of global R&D conducted by 7 European and 15 Japanese companies. Their objective was to identify 'best practice' and so construct a framework for future research.*

The authors' conclusions are as follows. Globalisation, that is decentralisation of R&D, has become a necessity for multinationals as a result of the localisation of competition, of product life becoming shorter than development time, and the need to locate laboratories near sources of new technological know-how.

Because foreign acquisitions often lead to the acquisition of laboratories, questions are raised about how best to integrate them with the administrative practices of the 'home' organization, whether to reorganize them or to close them down. When it is necessary to set up a new foreign-based laboratory deciding its exact location will require the weighing of factors such as whether the activities are to be market or process oriented, where on the R to D scale the activities will be placed, and how far direction of the laboratory's programmes and work will be decentralised.

Global management also demands special attention to the building of an open communication network among the laboratories, the best form of which has yet to be determined. The main concern in human resource management will be how to select and develop an internationally oriented management corps and how to train R&D professionals to communicate across sites.

If globally dispersed R&D laboratories are to be most effectively used then a new framework for their management needs to be developed. The authors believe that their findings should form a useful starting-point for this task.

1. INTRODUCTION

Management of research and development activities in laboratories located in different countries (i.e. global R&D management), is not a very widely studied topic. The reason is not that the importance of innovation to internationally operating companies has not been recognised. In fact

Reproduced by permission of Basil Blackwell Ltd. from *R&D Management, 19*, 2, 1989.

quite a lot of theory building about the multinational company goes back to Vernon (1966), who proposed with the product cycle theory the fact that the ability to innovate is the *raison d'etre* for multinational corporations. The recent literature on global competition stresses even more the importance of innovation for the multinational corporation in its struggle for survival.

Though innovation is thus recognised by many as having much practical importance to international management, the topic of innovations in multinational companies and more particularly the topic of international R&D has received little attention. Past research on multinational corporations has focussed more on strategy or structure, with most attention being paid to the determinants of headquarters-subsidiary relationships as opposed to their consequences (see for an overview Ghoshal & Bartlett (1986)).

Some efforts have been made to investigate certain isolated aspects of distributed R&D. Ronstadt (1977) has carried out an extensive analysis of the international R&D activities of 7 US multinationals. Behrman and Fischer (1980) report on structured interviews at 34 transnational corporations in the US, 16 in Europe and 6 in Japan. Hakanson and Zander (1986) have reported on four in-depth case studies of Swedish companies. Booz, Allen and Hamilton carried out in 1986 a survey of 16 multinationals to identify the most effective approaches for building global competitiveness in technology (Harris, 1987). All of these studies are studies of 'best practice'. None of them has even attempted to measure the relationship between performance and the practice used. In this paper, we will attempt to summarize the issues and problems in global R&D management, on the basis of these four studies, and our own case-based research. We will also propose a framework for further research.

2. THE RESEARCH PROJECT

Our own research consists at this stage of seven in-depth case studies of European companies operating multinationally, with research and development activities in more than one country. In each of these case studies, several executives involved in R&D activities were interviewed, and the results of these interviews were complemented with desk research, leading to extensive research cases. Part of the study was carried out in parallel with and sponsored by a Japanese research institute. As a consequence, we had access to data gathered in about 15 Japanese companies which had recently started R&D activities overseas.

The term R&D has to be handled with caution. Most of the laboratories we studied were development laboratories rather than research outlets. Only in a few cases did we have access to data on global research management.

Again, it should be mentioned that we did not attempt at this stage of the research to relate performance of the R&D network to the particular practice of R&D management. Our insights too are 'best practice' descriptions which have to be studied with caution.

3. THE STATE OF THE ART

3.1 The Need for International R&D: Why and Where

3.1.1 Why do companies locate R&D abroad? The evidence of R&D abroad is scant and based almost solely on US data. The existing statistics indicate that it is still not very common but that it is on the other hand growing. Some data seem to indicate that international R&D is more common for European companies than it is, even today, for US companies. The early internationalisation of European companies during the colonial period, and the fact that Europe consists of a patchwork of a few larger and many fairly small countries, make it all the more understandable why there are quite a few large European companies which have long-standing R&D laboratories in different countries. One should however not even in Europe overestimate the amount of research carried out abroad. In Sweden for example, the dominant share of R&D (86%) carried out by Swedish multinationals in 1984 was still located in Sweden.

Moreover, the fact that laboratories are located in different countries does not necessarily mean that these European companies have a truly global approach to R&D management. Often, in the past, European companies consisted of a 'confederation' of country subsidiaries, which were more or less independently operating, and had developed their own local development capabilities. The sum of these local development activities cannot always be added up to a global approach to R&D.

Though international R&D might not yet be an important activity from a macro-economic point of view, the strategic management literature indicates that the increasing global competition will require internationally operating companies to re-think the way they have organised their R&D. 'While traditionally many multinational corporations could compete successfully by exploiting scale economies or arbitrating imperfections in the world's goods, labour and capital markets, such advantages have tended to erode over time. In many industries, multinational corporations no longer compete primarily with numerous national companies, but with a handful of giants who tend to be comparable in terms of size, international resource access, and worldwide market position. Under these circumstances, the ability to innovate and to exploit those innovations globally in a rapid, and efficient manner has become essential for survival, and perhaps the most important source of a multinational's competitive advantage' (Ghoshal and Bartlett, 1987). From a management point of view the question of how to optimally manage the R&D function becomes all the more urgent.

These authors look at the globalisation in a pro-active way. A more conservative approach was equally prevalent in some of the Japanese companies we studied. The threat of retaliation activities by the US in the US/Japanese trade discussion, and the fear that the European integration after 1992 could lead to the possible creation of 'fortress Europe', i.e. the closing of the trade borders for outsiders to the big European market, has led many heavily exporting Japanese enterprises to invest in manufacturing facilities overseas. In a technology intensive world, where the speed of the response to market needs becomes an essential element of the competitive strategy, it is felt that pure marketing and manufacturing activities cannot be sufficient in this process of globalisation. Consequently, this process of globalisation will lead to an increase in the extent to which the company develops peripheral activities around its production facilities, e.g. process and product engineering, and ultimately R&D activities.

Another way of looking at what the trigger is for locating R&D abroad has been described earlier by De Meyer (1984). One of the reasons why a firm might consider creating R&D capabilities abroad is that the corporate central research is not able to provide the locally needed technology efficiently and effectively. This problem is in fact a trade-off between the costs associated with the exchange of information—from the parent to the subsidiary and *vice versa*, and associated with markets and/or technology—and the opportunity costs incurred by missed opportunities due to untransferred information on the one hand and the loss of economies of scale and critical mass in R&D on the other. Stated differently, a company will decide to internationalise its R&D activities when the information transaction costs become larger than the costs involved in duplicating the research facilities and organisation. Since information can be market oriented as well as technology oriented, the decision to internationalise R&D can be taken to be closer to the customer as well as to be closer to centres of technical or scientific excellence.

3.1.2 Types of global R&D laboratories. Ronstadt (1977) describes four types of international R&D activities. His model is based on the international product lifecycle and it classifies foreign R&D on the basis of their activities:

1. *Transfer Technology Units* or units established to help certain foreign subsidiaries transfer manufacturing technology from the parent while also providing related technical services for foreign customers.
2. *Indigenous Technology Units* or units established to develop new and improved products expressly for the foreign market. These products were not the direct result of new technology supplied by the parent organisation.
3. *Global Technology Units* or units established to develop new products and processes for simultaneous application in major world markets of the company.
4. *Corporate Technology Units* or units established to generate new technology of a long term or exploratory nature expressly for the parent.

The framework based on these four categories is attractive since it provides a trajectory for the logical evolution of an R&D laboratory overseas. It suggests how to start and develop an international network of laboratories, and it also brings a system of hierarchy to the network of laboratories. But Ronstadt makes the point that the US companies he studied had started their international R&D in all four categories, and that there is no reason why one would have to start with group one. Once started, there seems to be evidence that the vast majority of R&D investments follows the evolutionary pattern from technology transfer unit over indigenous technology unit to global technology unit. This model is of course in agreement with the theory about the international product lifecycle. Globalisation of competition has however brought some doubts about the validity of this model, and we probably have to use Ronstadt's model with necessary caution (De Meyer and Schuette, 1989). The types of laboratories he describes probably still exist, but the evolutionary pattern he sees might have changed.

Behrmann and Fischer (1980) found, for example, that more than one-half of the foreign R&D groups of the American transnationals they studied were established through the evolution of skills, capabilities, and missions, from an initial emphasis on technical support to manufacturing and marketing to applied R&D. This is similar to Ronstadt's model. But foreign laboratories with (global or regional) new product responsibilities (including exploratory research) were, however, more likely to be established through direct placement rather than evolution.

Moreover, Ronstadt's model does not provide a useful tool when it comes to the management of laboratories which are 'created' through acquisition of foreign companies. In these cases, one can end up with laboratories which are at a totally different stage than the one which the central laboratory is able to manage, and some regression to previous stages is not inconceivable.

The Swedish study (Hakanson & Zander, 1986) summarises the reasons for the increasing shares and volumes of foreign R&D as follows:

• The evolution of technical support functions at foreign subsidiaries to encompass more advanced product development tasks. Entrepreneurial subsidiary managers were able to exploit local market opportunities and attract and retain qualified technical personnel.
• Increasing reliance on acquisitions as a strategy for internal growth.
• International rationalisation of production, i.e. the establishment of specialised manufacturing units with groupwide supply responsibility.
• Difficulties in recruiting qualified personnel on the tight Swedish labour market.

- The exploitation of foreign entrepreneurial and technical talent, sometimes in compensation for stagnating R&D at home.
- Advantages of proximity to customers and foreign research establishments.

These reasons include, apart from the market oriented reasons, also explicit supply reasons of availability of personnel (technical or entrepreneurial) or the proximity to the source of technological know-how. They emphasize that more than a few of the foreign R&D laboratories were the byproduct of acquisitions. Ronstadt mentions also that of the 55 R&D investments he studied, 13 were 'incidental' because they were simply part of a company which was acquired for other reasons than the technology. The Booz, Allen & Hamilton survey comes to similar conclusions, but adds explicitly the need to meet (or bypass) national regulatory demands.

In our own case studies it became apparent that all the reasons mentioned in the Swedish study have played an important role. In five of the cases, markets were a primary determinant in locating R&D in different countries. But the lack of researchers, for example, in the home countries was definitely a secondary reason. For developments in more advanced technologies such as genetic engineering, too, lack of researchers in the home country and proximity to sources of technology in the US have played a major role. The proximity to sources of technology seems to be a reason which is increasing in importance. An interesting aspect of these types of sources appeared to be that their number is getting higher. Where, for example, for microelectronics it was quite obvious that in the 1960s, Boston and Palo Alto were sufficient to know what was going on, today there seem to be more places where knowledge in this field is created.

Summarising one can say that internationalisation of R&D activities has to do with a range of factors of market development, supply of technology, and is often triggered by acquisitions. Where the international product lifecycle could explain to a large extent internationalisation of R&D in the sixties and seventies, we need today a model which pays more attention than before to the role of supply of technology and global product development. In the concluding section, we will translate some of these findings into research propositions.

3.1.3 Selection of location. The criteria for the selection of the location are of course quite closely related to the reasons for going abroad with R&D. As Behrman and Fischer stress 'the most powerful inducements to locate R&D in a particular foreign location appear to be the presence of a profitable affiliate in the foreign country, and a growing and sophisticated market with an adequate scientific and technical structure. The primary obstacles to locating R&D abroad appear to be the firms' perceptions of the economies of centralised R&D and the perceived difficulties of assembling an adequate R&D staff in foreign countries.' In no instance was saving money on doing research a primary inducement to decentralise R&D in different countries.

Other reasons that can be found in the literature or which were derived from our own cases are (not in order of importance):

- Proximity to a manufacturing site, to be able to share costly overheads and to have an effective transfer of technology between R&D and manufacturing.
- The availability of adequate local universities, mainly as a stable supply of professionals, and sometimes for the availability of analytical testing or small pilot plant facilities.
- The ability to build up a critical mass of local researchers is most important in those cases where the laboratories carry out global technological research. Although there is considerable variation in the estimates of critical mass, it is clear that it varies with the scientific orientation of an industry and the type of R&D to be performed. Generally consumer

oriented industries and process oriented industries require the least critical mass. Estimates vary from 25–30 technical people for paints and chemicals to 100–200 technical people for pharmaceuticals.

- The attractiveness of sources of technical excellence, e.g. universities or research institutes, advanced customers or suppliers, etc.
- Specific environmental conditions, in particular for food, chemical or agricultural research.
- Government requirements to increase the local technological content of the firm's activities. Though it is played down as a reason for the choice of a particular location, one can find that in the case of pharmaceutical development or products having an impact on the environment, local clinical testing is required in order to meet host-country regulations. These firms usually also mention, however, positive reasons such as speeding up the approval procedures if one can collaborate with local regulatory agencies, or the wisdom of using foreign academic researchers who might be on the local boards of health, etc.
- Excellent communication systems: travel conditions were mentioned, but increasingly the quality of the electronic communications network is envisaged as an asset to a particular location.
- Work permit regulations for expatriates are often mentioned as a minor, though explicit element of the selection decision.

3.2 The Management Challenge

We have no record of companies which would indicate that it is easier to do R&D on a global scale than in a geographically centralised approach. Globalisation of R&D is typically accepted more with resignation than with pleasure. Risks of cost escalation, loss of economies of scale, difficulties to reach a critical mass, or risk of unintentional duplication of research are often mentioned as factors which inhibit firms from internationalising their R&D. In one of our own cases, internationalisation was almost described as an unavoidable nightmare, closer to a marketing gimmick than to an effectively contributing R&D outlet.

The two core management problems as we perceive them through the literature and the case studies are:

- a. How to find the right balance between (i) a central control of the activities to avoid inefficiencies and unintentional duplication and (ii) a level of autonomy which is high enough to allow for an optimal deployment of local entrepreneurship and technical competence.
- b. How to optimise the flows of information between the different laboratories and the individual researchers in those laboratories.

3.2.1 Central control versus autonomy: management style. The Booz, Allen & Hamilton survey puts the management of a network of laboratories into the context of integration. They see primarily two approaches—the 'hub' model and the 'network' model. In the hub model, the home lab retains leadership in all technologies; centralized decision making is the norm. In the network model, individual laboratories focus on different missions.

To decide how to deploy technological resources, participants in the Booz, Allen & Hamilton survey indicated that they generally analyzed three factors—internal efficiency, market proximity requirements, and external constraints. If the demand for internal efficiency is high, participants favour centralized resources and top-down decision making for several reasons: scale advantages and more effective use of assets reduce costs. Multidisciplinary interaction is optimized. And internal communication is made easier.

When market proximity is critical or when external constraints are of prime consideration, companies tend to adopt the decentralized model.

Behrman and Fischer define four managerial styles influencing R&D activities: (1) absolute centralisation, (2) participative centralisation, (3) supervised freedom and (4) total freedom. They have found only a few examples of the first and the fourth types. The two dominant (and as is suggested implicitly in their description the two most successful) are the second and third types.

What they describe as 'participative centralisation firms' tend to exert strong centralised authority over the funding, programmes, and often even over project selection decisions faced by the overseas subsidiaries. There is however some evidence of genuine participation by the overseas subsidiaries in the management of R&D activities.

'Supervised freedom' firms are characterised by both a number of R&D laboratories abroad and a tendency to place primary responsibility for operational decisions in the hands of foreign R&D management. Coordination appears to be far less formal than attempted by the participatively centralised firms and tends to rely on good personal relationships and lots of travel.

Their framework consists in fact of four discrete points on a continuum ranging from a confederation of non-integrated R&D laboratories to a central R&D laboratory which happens by chance to have its activities in different geographical locations. It our own data, the management style was scattered along this dimension and it became clear that the top R&D manager's attitude towards the desirable position on this dimension permeated his/her whole management approach. The choice of where to position oneself on the scale from absolute freedom to absolute control appears to us to be the central management decision in global R&D management. Coordination and control systems, communication systems, planning, seem all to be a consequence of this particular choice.

If our hypothesis should prove to be correct, the challenging question becomes, of course, what are the criteria which guide the top R&D manager in making this choice? Behrman and Fischer make no comments on the success of either of the forms of organisation they described. They conclude however that the scientific orientation of a firm appears to strongly influence the choice between both. Firms with a strong science-orientation tend to employ participatively centralised management styles. Most of the companies which started their foreign R&D as a direct placement rather than as an evolution from technical services, seemed to favour this participatively centralised management style. Consequently, one can say that the position of the technological work carried out by the laboratory *vis-à-vis* the state of the art is a first factor determining the position on this scale.

In our own case studies, three other factors seem to play a role. One of them is a conglomerate of influences which probably can best be defined as managerial culture, or the company's and the manager's basic attitude towards centralisation. In some of the Swiss/German firms we studied, the whole company seemed to be permeated by a tendency towards centralisation, which was reflected in the R&D management style. The second factor has to do with time. The higher the time pressure, i.e. the pressure to shorten the response time to the market's requirements, the higher the tendency seemed to be to go to centralisation. The third factor has to do with the size of the foreign laboratories. The smaller the foreign laboratories, the higher the control exercised over them.

3.2.2 Central control versus autonomy: organisational structure. Traditionally one finds in the literature on the organisation of decentralised (not necessarily internationally) research laboratories three models, i.e.

a. The functional organisation where the several R&D laboratories report through the R&D function to the CEO, and where central R&D has a strong coordinating function.
b. The divisionalised organisation where each division has its own divisional R&D reporting through the division manager to the CEO. In these cases a central R&D can have a coordinating and advising role.
c. The matrix organisation where the subsidiary R&D manager reports both to a divisional and a central R&D manager.

These three approaches can of course easily be translated into an international R&D organisation. Division manager can in such cases be replaced by country manager. In some cases the matrix structure can become a three-dimensional structure in which the local R&D manager has to report to central R&D, the local country manager, and a product or divisional manager.

Hakanson and Zander (1986) propose on the basis of their Swedish study as one of their major conclusions that these traditional practices do not suffice to achieve the required level of international coordination and integration of R&D. They see an evolution to what they call *integrated networks*, characterised by tight and complex controls and high subsidiary involvement in the formulation and implementation of strategies. As a consequence of the strategic allocation of tasks between specialised units, heavy flows of technology, finance, people and materials tie subsidiaries to each other and to the parent. They see as a consequence the requirement for new roles and capacities for headquarters, divisions and subsidiaries. In fact they have developed a somewhat adapted version of the supervised freedom concept of Behrman and Fischer. They summarise their recommendations as follows:

a. The central task of corporate level R&D staff is to act as a liaison between the R&D organisation and corporate management, i.e. monitoring the R&D portfolio of the group to ensure its conformity with overall corporate strategy and to explain technological threats and opportunities in the formulation of corporate strategy.
b. Divisional R&D staff carries the responsibility for the bulk of the R&D effort and must ensure worldwide coordination of R&D within its product areas. A central task in this context is to allocate R&D responsibilities in a way that both matches the technical capacity of different units and minimises the need for close and costly control.
c. Line responsibility for foreign R&D units should rest with local subsidiary management with a great amount of discretion as to the allocation of R&D funds. Only in this way will decision processes be flexible enough to permit the rapid exploitation of new business opportunities.

They describe a fairly organic type of organisation which is strongly dependent on an extensive informal communication network, a great deal of lateral contacts, more or less formal coordination of committees of peers and a strong common corporate goal which provides the cement which is needed to have all subsidiaries evolving in the same direction.

One should be careful with their conclusions. They are based on a very limited number of cases, and the recommendations have no relation to a direct performance measure. However the concept of the integrated network as opposed to a more traditional structure clearly deserves some reflection.

Comparing our cases with these proposals one can see that none of them are pure forms of one of the organisational structures which are discussed above. We have found limited matrix structures with strong functional or divisional components, integrated networks, purely functional structures and structures which seem to organically move over the years, following the redistribution of power going on in other functions such as marketing and sales. It is fair to say that none of the cases we studied were pure examples of what management theory would describe. They were in almost every case a mixed form. The value of Hakanson & Zander's framework is probably that they have explicitly recognised the messiness of real organisations, and try to explain how the organisations work in those circumstances.

3.2.3 Communication flows. Communication flows have a twofold role in international research and development. As is stressed by Hakanson and Zander, but also mentioned in countless other publications, communication has an important coordinating role. In this sense, it is the variable which can be fine-tuned to influence the position on the managerial style dimension. But beyond this, in R&D communication is at the core of the activities (Allen, 1977). One could argue that management of R&D is to a large extent the management of the information flows between the researchers and between the research team and the outside sources of information.

Management of Global R&D requires a careful monitoring, stimulation or limiting of the flow of information, from corporate headquarters to the subsidiaries, and *vice versa*, but also between the different subsidiaries. To a large extent these communications can be routinised and one can rely on impersonal media, letters, telexes, reports, etc. Each of our case studies indicated that the companies have developed quite elaborate procedures, ranging from traditional written media, to the sophisticated deployment of worldwide accessible computerised databases.

But in the area of R&D the personal face-to-face communication remains of primordial importance. Indeed personal contacts are critical in several stages of the innovation cycle. Time and again it was stressed during the interviews leading to the case studies that lateral information flows had to be stimulated. Tools which were used by the companies we have studied were:

- a policy to stimulate travel and constant telephone contacts between the subsidiary managers and between the technological specialists;
- regular formal meetings or internal seminars with extensive informal 'appendices';
- creation of a company culture which stimulates a very open information exchange;
- organisation of international working groups, project teams, etc. leading to intense personal interaction between researchers of different countries;
- an active policy of job rotation of scientists and managers between different countries;
- language training.

One would hypothesize that some of the person-to-person communication will be replaced in the near future by real-time communication through electronic networks such as video-conferencing, computer conferences, electronic mail, etc. Confronted with that hypothesis, most of the interviews accepted this, but most if not all of them indicated that there existed something which we could define as a 'half-life time' of confidence in electronic communication.

To be able to collaborate on research projects the geographically decentralised members of a research team need to trust each other. This trust can only be created through face-to-face encounters. Once separated, the team members can go on working with each other through electronic means, but like radiation, the trust they have in each other will gradually decrease. When this trust drops below a certain level, a new injection of confidence is needed, and this can only be achieved through face-to-face meetings. What the length is of the half-life time of confidence is not at all clear, but most of the companies with extensive experience with electronic communication systems appeared to have experienced this phenomenon.

3.3 International Human Resource Management

Managing R&D projects is first and foremost managing R&D professionals. Managing global R&D requires managing R&D professionals with a different cultural and educational background and managing the transfer of R&D 'expatriates'. The management of intercultural teams does not seem to pose too many problems, when it comes to researchers: the scientific culture seems to dominate local culture. To manage the laboratories two options are conceivable: local managers or expatriates.

Particularly during the start-up phase of an R&D facility, managers and employees are transferred from the parent company to the R&D laboratory. Edstrom and Galbraith (1977) developed a typology of transfers which is helpful in developing a transfer strategy and also for manpower and career planning.

- Transfer for staffing due to lack of local personnel to fill a given position;
- Transfer for management development. Head office employees can be transferred to positions in subsidiaries to learn how to manage in a foreign environment or to learn specific skills which might exist in a particular laboratory.
- Transfer for organizational development.

However, two things have to be kept in mind when transferring parent or third country nationals to a foreign research site:

1. Extensive literature exists on the high failure rate of expatriate managers. The percentages for premature termination of assignments vary between 10%–35% (variation in respect of the managers' parent country and in respect of the host country, e.g. 9 out of 10 expatriates were found to be significantly less successful in Japan than in previous assignments in the US (Zeira & Banai 1984). The reason most frequently found for this outcome is the inability of the spouse to adjust to the new environment. Pre-departure counselling and training can alleviate some of the pressures for the family and prevent severe cases of culture shock.
2. Using expatriate managers to lead a foreign R&D facility blocks the opportunities for promotion of the host country nationals and therefore often results in a decrease in their identification with the organisation. The conviction is intensified with each new rotation of their foreign superiors (Zeira & Harari, 1979). Such a negative promotional situation can, of course, be avoided through actively reinforcing international careers throughout the organization, i.e. host country nationals have the opportunity to move beyond the regional level thus pursuing a global career similar to the headquarters' managers and scientists.

When it comes to selecting the manager for an international research laboratory, the common approach is primarily to look for technical competence, which almost always prevents immediate failure on the job. Selectors play safe by placing heavy emphasis on technical qualifications and little on the individual's ability to stimulate, develop and manage researchers. One of the interviewers summarized that they would always be looking for a technological 'star' to manage an international research laboratory.

Parallel to on-the-job individual and organizational development activities, off-the-job activities such as joint training programmes and workshops have to be specifically developed in order to build an international network of scientists and researchers.

In all of our cases, scientists and researchers were included in the routine management training activities of the company. Of course, this gave them the opportunity to meet people from other departments in the organization. Development activities tailored to the needs of R&D employees were limited to technology updates and in some cases to project management techniques. The opportunity to meet fellow scientists in a nonresearch related environment in order to build an informal network is thus very limited in light of the fact that managing scientists and researchers is usually viewed by them as very different and demanding.

4. TOWARDS A NEW FRAMEWORK

The previous sections gave an edited summary of what the literature indicates on management of global R&D. Through our own case studies and access to insights on selected Japanese companies, it became clear, however, that our view on management of global R&D will need a different framework in the near future. We will make an attempt here to summarise some of the elements of such a framework in ten assertions which can be used as hypotheses for further research. There is a big danger in this exercise. While case studies provide ample and verifiable data on the past—and are as such an acceptable methodology to understand frameworks as they were successfully or unsuccessfully applied in the past—they often only provide vague and by definition unverifiable options on what is to be expected. Like every forecasting exercise, this one too is full of pitfalls.

A. *On the reasons for globalisation of R&D*

Assertion 1: The accelerated trend towards globalisation of European and Japanese companies has turned what used to be a marginal characteristic of the economy into a key building block of a global competitive posture: international decentralisation of R&D activities has become an essential component of the global firm.

Assertion 2: The sequence suggested by the international lifecycle of sales and marketing, production, technology development and finally research is perhaps still applicable. What has changed is the duration of the period during which one rides down this cycle. Whereas in the 50s and 60s one could have 25 years to go through the cycle, it appears that today it has to be run through in a far shorter period. In earlier periods, one could wait to start up production until sales had grown into a mature position, and one could delay the start of development until production had grown into maturity. The pressure to shorten this time frame leads to a situation where R&D already has to be initiated before one knows the results of production or sales internationalization. Creation of a laboratory under these circumstances has to happen under higher uncertainties, and with less support of an infrastructure already in place.

Assertion 3: Supply of technology will become an increasing important reason for globalisation of R&D. Two elements have, however, changed with respect to this reason. Firstly, the production of technological know-how in research institutes or universities is less concentrated in a few centres of excellence than it used to be. Secondly, in some cases the normal diffusion process of scientific knowledge through conferences and publications in refereed journals, appears to be too slow a process. As a consequence, some companies seem to think that the diffusion of technological know-how is faster through their own channels than through the usual channels of scientific community. Thus, they prefer to create a research centre close to the sources of technological know-how and to diffuse it internally, than to wait until this know-how has spread through the international scientific community by means of conferences and publications. One can expect these companies to have a network of more numerous though smaller laboratories.

B. *On the creation of R&D laboratories abroad*

Assertion 4: Acquisition strategies will lead to an increasing number of laboratories being absorbed. Tools to integrate laboratories after acquisition consist of exchange of researchers, common budgeting and planning, reorganisation or closure of the laboratories. The choice between these different possibilities will be determined by variables such as (a) proximity of the technological activities of the acquired laboratory to the acquiring laboratory; (b) the strategic importance of the acquired laboratory's technological strengths to the acquiring company; (c) the areas of strength of the acquired laboratory on the scale of technological development to fundamental research.

Assertion 5: The technology-driven approach to globalisation of R&D can be based on two different categories of technologies. In some cases we saw the creation of foreign laboratories for technologies related to the existing technological competences of the firm. In other cases, we saw the creation of laboratories specialising in unrelated technologies. One example of this was the creation of an overseas bio-engineering venture by a chemicals firm. It will be clear that the degree of risk and the difficulties encountered in the second type of development are expected to be much larger than in the first type.

C. *On the management of an international network of R&D laboratories*

Assertion 6: Location of global R&D activities will be determined by two categories of factors: (a) what is the orientation of the activities, i.e. towards the market (product) or towards the process, and (b) the *type* of activities, i.e. where the laboratory is positioned on the scale from technical development to fundamental research. Locations close to production sites, customers, research institutions, sources of researchers or simply close to the world experts in the field, will be determined by those two factors.

Assertion 7: The key management decision in global R&D management is the choice of where one wants to position oneself on the scale of absolute centralisation of the management process to absolute freedom of the management process. This choice determines the type of organisation structure, the patterns of formal and informal communication and the human resource management. This choice is not one which is common to all laboratories of the firm, but will be different from one laboratory to another, depending on the types of activities they perform.

Assertion 8: The choice of centralisation versus freedom is a dynamic choice, i.e. it can change over time. It is among other influences determined by the rate of change of the technologies which are developed, the time pressure to deliver results, the managerial culture of the company and the size of the individual laboratories.

Assertion 9: Global R&D management will require new types of organisation structures. The most frequently quoted type of organisation is that of a network of peer laboratories. The precise mechanisms operating in this network are still not well specified.

Assertion 10: The core foci in human resource management in global R&D will be the grooming and selection of the laboratory managers and the training of R&D professionals to increase the exchange of information across sites.

5. CONCLUSION

Global R&D management will be a major element of the management of globally operating companies. International networks of laboratories are not totally new and the literature provides some details on the management of those laboratories. But on the basis of our own case studies it appears that a new model for the management of such a network of laboratories is needed. We have provided in this paper a number of assertions which could lead to such a new framework.

ACKNOWLEDGMENT

Part of this research was sponsored by Mitsubishi Research Institute (Tokyo).

REFERENCES

Allen, T. J., (1977), Managing the Flow of Technology, M.I.T. Press, Cambridge, Ma.

Behrman, J. N., Fischer, W. A., (1980), Overseas Activities of Transnational Companies, Oelgeschlager, Gunn and Hain, Pub. Co., Cambridge, Ma.

De Meyer, A., (1984), Internationalisation of Research and Development, Conference proceedings, EIBA conference, Rotterdam, December.

De Meyer, A., Schuette, H., (1989), Trends in the Development of Technology and Their Effects on the Production Structure in the European Community. *INSEAD Working Paper* 89/10.

Edstrom, A., Galbraith, J., (1977), 'Transfer of Managers as a Coordination and Control Strategy in Multinational Firms', *Administrative Science Quarterly*, Vol. 22(2), pp. 248-263.

Ghoshal, S., Bartlett, C. A., (1987), Innovation Processes in Multinational Corporations, Proceedings of the Symposium on Managing Innovation in Large Complex Firms, INSEAD, Fontainebleau, September.

Harris, J. M., 'The Global Management of R&D Resources', *Outlook*, Vol. 11, New York.

Hakanson, L., Zander, U., (1986), Managing International Research and Development, Mekanforbund, Stockholm.

Ronstadt, R., (1977). Research and Development Abroad by U.S. Multinationals, Praeger Publishers, New York.

Vernon, R., (1966), International Investment and International Trade in the Product Cycle, *Quarterly Journal of Economics*, May.

Zeira, Y., Banai, M., (1984), 'Present and Desired Methods of Selecting Expatriate Managers for International Assignments', *Personnel Review*, Vol. 13(3), pp. 29-35.

Zeira, Y., Harari, E., (1979), 'Host Country Organisations and Expatriate Managers in Europe'. *California Management Review*, Vol. 21(3), pp. 40-50.

Part Four

Review and Questions

Review

Contractor and Narayanan offer a framework that incorporates technological dimensions in strategic planning. Central to their argument is that technology cuts across many products and national boundaries and cannot be treated as a profit center. Technology planning and strategy must be multidisciplinary, drawing contributions from several parts of the organization. Specifically, technology strategy should (1) be synchronous with global manufacturing and global marketing strategies, (2) take into account a company's involvement in multiproducts and multinations, (3) guide a company toward an efficient avenue of technological development, and (4) enable the company to utilize effectively technical assets across nations.

The planning process begins at a company level with an audit of the current portfolio of company technology and a scan of technology external to the company. This technological audit helps the company formulate its intellectual property strategy, highlight its technological gap, and identify "stars" and "dogs" in its technological portfolio.

The second stage of planning is at the product level and concerns the development and commercialization of products from one specific technology. At this stage, the items that need to be evaluated are the time-cost trade-off, the company's competitive position, the means of acquiring technology, and globalization issues.

The final stage is at the country level, where managers must determine an optimal utilization of developed products through different business arrangements in individual countries.

Increasingly, MNCs are decentralizing R&D activities. According to de Meyer and Mizushima, market development is the primary determinant in decisions to locate R&D activities abroad. Global product development, technology supply, and acquisition are additional drivers. Internationalization of R&D activities poses significant challenges to R&D managers, in particular, with respect to management style, organizational structure, communication process, and human-resource development. First, managers must strike a balance between central control and autonomy in R&D activities. Second, they have to develop new roles and capabilities among headquarters, divisions, and subsidiaries that are not offered in a pure form of organizational structure. Third, they have to plan for utilizing different means of communication between headquarters and subsidiaries and among subsidiaries. Finally, they must design a development program for human resources that is oriented to a specific group of organizational members, namely, scientists and researchers.

De Meyer and Mizushima share the belief with Contractor and Narayanan that the efficiency and speed with which MNCs exploit innovations are critical to their success and competitiveness. In these complementary analyses, de Meyer and Mizushima focus on coordinating research and development activities in various locations, whereas Contractor and Narayanan emphasize the development as well as transfer and utilization of technology. Issues raised by de Meyer and Mizushima can be applied to the Contractor and Narayanan planning framework, and vice versa. For example, the globalization issues raised by Contractor and Narayanan can apply to the balance between central control and local autonomy discussed by de Meyer and Mizushima. Also, the structural issues raised by de Meyer and Mizushima can be applied to the coordination of technology used across nations that is addressed by the Contractor and Narayanan model.

Both papers offer *normative* frameworks for global R&D management. For these models to be fully utilized, we need to operationalize R&D and technology. In addition, we need to develop such measurements as R&D capital budgeting and R&D effectiveness. Linkages between practice and performance of technology strategy are also important. In sum, there remain many practical issues of implementation.

Questions

1. What planning tools can companies use in place of, or in addition to, capital budgeting when technology is considered?
2. How can one measure technology in terms of return on investment? How can one measure the success of technological planning?
3. Given that a specific technology has multiple applications and that multiple technologies are used in specific product development, how can a company coordinate different technologies at the development stage?
4. What implications do the models of de Meyer and Mizushima and Contractor and Narayanan have for strategic planning processes and for strategic planners?
5. What implication do the models of de Meyer and Mizushima and Contractor and Narayanan have for international strategy?
6. Is the globalization process of R&D investment "evolutionary" or "direct placement"?
7. What is the relative importance of technology supply, global product development, and market development in the internationalization of R&D activities? What additional factors can influence company decisions to locate R&D abroad?
8. What are the criteria affecting management styles in R&D activities?
9. What is the relationship between technology strategy, practice, and corporate performance?

Part Five
Forming International Strategic Alliances

Chapter 12

Competition vs. Cooperation: A Benefit/Cost Framework for Choosing Between Fully-Owned Investments and Cooperative Relationships

Farok J. Contractor
Rutgers University

Peter Lorange
University of Pennsylvania

INTRODUCTION

How should a company choose between the options of investing in a fully-owned operation versus entering into a cooperative arrangement involving another international firm? The basic intent of this paper is to develop a framework for answering this question. The framework can be used in either a strategic planning sense or in a project cash flow sense, to enable the analyst to select one of the options.

In the last few years, there appears to have been a proliferation of international joint ventures, licensing, co-production agreements, joint research programs, exploration consortia, and other cooperative relationships between two or more potentially competitive firms. Contrast this with the traditional preference of international executives to enter a market or line of business alone. The latter seems to have been particularly true for larger multinationals, especially those based in the United States although for firms based in Japan, Europe and developing nations there has always been a somewhat higher propensity to form cooperative relationships (United Nations, 1978; Stopford and Haberich, 1976). Traditionally, cooperative arrangements were often seen as second best to the strategic option of going-it-alone in the larger firms. Licensing, joint ventures, co-production, management service agreements, etc., have been viewed as options reluctantly undertaken under external mandates such as government investment laws, or to cross protectionist entry barriers in developing and regulated economies.

What makes the recent spate of cooperative associations different is that they are being formed between firms in industrial free-market economies where there are few external regulatory pressures mandating a link up. Instead of the traditional pattern of a large "foreign" firm trying to access a market by associating itself with a "local" partner, many recent partnerships involve joint activities in several stages of the value-added chain, such as production, sourcing and R&D.

Reproduced by permission of Management International Review from *Management International Review*, Special Issue, 1988.

These associations often involve firms of comparable rather than unequal size, both may be international in scope, and each may make similar rather than complementary contributions. Further, the territorial scope of these new cooperative ventures is global, rather than restricted to a single country market as in the traditional pattern of joint ventures and contractual agreements.

Before we discuss the main issue treated in this paper, namely a model to assess the relative benefits and costs of cooperative arrangements over fully-owned subsidiaries, let us take a brief look at data on how common cooperative agreements are, and at at their various forms.

THE INCIDENCE OF COOPERATIVE ARRANGEMENTS

How important are cooperative arrangements such as joint ventures and licensing, compared with fully-owned foreign subsidiaries? For U.S.-based companies, arrangements involving overseas "partners," licensing or local shareholders, outnumber fully-owned subsidiaries by a ratio of 40 to 1. Compared with the approximately 10,000 fully-owned foreign affiliates, there are 14 to 15 thousand affiliates in which the U.S. parent's share is *less* than 100 percent. Of the latter, in about 12 thousand affiliates, the U.S. parent has a 10 to 50 percent equity position, i.e., minority affiliates roughly equal majority and fully-owned affiliates put together.[1] In addition, there are at least 30,000 overseas licensees who have received American technology but where U.S. firms have negligible or no equity stake. (See U.S. Department of Commerce, 1981 and 1985). The fact remains that many of the cooperative ventures, particularly those in which the U.S. company has a minority stake, are rather small affairs. Hence, the above picture can be misleading. By indexes such as assets or number of employees, the fully-owned foreign subsidiaries of U.S.-based multinationals continue to account for over two-thirds of the *value* of American foreign investment, even if these subsidiaries are vastly outnumbered by the shared equity arrangements. Companies based in Europe and Japan are said to have a higher propensity than U.S. firms to enter joint ventures and licensing agreements. But the data remain fragmentary and incomplete, making it hard to verify global patterns of cooperative activities. They are ubiquitous however and are being increasingly factored into global strategy.

TYPES OF COOPERATIVE ARRANGEMENTS

Between the extremes of spot transactions undertaken by two firms, on the one end, and their complete merger, on the other hand, lie several types of cooperative arrangements. These arrangements differ in the formula used to compensate each partner, i.e., the legal form of the agreement, as well as the strategic impact on the global operations of each partner. Table 1 ranks these arrangements in order of increasing inter-organizational dependence which is generally, but not necessarily, correlated with strategic impact (Pfeffer and Nowak, 1976).

For instance, technical training and "start-up" assistance agreements are usually of short duration. The company supplying the technology and training is typically compensated with a lump-sum amount, and will thereafter have minimal links with the start-up company, unless, of course, there is an additional licensing agreement. Similarly, patent licensing involves a one-time

---

[1]These estimates are drawn from U.S. Department of Commerce (1981). In the latest benchmark survey of the Commerce Department (U.S. Department of Commerce, 1985) the numbers of all foreign affiliates and U.S. parents appear to have dropped dramatically from the five years previous survey. But this is a statistical data collection anomaly rather than a fact. For further details on this issue see the appendix to Chapter 1 in Contractor, F., and Lorange, P., *Cooperative Strategies In International Business* (Lexington, Mass.: Lexington Books, 1987).

Table 1
Types of Cooperative Arrangements

	Typical compensation method	Extent of interorganizational dependence
• Technical trainings/start-up assistance agreements	L	Negligible
• Patent licensing	r	
• Production/assembly/"buyback" agreements	m	Low
• Franchising	r; m	
• "Know-how" licensing	L; r	
• Management/marketing service agreement	L; r	
• Non-equity cooperative agreements in		Moderate
— Exploration	$\pi_i = f(C_v \times P_v)$	
— Research partnership	$\pi_i = f(C_v \times R_i)$	
— Development/coproduction	$\pi_i = f(C_i \times R_j)$	
• Equity joint venture	α	High

Key: α = Fraction of Shares/Dividends; r = Royalty as % of Turnover; L = Lump-Sum Fee; m = Markup on Components Sold, or Finished Output Brought Back; π_i = Profit of Firm P in Non-Equity Joint Venture; C_v, R_v = Costs and Revenues of the Venture; C_i, R_i = Costs and Revenues of the Firm i; R_j = Revenues of Dominant Partner.

transfer of the patent right. Compensation, however, is often in the form of a running royalty expressed as a fraction of sales value. In component-supply, contract assembly, "buy-back" and franchising agreements, the principal form of compensation for both partners is the mark-up on the goods supplied, although there could be a royalty arrangement as well, as in the case of franchising. The interdependence between the partners is thus becoming somewhat greater because of delivery, quality control and transfer pricing issues associated with the supply of materials, as well as due to the global brand recognition in franchising.

Know-how licensing and management service agreements assume a closer degree of continuing assistance and organizational links. Studies show that most licensing involves the transfer of know-how and proprietary information (Contractor, 1984). It is not simply a matter of transferring a patent right or providing start-up training. It involves extended links between the two firms and ongoing interactions on technical or administrative issues. Payment in these cases will typically be in the form of a lump-sum fee plus running royalties.

The term "joint venture" usually connotes the creation of a separate corporation, whose stock is shared by two or more partners, each expecting a proportional share of dividends as compensation. But many cooperative programs between firms involve joint activities without the creation of a new corporate entity. Instead, carefully defined rules and formulae govern the allocation of tasks, costs and revenues. Table 1 gives three examples. Exploration consortia often involve the sharing of the venture's costs and revenue from a successful find, by formula. By comparison, the costs of a research partnership may be allocated by an agreed upon formula, but the revenue of each partner depends on what each company independently does with the technology created. In co-production agreements, such as the Boeing 767 project involving Boeing and Japan Aircraft Development Corporation (itself a consortium of Mitsubishi, Kawasaki and Fuji), each partner is responsible for manufacturing a particular section of the aircraft. Each partner's costs are therefore a function of its own efficiency in producing their part. However, revenue is a function of the successful sales of the 767 by the dominant partner Boeing (Moxon and Geringer, 1985). Each of these examples involves different risk/return tradeoffs for the parties.

CHOOSING BETWEEN A COOPERATIVE ARRANGEMENT
AND A WHOLLY-OWNED OPERATION

The decision of whether to enter into a cooperative arrangement or whether to expand via a wholly-owned operation is often a critical issue in international strategy. We now introduce a framework for a cost/benefit analysis comparing the two options.

A cooperative venture may have the effect of increasing the project's revenues and/or decreasing costs over what could have been earned by a fully-owned subsidiary; on the other hand certain drawbacks endemic to cooperative relationships might decrease revenues and/or increase costs over the level of a fully-owned operation. We assume that a company has made projections for the revenues, costs and profitability of a fully-owned operation and a cooperative mode alternative. Using this as a base of reference, we make the following axiomatic statement:

A Cooperative Venture (CV) is Preferred over Fully-owned subsidiary when

$$[(R_1 + R_2) + (C_1 + C_2)] - [(R_3 + R_4) + (C_3 + C_4)] > (1 - \alpha)\pi_{CV}$$

Incremental	−	Incremental	>	Share of
Benefit of		Cost of a		Other Partner's
a CV		CV		Profit in Venture

and/or

if risk is reduced significantly through cooperation

where α = Profit share of firm doing the analysis
      $1 - \alpha$ = Profit share of other partners, $(0 < \alpha < 1)$.

That is to say, a cooperative mode is preferred over the go-it-alone option when the net benefit of the former over the latter is greater than the share of profit of the other partners. Our firm is then better off by cooperating, especially if in so doing, risk is reduced. (We will discuss how operating risks are reduced by cooperation in a later section.)

The terms are defined as under: *A cooperative venture, compared with the fully-owned subsidiary will create Incremental Benefits and Costs.* These are defined in more detail in Tables 2 to 6.

By "direct" is meant the revenue and cost increments directly impinging on the project itself. By "indirect" is meant the effect of undertaking the cooperative venture on the *rest* of the global enterprise, i.e. on other divisions of the company, on affiliates in other countries, and on overall

Table 2
Increased Revenue from Cooperative-Venture (CV) Mode

Direct (R1)	Indirect (R2)
• Other partner's knowledge of market • Other partner's intangible assets such as technology, patents, trademark • Other partner's ties to government or important buyers • One less competitor; hence larger market share • Faster entry improves NPV • Access to market otherwise foreclosed	• More complete product line helps overall sales • Technical or new product ideas learned from other partner, diffused to other parts of company • Markups on components, or product

strategy. The "direct" and the "indirect" revenues and costs do not always have the same directional effect. A licensing agreement or a joint venture for instance, may in itself be directly profitable, but it can be indirectly harmful if it creates a *future* competitor, perhaps in a third country.

The analytical framework applies to all types of cooperative arrangements. We now examine the incremental benefits and costs of cooperation in more detail.

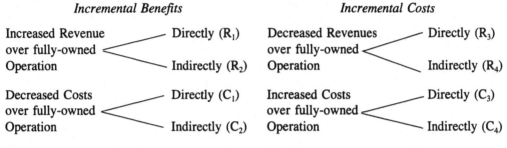

Incremental Benefits	*Incremental Costs*

Increased Revenue over fully-owned Operation — Directly (R_1) / Indirectly (R_2)

Decreased Revenues over fully-owned Operation — Directly (R_3) / Indirectly (R_4)

Decreased Costs over fully-owned Operation — Directly (C_1) / Indirectly (C_2)

Increased Costs over fully-owned Operation — Directly (C_3) / Indirectly (C_4)

(For definitions of R_1 to R_4 and C_1 to C_4 see Tables 2 to 6)

BENEFITS OF COOPERATIVE VENTURES

Increased Revenues from Cooperation (R_1 and R_2)

The benefits of cooperative ventures are summarized in Tables 2 and 3. Among the reasons why cooperative project revenues can be greater than a single-owner operation are the other partner's market knowledge, technology, market access, ties to important buyers and government, and faster entry and payback. Besides there is the obvious, but sometimes important, fact that market share is larger because now there is one less competitor.

Market access, or the other partner's market knowledge remain important factors in both socialist, developing and industrial country markets. In weapons systems NATO encourages or requires tie-ups among defense firms, so that arms purchasing nations get some value added in their economies as well as receive technology (Mariti and Smiley, 1983). The AT&T/Philips joint venture is predicated in part on AT&T's relative inexperience in international markets familiar to Philips. The Boeing-JADC co-production agreement (involving three Japanese firms) is partially based on the idea that sales of the 767 would be augmented in Japan over what may have been possible had Boeing produced the airplane alone. For the Japanese market, even though MITI

Table 3
Decreased Costs from Cooperative-Venture (CV) Mode

Direct (C_1)	Indirect (C_2)
• Economies of scale from larger market shape	• Productivity and technical improvements diffused to other parts of company
• Rationalization based on each partner nation's corporative advantage	
• Government incentives/subsides given to CV's only	
• Using slack/underutilized equipment or design capabilities in each partner lowers capital cost and overheads	
• Fewer headquarter personnel deputed	
• Access through partner to cheaper inputs	
• More productive technology or administrative methods contributed by one partner	

(Ministry of International Trade and Investment) no longer requires joint ventures with Japanese firms as a precondition of entry, foreign investors most often find it expedient to take a local partner who knows local distribution methods (Abegglen, 1982; Reich, 1984). Even when the product itself is simple, such as a commodity or chemical, distribution practices and industrial buying methods appear arcane to non-Japanese. This is an important reason for nearly a thousand joint ventures formed between U.S. and Japanese companies.

The market access motivation is often paramount in patent licensing, since a patent is a territorial monopoly. This right is conveyed to the licensee. As Telesio (1977) and Contractor (1985) show, the territory-allocation issue is very important in licensing in the pharmaceutical and chemical industries.

For small-sized companies lacking international experience, their initial overseas expansion is often more likely to be a joint venture especially when the firm is from a middle-income or developing country. Dunning and Cantwell (1983) show that the lower the GDP per capita of the host nation originating a multinational firm, the more likely will it use joint ventures in its initial international expansion. Firms often have production capability, but lack knowledge of foreign markets for which they depend on their partners. Embraer is a successful Brazilian aircraft manufacturer, helped by its joint venture with Piper. It makes small commercial jets as well as fighters: Initially intended for the Brazilian market, Embraer is now a strong exporter, landing orders even in the most critical market, the United States. Another example is the practice of allying with a prominent retail chain in a new country targeted for expansion, or licensing a well-known trade name in order to enter a new market. When Japanese companies like Casio lacked experience in the U.S. market, they formed a cooperative promotional campaign with established U.S. retail chains. When Murjani, a Far-East based apparel manufacturer first entered the U.S., it was by licensing the Gloria Vanderbilt label. Intriguingly, over time, the Murjani name increased in type size, in the advertisements. Today, they go-it-alone in many markets.

Strategic alliances in the pharmaceutical and bio-technology fields, also have a technological synergy rationale. Contractor (1985) describes cross-licensing agreements. By pooling patents, a superior product is expected. In general, it is important to consider joint ventures as vehicles to bring together complementary skills and talents which cover different aspects of state-of-the-art know-how needed in high technology industries. Such creations of "eclectic atmospheres" can bring out significant innovations not likely to be achieved in any one parent organization's "monoculture" context.

A patent however is not merely a right to a process or design, it is also a right to a *territory*. Often, the marketing or territorial right is as important an issue as technological synergy. Research partnerships have a similar intent.

Faster entry into a market may be possible if the testing and certification done by one partner are accepted by the authorities in the other partner's territories. One partner may cede the rights to a partially developed process to another firm able to commercialize the technology faster, the fruits of the development to be shared in a joint venture. This is a typical pattern among smaller and larger firms (Doz, 1986). A medium-sized company that has invested heavily in developing a new technological break-through may not have on its own, production or global marketing resources to secure a rapid, global dissemination of its use, to achieve a quick or adequate payback for its investment. A joint venture or licensing approach can thus be an important vehicle in achieving such dissemination and realistically getting the necessary payback quickly. This is especially true for smaller firms lacking the internal financial or managerial resources to make their own investments, and important for industries with short product cycles, or rapid technology turnover.

Paradoxically, this is also true in giant firms which are diversified. Take GE as an example, with scores of foreign affiliates, but with several hundred licensing or production contracts and minority joint ventures. The potential country/product combinations for a company with the number of products GE has, run to over ten thousand. Not even a giant firm can invest in all of these. Direct investment in fully-owned subsidiaries is reserved for the most interesting combinations; many of the rest are handled by cooperative ventures. Stopford and Wells (1972) confirm in their study that the propensity to form joint ventures is higher when the entry entails product diversification. Berg, Duncan and Freidman (1982) indicate that large average firm size and rapid growth in an industry correlate positively with joint venture formation.

Indirect benefits (R_2) of a cooperative venture (over a single owner operation) include technical or new product ideas learned from other partner and diffused to other parts of the company (Lyles, 1986). This is likely to have been one motive for General Motors to associate with Toyota—the hope that more productive methods and better quality control could be learned from the Japanese partner. Another GM motive may have been a fuller or more complete product line. Instead of abdicating the smaller-sized end of the automobile business, joint ventures provide American producers with a means of offering a complete range of cars in the showroom. (This is important not only for the conventional marketing reason of overall impact on consumers, but because trading-up as family incomes rise is an established fact of the business.) Pharmaceutical cross-licensing agreements whereby two companies swap patented drugs and territories, are partially predicated on the same idea. Each company is able to offer a fuller range of drugs, in their country, often using the same distribution and marketing fixed costs. Or at least, to each partner, the incremental cost of adding the extra drugs plus the net royalty cost is less than the incremental revenue, so derived.

Another indirect benefit of cooperation is the possibility of having other divisions of the company handle (for a markup) products from the partner organization. While the international division of a company which formed the partnership accounts for only the direct revenues and costs, it may be the product division which derives this indirect benefit. Hence the importance of an overall framework of strategic assessment, which looks at the situation for the whole company. Seen in isolation, a cooperative venture may only be a simple start-up, technical training agreement or a standard patent license. But if the effect of this cooperative move is that it creates a long-term customer for a part or active ingredient, the strategic impact goes beyond the arrangement itself. Examples of this kind are frequently found, in the pharmaceutical industry's licensing practices or in automotive assembly agreements, where the nominal royalty accruing to the headquarters technology licensing group typically will be vastly exceeded by the profit margin earned by the division that supplies the active ingredient for the drug, or the automotive parts (Contractor, 1985).

Reduced Costs from Cooperative Venture Mode (C_1 and C_2)

Important benefits of a cooperative form over a go-it-alone option are reduction in costs, directly and indirectly. (See Table 3.)

Among the reasons why project costs may be lower under a cooperative form are economies of larger scale and rationalization; government incentives available to joint ventures and licensing (but not to fully-owned subsidiaries); lower capital investment and overheads by utilizing slack capacity in the partner firms; and finally, cheaper inputs and more productive methods acquired through the partner. Indirectly, other parts of the company might gain cost advantages from productivity gains and other efficiency improvements learned from the other partner. This was probably an important consideration for GM when it linked up with Toyota.

Joint ventures lower the total capital cost of a project and reduce the slack production and administrative capacity of each partner. This is similar to the cost sub-additivity factor in the economics of cooperative advertising or electric utility pools (Herriott, 1986). To serve a region, electric companies get together in power-sharing arrangements which enable *each* company to install a lower maximum capacity than it would have installed independently. In our analysis, production rationalization can occur when two companies in an industry cooperate. This means that components or sub-assemblies are no longer made in two locations with unequal costs. Production of this item is transferred to the lower cost location in one of the partner firms. But there is an added advantage. Because volume in the other location is now higher, *further* reduction in average unit cost is possible due to economies of larger scale. Many international joint ventures in the automobile business are based on this cost-reduction factor.

Another example is a licensing/franchising operation for the servicing of marine engines and boats in ports over the world. Ships are drawn to the internationally recognized "brandname" for the service facility so that they can enjoy an identically high standard of service anywhere. Moreover, there are important economies of scale in centralized engine rebuilding, parts inventories and training, savings which are passed on to the franchise holder, and thence to the customer.

The synergistic effect of joint ventures was confirmed by McConnell and Nantell (1985) who show that the value of the shares of over 200 firms listed in the New York and American stock exchanges, was increased for those companies that had undertaken joint ventures.

THE "COSTS" OF COOPERATION

Decreased Revenues from Cooperative Venture Mode (R_3 and R_4)

We now examine the possible detrimental effects of cooperative modes as compared with fully-owned investments. The incremental costs of cooperative ventures are summarized in Tables 4 and 5.

As opposed to fully-owned investments, the firm may be constrained by its association and suffer a relative decline in revenues because it does not have the freedom to expand into certain lines of business, or because end-product prices set in collaboration with the partner may be lower than they would like them to be. Contractor (1983; 1985) shows in an algebraic negotiations model that the optimum price for the end-product is different for the two partners in a joint venture or license, in many conditions. This is also observed in practice.

In general, as joint ventures evolve, the relative benefits derived by the partners is frequently not commensurate with their original contributions. According to Hamel, Prahalad and Doz (1986), Japanese firms plan ahead to increase the benefits they extract from an alliance across the "collaborative membrane," leaving the European or American partner in a worse strategic posi-

Table 4
Decreased Revenue from Cooperative-Venture (CV) Mode

Direct (R_3)	Indirect (R_4)
• CV Associated does not allow firm to expand into certain lines of business in the future	• Partner's desire to export decreases sales made by other affiliates in international markets
• Partner reaps the benefit of future business expansion, not proportional to their future contribution	• Partner becomes more formidable competitor in the future
• Setting lower price at behest of partner	

Table 5
Increased Costs from Cooperative Venture (CV) Mode

Direct (C$_3$)	Indirect (C$_4$)
• Cost of transferring technology/expertise to partner • Increased coordination/governance costs • Pressures from partner to buy from designated sources. Or sell through their distribution channel. • Global optimization of MNC partner may not be possible for — Sourcing — Financial flows — Tax — Transfer pricing — Rationalization of production	• Slight increase in headquarters administrative, legal and other overheads • Opportunity costs of executives or technicians deputed to CV

tion. In their view the Japanese often look upon partnerships as a cynical competitive move, based on tactical expediency.

Indirectly, global revenues frequently decline because the partner's desire to have the venture export cuts into the sales of the firm in other countries. In general, revenue declines could occur in the future if the partner turns into a global competitor, having learnt the technology or skills.

The worry of "creating a future competitor" is often overblown, but must be considered when entering into any venture or transferring technology to another firm. Much depends on the industry and the circumstances. Let us consider two opposite examples. One is a chemical company helping to set up a PVC-plastic plant for a Korean firm. The technology is mature, if not widely known in its most efficient production form. The PVC industry is globally decentralized. Delivery to customers from local sources is a more common pattern than imports. Hence there is little reason to fear that the company receiving the assistance will become a global competitor, or otherwise impinge upon the strategy of the firm supplying the technology (except in that one country).

The opposite case of the "junior" partner turning eventually into a global competitor is well documented (but only for Japanese firms). Reich (1985) or Abegglen (1982) relate many examples, including the celebrated stories of Western Electric licensing transistor technology to Sony for $25,000 in 1953 and RCA assisting Japanese companies to make color-television receivers. Apart from Japan, there is no empirical evidence to show how significant this problem is in cooperative agreements. One has to assess whether the partners are mutually inter-dependent and vulnerable later on. Much depends on the duration of the arrangement, the ability of each partner to "go-it-alone" on its expiration, and independently keep up with technical changes in the industry; the territorial or other constraints written into the agreement; and whether the industry is characterized by global production-integration efficiencies or characterized by decentralized adaptation at the country level.

In industries which are "configured" to be country-based or globally decentralized (Porter, 1986), cooperative ventures are less dangerous in terms of creating global competition; but this is true only if the partner is a "local" firm unlikely to make their own direct investments in other countries. Otherwise, even if the industry is territorially fragmented or "multi-domestic", an improved technology can be easily spread by a partner already global in scope. It may take time though. Competition from a former joint venture partner or licensee is likely to be felt sooner, and in greater intensity, in geographically concentrated industries.

Overall, the opinion of the Office of Technology Assessment or of authors such as Contractor (1985) is that U.S. technology transferred to overseas licensees or joint-venture partners does not induce a pervasive competitive threat, barring a few notable cases. The technology receiving organization is often local in orientation, or remains one-step behind; the rate of technical change may be rapid enough to diminish the danger from one transfer; or the terms of the agreement itself may limit the other partner via patents or other restrictive clauses. The potential threat can be dealt with through careful creation of a "black box position" for one-self, emphasizing not only legal and patent protection, but also maintaining control over the venture through staffing, maintaining one's strong independent research momentum, and through linking the partner up through a complex system of relationships.

Increased Costs from the Cooperative Mode (C_3 and C_4)

Costs of a cooperative venture may exceed that of a fully-owned, internalized operation because of the extra elements of having to negotiate and transfer technology and administer an enterprise jointly with another firm. This is, in brief, the "transaction costs" and "governance cost" argument, pioneered by Williamson (1975). Buckley and Casson (1976) and Rugman (1982) place considerable emphasis on the relative efficiencies of "internalized" expansion of the multinational firm, unencumbered by partners.

For a multinational firm, costs rise when global optimization is not possible with respect to sourcing, finance, tax, transfer-pricing and distribution because of the divergent objectives of the partner. A large literature describes these disadvantages. This is typified by Stopford and Wells (1972), Killing (1983), Gullander (1976) and Reich (1985).

Indirectly, a cooperative venture can increase costs to corporate headquarters in legal and administrative overheads for the extra costs of negotiating and monitoring agreements. Many firms with extensive licensing and joint venture agreements need to support larger legal departments than they would otherwise.

RISK REDUCTION BENEFITS OF COOPERATIVE VENTURES

Cooperative ventures reduce a partner's risk by (a) diversifying or spreading the risk of a large project over more than one firm, (b) enabling diversification in a product portfolio sense, (c) enabling faster entry and payback, (d) cost sub-additivity: the cost to the partnership is less than the cost of an equivalent investment undertaken by each firm alone, and (e) reducing political risk in some cases.

A large project such as a new car or airplane is a multi-billion dollar undertaking. Joint production such as the Boeing 767 Project spreads the risk of failure (and the potential gains) over more than one party. This applies also to exploration consortia. We have seen how product portfolio diversification via partnerships such as the GM/Toyota venture reduces market risk; how the total capital investment of a project can be reduced by rationalization and scale economies from a joint venture; and how the experience of both partners, sharing of markets and test results make for quicker entry and payback. All of these reduce risk, besides reducing costs.

The risk sharing function of coalitions is especially important in research-intensive industries like computers where each successive generation of technology costs much more to develop, while at the same time product cycles shrink, leaving less time to amortize the development costs.

Another dimension of risk reduction has to do with containing some of the political risk by linking up with a local partner. Such a partner may have sufficient political clout to steer the joint venture clear of local governmental action or interference (Stopford and Wells, 1972; United Nations, 1978).

Multiple partnerships for risk-diversification purposes are found in many high-tech areas; companies have a stake in many ventures with several potential competitors, in several technologies at various stages of development—almost like dancing with multiple partners, or a loose network (Miles and Snow, 1986). The strategy is to maintain a stake and potential payoff from several (sometimes speculative) projects. This limits risk per venture, while diversifying it over several. The cooperative venture is, in many instances, viewed as a "guinea-pig", perhaps to be brushed aside should it come up with an interesting discovery or market success (Table 6). Especially for medium and small size firms, cooperative ventures may be the only way to reduce risk to tolerable levels, in such industries.

CONCLUSIONS: THE VALUE AND LIMITATIONS OF THE ANALYTICAL FRAMEWORK

This paper presented a benefit/cost framework to enable a firm to choose between competing on a "go-it-alone" basis, versus cooperating with another company in a joint venture, licensing, or other negotiated agreement. The framework detailed direct and indirect, incremental benefits and costs of a cooperative association over a fully-owned investment. The incremental net benefit of a cooperative venture over a go-it-alone alternative has to be not only positive, but moreover, be large enough to cover the other partners' share of the profits in order for the cooperative alternative to be chosen. Or the risk of the cooperation alternative has to be so substantially below the go-it-alone option that the former will be chosen. This must occur in a large number of cases, judging from the prevalence of joint venture, licensing, franchising, management, joint exploration, research partnerships and other contracts in international business.

The above approach can be used to analyze any cooperative venture. In some cases, actual cash flow calculations have been made for the comparison (Contractor, 1985), but at the least, the framework provides a useful strategic planning exercise, which helps to plan negotiation terms with prospective partners. It helps to focus attention not merely on the direct effects of the cooperative venture, but on its indirect and future effects on other parts of the company, so that the overall picture emerges.

The present analysis compares only two options at a time, such as a fully-owned subsidiary or a joint venture *ex ante*. It cannot predict success or failure; it is simply a planning tool. Quantification of every factor may be difficult and tenuous, except in simple cases; but much the same

Table 6
Risk Reduction

- Lower capital investment at stake
  - Partial investment
  - Excess capacity utilization
  - Economies of scale
  - Economies of rationalization and quasi-integration
- Faster entry/certification
- Use CV as guinea-pig
- For large risky projects
  - Limit risk per venture
  - Diversify risk over several
- Lower political risk
- Medium and small sized firms

drawback applies to capital budgeting exercises involved in project planning and projecting future cash flows. At a minimum, the framework provides a useful strategy checklist.

International executives need to acquire a new set of skills since they already negotiate and run far larger numbers of cooperative arrangements with other firms, than fully-owned subsidiaries. In a closed global administrative system, efficiency and optimization require centralized control over fully-owned operations. Some industries with homogeneous products or technological standardization may be moving in that direction (Levitt, 1983). In other industries, because of local mandates, marketing and cultural variation, entrenched competitors, and high development risk, among several factors discussed in this paper, cooperative forms of international business organization can frequently be superior. The educated executive must therefore know both arts, of centralized control as well as external negotiation and cooperation.

REFERENCES

Abblegen, J., "U.S.-Japanese Technological Exchange in Perspective, 1946-1981," in Uehara, C. (ed.), *Technological Exchange: The US-Japanese Experience* (New York; University Press, 1982).

Berg, S., Duncan, J., and Friedman, P., *Joint Venture Strategies and Corporate Innovation* (Cambridge, Mass.: Oelgeschlager, Gunn and Hain, 1982).

Boston Consulting Group, "Strategic Alliance," Working Paper #276, 1985.

Buckley, P. J. and Casson, M. *The Future of the Multinational Enterprise,* (New York: Holmes & Meir, 1976).

Contractor, F. J., *Licensing in International Strategy: A Guide for Planning and Negotiations,* (Westport, CT: Greenwood Press, 1985).

Contractor, F. J., "Technology Licensing Practice in U.S. Companies: Corporate and Public Policy Implications of an Empirical study," *Columbia Journal of World Business,* Fall 1983, pp. 80–88.

Contractor, F. J., "Technology Importation Policies in Developing Countries: Some Implications of Recent Theoretical and Empirical Evidence," *Journal of Developing Areas,* July 1983, pp. 499–520.

Doz, Y., "Technology Partnerships Between Larger and Smaller Firms," (draft paper, August 1976).

Dunning, J. and Cantwell, J., "Joint Ventures and Non-Equity Foreign Involvement by British Firma with Particular Reference to Developing Countries: An Exploratory Study," working paper, University of Reading (Economics Department), 1983.

Gullander, S., "Joint Venture and Cooperative Strategy," *Columbia Journal of World Business,* Winter 1976, pp. 104–114.

Hamel, G., Doz, Y. and Prahalad, C., "Strategic Partnerships: Success or Surrender?" paper presented at the Rutgers/Wharton Colloquium on *Cooperative Strategies in International Business,* October 1986.

Herriott, S. R., "The Economic Foundations of Cooperative Strategy: Implications for Organization and Management," working paper, University of Texas, 1986.

Killing, J. P., *Strategies for Joint Venture Success,* (New York: Praeger, 1983).

Levitt, T., "The Globalization of Markets," *Harvard Business Review,* May-June, 1983, pp. 92–102.

Lyles, M. A., "Learning Among Joint Venture Sophisticated Firms," paper presented at the Rutgers/Wharton Colloquium on *Cooperative Strategies in International Business,* October 1986.

Mariti, P., and Smiley, R. H., "Cooperative Agreements and the Organization of Industry," *Journal of Industrial Economics,* June 1983, pp. 437–451.

McConnell, J., and Nantell, J. R., "Common Stock Returns and Corporate Combinations: The Case of Joint Ventures," *Journal of Finance,* Vol. 40, pp. 519–536.

Miles, R. F., and Snow, C.C., "Network Organizations: New Concepts for New Forms," *California Management Review,* Vol. 28, No. 3, Spring 1986.

Moxon, R. W. and Geringer, J. M., "Multinational Ventures in the Commercial Aircraft Industry," *Columbia Journal of World Business,* Summer 1985, pp. 55–62.

Pfeffer, J., and Nowak, P., "Joint Ventures and Interorganizaitonal Interdependence," *Administrative Science Quarterly,* Vol. 21, September 1976, pp. 398–418.

Porter, M. E., "The Changing Patterns of International Competition," *California Management Review,* Vol. 28, No. 2, Winter 1986.

Reich, R. B., "Japan Inc., U.S.A." *The New Republic,* November 26, 1984, pp. 19-23.

Stopford, J. M., and Wells, L., *Managing the Multinational Enterprise,* (New York: Basic Books, 1972).

Telesio, P., *Foreign Licensing Policy in Multinational Enterprises,* D.B.A. dissertation, Harvard University, 1977.

United Nations (Economic and Social Council), *Transnational Corporations in World Development: A Re-Examination,* (New York: United Nations, 1978).

United States Department of Commerce, *U.S. Direct Investment Abroad, 1977* (Washington D.C.: U.S. Government Printing Office, 1981).

United States Department of Commerce, *U.S. Direct Investment Abroad, 1982: The Benchmark Survey* (Washington, D.C.: U.S. Government Printing Office, 1985).

Williamson, O. E., *Markets and Hierarchies: An Analysis and Antitrust Implications,* (London: Free Press, 1975).

Chapter 13

The Role of Technology in the Formation and Form of Multinational Cooperative Arrangements

C. Christopher Baughn and Richard N. Osborn
Wayne State University

Abstract *An analysis of new cooperative arrangements between U.S. and Japanese industrial firms suggests that technology plays an important role in linking firms, in facilitating strategic positioning, and in influencing the form of the linkage. Firms with a similar emphasis on R&D are more likely to engage in such alliances. Japanese firms appear more likely to use these alliances as a means to enhance involvement in industries of high technological intensity. The form of the linkage appears to be influenced by the technological intensity of the arrangement's product and the intention to conduct joint R&D.*

With the increasingly rapid pace of technological development across Japan, Western Europe, and North America coupled with the globalization of markets, scholars are reconsidering the factors underlying the survival and growth of multinational corporations. Many are calling for multinationals to develop global strategies (e.g., Hamel & Prahalad 1985; Porter 1986; Ghoshal 1987). These strategies often include the formation of alliances with firms based in different developed nations (Perlmutter & Heenan 1986; Harrigan 1987). Unfortunately, comparatively little is known about which firms link, the extent to which such alliances facilitate technological positioning, or conditions influencing their basic forms of governance.

The purpose of this article is to explore some of the key technological factors underlying (a) who will join in forming a new multinational cooperative relationship, (b) the technological positioning of the partners, and (c) the overall structure for the new relationship. The empirical analyses involve new cooperative arrangements between U.S. and Japanese firms during the three year period from 1984 through 1986.

TECHNOLOGY AND MULTINATIONAL COOPERATIVE RELATIONSHIPS

Traditionally, analyses of multinational cooperative arrangements concentrated on relationships formed by large multinationals from a developed nation with a smaller, often less technologically

Reprinted from *The Journal of High Technology Management Research*, Vol. 1, No. 2 (1990). By permission of JAI Press Inc.

sophisticated, firm from a developing country (Connolly 1984; Beamish 1985). The dominant multinational often sought cheap labor, inexpensive sources of raw materials and components, less restrictive governmental regulations and/or access to a foreign market. American multinationals historically pressed to accomplish these ends through wholly-owned subsidiaries (Hennart 1988). The development and form of the arrangement, however, was often controlled by the government of the less developed nation. For instance, host governments, through foreign investment laws or limits on the amount of royalty payable on licensing agreements, have often restricted firms to using joint ventures (Zimmerman 1985; Beamish 1985).

The industries involved in such arrangements tended to be in the "mature" stage of their life cycle, where cost advantage rather than product differentiation-based technological considerations were salient. In contrast, new cooperative arrangements often involve two or more large multinationals and advanced technologies including computers, robotics, electronics and semiconductors (Porter 1986; Auster 1986). Further, a number of the ventures have announced ambitious R&D programs involving the technical cores of the two parent firms (Osborn, Olson & Hanada 1985).

These changes in the nature of international alliances reflect the escalating speed and scope of technological innovation, as well as the increasing number of technologically advanced competitors around the world. Global competition has been fueled by and promotes the commercialization of new technology (Porter 1986). Historically, firms in the later stages of the industry life cycle could, through the use of standardized manufacture, recover the costs of research and development and realize substantial profits (Abernathy, Clark, & Kantrow 1983; Roussel 1984). New technologies, however, are causing rapid product obsolescence, shortening product life cycles and the time available for realizing return on investment (Astley & Rajam 1988; Powell 1987). Between 1982 and 1985, for example, three generations of floppy and Winchester disk drives were introduced in the computer industry (Bahrami & Evans 1987). International alliances may be formed to help in rapid global commercialization of new products to recover R&D investment.

The rising costs of technological development and the high risks of failure provide incentive for firms to share development costs and knowledge (Ouchi & Bolton 1988). Further, as products are increasingly developed which combine technologies from different industries (such as computers with communication equipment or optics with medical equipment) different organizational competencies may be required.

Collaboration in the early stages of product development may also serve the function of joint development of industry standards (Harrigan 1985). With the continued blurring of industry boundaries, the importance of establishing a common technological and commercial standard may outweigh the traditional emphasis on being in sole possession of proprietary technology (Astley & Rajam 1988).

Partner Selection

To the extent that technological changes underlie alliance formation among firms in developed nations, one would expect to see technological factors relating to partner selection. Firms would be expected to link with others having complementary technical abilities. Technological competence may serve to make a firm a desirable partner. Technological assets, however, may allow such a firm to be particularly selective in its choice of partners. Marked disparities in the technological capabilities of linked firms would therefore not be expected unless the less technologically capable partner had other resources (such as access to distribution channels) to offer.

Cooperative Alliances and Technological Positioning

While interorganizational linkages can be utilized in technology development and transfer within an industry, they may also be an important mechanism for allowing a firm to adjust its overall technological positioning by increasing its involvement in *other* industries. As part of GE's global strategy, for example, it sold its consumer electronics business in Europe to Thomson SA of France. GE then bought Thomson CGR, Thomson's medical equipment business. This purchase, coupled with GE Medical Systems Asia, enhances GE's stance in the market for CAT scan, magnetic resonance, and other medical equipment (Main 1988). Such positioning is possible through a variety of transaction forms, including partnerships, joint ventures, and licensing agreements, among others. One of the key elements in the development of the Japanese auto industry, for example, was a 1953 licensing agreement between Isuzu of Japan and Rootes of Britain that ran through 1964 (Franko 1983).

The U.S., Japan, and many Western European nations see their economic futures relying on industries and products utilizing more research and development, high value added services, and education (De Benedetti 1987). Indeed, a particularly sobering aspect of Japanese competitive strength is that it has steadily proceeded up the technological scale from textiles and steel to cars and consumer electronics, and now to micro-electronics and robotics (Franko 1983). This represents a progression to industries of high technological intensity—industries in which the percentage of companies' revenues allocated to R&D is large (Doz 1986). It is therefore important to examine whether the alliance involves a product area that is different from the core businesses of one or both partners. We would be particularly interested in those linkages involving products of higher technological intensity than that of the firm's primary industry.

Forms of the Arrangements

A key challenge in creating alliances is to establish a workable structure for the cooperative relationship. While governmental influence in restricting the form of involvements still exists, a wide variety of transactional forms are utilized among firms from developed nations. These include licensing agreements, supply arrangements, marketing tie-ups, joint ventures, and partnerships, among others. These inter-organizational linkages may be seen as potentially occupying any position along a continuum ranging from informal, arms-length transactions to full mergers. Prior work on multinational cooperative relationships suggests that the distinction between the joint venture form (shared equity in a new entity) and other contractual agreements is particularly important (Harrigan 1987; Porter 1986). While different forms may serve as alternatives in accomplishing the same end, they may involve different risks and transaction costs (Hennart 1988).

New multinational cooperative relationships are often fragile because they face an unusually complex set of challenges (Franko 1971; Zimmerman 1985). These alliances are (a) multinational, (b) are often involved in advanced technological areas, (c) constitute partial extensions of two or more parent firms, and (d) may need to survive as quasi-independent business entities in highly competitive global markets. In light of the fragile nature of these relationships and the caution firms will likely take in developing them, one would expect that relationships will tend toward the informal, market-mediated forms rather than the joint venture.

We have also noted that changing technology is a driving force behind globalization and the development of new cooperative relationships. In high tech areas involving increased rates of technological change, more flexible inter-organizational relationships may be desired (Ettlie 1986). Harrigan (1985) further notes that cooperative relationships *other* than joint ventures were frequently adopted when the arrangement involved a product line or area of technology that was of vital strategic importance. It appeared that some knowledge was too sensitive to be shared through joint ventures. Concerned with "bleedthrough" (the dissemination of technological information through the joint venture to a rival parent firm or perhaps to a third party), many firms preferred more arms-length arrangements to protect technological assets.

Williamson (1975) suggests that the form of the transaction should be efficient and still protect the parties from exploitation. Market transactions such as supply contracts, marketing agreements, and cross-licensing arrangements are often more efficient in linking corporations (Zimmerman 1985). They involve less of a commitment, permit flexibility over the long term, and may be less expensive than integrating the operations of two highly diverse corporations via a new legal entity. One might well expect market agreements to be preferred in high tech areas (cf. Jauch & Osborn, 1981).

Such market-mediated mechanisms may fail or become too cumbersome, however, under conditions of technological uncertainty (Williamson 1975). The difficulties of market exchange as a means of appropriating returns to knowledge are well-known, and have been used as a basis for explaining the diversification of firms having high R&D investments (Penrose 1959). If two firms decide to jointly develop new products and processes, it is likely they will attempt to develop an arrangement that increases the chances of R&D success and allows each to capture the benefits of successful commercialization. In such cases the joint venture form may be desirable. The joint venture may allow the partners to reap the potential benefits of technological development with more confidence that new knowledge, products, and processes will be shared. Market-mediated governance mechanisms may not provide adequate control over the myriad of complex, judgmental tasks in R&D. In R&D individuals often need to interact to develop new ideas and a special language for problem identification and problem solving. Here a hierarchy, such as a joint venture, can promote teamwork and successful technological development (Osborn, Olson, & Hanada 1985).

The decision to engage in joint R&D may also signal a commitment to a long-term relationship among the parent firms. For example, joint R&D may be associated with joint production and marketing across major international markets to insure that both parents can effectively compete on a global basis (c.f., Porter 1986; Jelnick & Burnstein 1982). Non-separable tasks in the process of technological commercialization may favor a hierarchy particularly where individuals of different cultures may need to interact.

Summary

The analysis above has linked technological concerns with three important aspects of alliances among firms from developed nations. Given the technological conditions surrounding alliance formation, technological prowess would be likely to make a firm a more attractive partner. Firms with a comparable emphasis on R&D would be more likely to form an alliance. While firms may be selected on the basis of product-specific expertise, leading to ventures in which the product is identical with the core industry of the parent, alliances may also be used to expand involvement in other industries. Finally, preferences as to the form of the arrangement are seen as being shaped by technological factors. The form of new international linkages will likely reflect the conflicting tensions involved in establishing transactions that are efficient and flexible, provide for protection from exploitation, and are able to withstand or overcome technological uncertainties. As the technological intensity of the product of the arrangement increases, firms may be more likely to opt for market mediated mechanisms (agreements versus joint ventures). When intending to conduct joint R&D, however, firms may opt for the quasi-hierarchy provided by the joint venture.

Examination of factors influencing the formation and form of international alliances have typically relied on case studies rather than empirical analyses. This work is an attempt to empirically assess the impact of technological factors on recent alliance development over a wide range of industries and interorganizational forms.

SAMPLE AND MEASURES

Announcements of U.S./Japanese cooperative arrangements published in the *Japanese Economic Journal* and the *Asian Wall Street Journal* during the three year period from January 1984 through December 1986 were identified. All announced cooperative ventures except those involving government agencies and universities were noted. The announcements generally included the form of the arrangement, its stated purpose (including plans for joint research and development) and listed the partners.

Two hundred and seventy cooperative arrangements were recorded during the 1984–1986 period. A wide variety of arrangements were announced, including informal agreements and contractual ties involving marketing, licensing, original equipment manufacture, and technical assistance. Such agreements outnumbered joint venture formation (equity contributions by partners in a new legal entity), though joint ventures were the most common single form of cooperative arrangement, constituting 35 percent of the announced linkages. Among the 270 ties noted above, the overwhelming majority (248) involved two host firms.

An index of the technological intensity of the arrangement's product was derived using the R&D/sales average for firms in U.S. industries producing that product over the three year (1984–1986) period. This information was obtained from *Business Week* surveys, based on Compustat data for that period. To measure technological positioning we simply noted whether the product of the announced linkage was associated with industries of the same, higher or lower R&D/sales expenditure than that of the firm's primary industry. Information regarding individual firm's commitment to R&D (R&D/sales) was obtained through the *Business Week* survey for U.S. companies and from the *Japan Company Handbook* for Japanese firms. Figures reflecting individual firm's R&D position in 1985 (the middle year of our study period) were used for all firms.

Table 1 shows a break-out of the cooperative ventures between U.S. and Japanese firms by industry/technology area based on the product of the announced cooperative arrangement. Once the product was identified we then found the U.S. industry R&D/sales average for firms producing that product, as described above.

We have ordered the industry/technology areas in the table in roughly ascending order of R&D expenditures as percent of sales. That is, from steel to semiconductors, one finds an increasing emphasis on developing new products and processes with increasingly heavy commitments to R&D. The product areas following "semi-conductors" are those where we identified products for which industry-wide R&D data were not provided in the *Business Week* surveys.

Although the product areas covered by these arrangements cover a wide span, the number of new cooperative ventures involving high tech areas is consistent with an emphasis on technology. In computers, semiconductors, telecommunications, and precision equipment there were seventy-four new arrangements announced during the three year time period. Fifty-six (approximately one in five) of the 270 linkages involved an announced intention to conduct joint research and development.

Table 1
Announced New US/Japanese Cooperative Arrangements
1984–1986

Industry/technology area	Frequency	3 Year US Average R&D/sales (1984–1986)
Steel	7	.5%
Oil/petroleum	4	.7
Textile/apparel	2	.8
Food/beverage	6	.9
Metals/metal prod.	12	1.5
Appliances	4	1.6
Auto parts	16	1.9
Tires/rubber	3	2.5
Misc. mfg.	7	2.7
Machines/ind. parts	16	3.1
Automotive	13	3.5
Chemicals	25	3.6
Electronics	9	4.4
Telecommunications	19	4.4
Aerospace	4	4.5
Precision equipment	16	6.4
Pharmaceuticals	6	7.6
Computers	28	7.8
Software	7	7.9
Semiconductors	11	10.4
Banking	17	
Biotech	6	
Broadcasting/Info Sv	7	
Construction	5	
Nuclear	4	
Robotics	5	
Other	11	
TOTAL	270	

RESULTS AND DISCUSSION

To assess the role of R&D commitment in linking firms, data concerning pairs of U.S. and Japanese industrial firms forming cooperative arrangements were correlated. R&D/sales data were available for eighty-four two-party arrangements of larger industrial firms. Arrangements involving banking firms or Japanese trading companies were not included. Positive correlations were found between U.S. and Japanese partners' R&D/sales figures ($r = .43$, $p < .01$). The correlations between the R&D/sales for the partners remain significant whether those arrangements involve parent firms in the same industry ($r = .56$, $p < .01$) or from different industries ($r = .31$, $p < .05$).

Technological Positioning

A total of 112 two-party industrial arrangements were found for which the primary industry of both the U.S. and Japanese partners, as well as of the product of the linkage, were identified. These arrangements were to be transacted through a variety of forms, including technology and licensing agreements, partnerships, and marketing agreements. The most common type of linkage was the joint overture, comprising forty of the 112 arrangements.

Table 2 provides an overview of firms' technological positioning through U.S./Japanese cooperative alliances during the three year period covered by this study. As shown in Table 2, approximately half (55 of 112) of the linkages involved products which constituted the core business area of *both* the U.S. and Japanese firm. About 70 percent of the linkages (78 of 112) were within the core business area of the U.S. firm involved in the arrangement, and some 61 percent (68 of 112) of the linkages involved products within the core business area of the Japanese firm. Overall, this suggests that the U.S. and Japanese firms generally see the alliances as providing a more effective way of continuing and geographically expanding the scope of their current line of business rather than serving as a means to diversify their product line or simply to acquire components through a form of vertical integration.

Examination of the patterns of involvement in transactions *outside* the primary business of the parent firms suggests differing strategies of the U.S. and Japanese counterparts. In those linkages involving products outside the firms' primary business area, the U.S. firms were as likely to move down as up on the positioning scale. General Motors, for example, saw benefits in establishing a joint venture with Akebono to produce brakes, a product generally involving less R&D activity than that associated with automobile production. During the same time period, however, GM also established a joint venture with Fanuc, involving high tech robotics.

Japanese firms were far more likely to be involved in product transactions of higher-than-core business technological intensity when outside their core industry (thirty higher versus ten lower). Results of statistical testing of the null hypothesis of equiprobability for directionality of Japanese involvement were significant ($x^2_1 = 13.09$, $p < .001$). In 30 percent of the linkages the product was of comparatively high technological intensity for the Japanese partner, while this was the case for the U.S. firm in only 14 percent of the linkages. It does appear that cooperative alliances are being used more often by Japanese than U.S. firms to increase activity in products and

Table 2
Technological Intensity of Alliance Product Relative to Firm's Core Industry

		Japanese firm						
		Lower		Same		Higher		
U.S. Firm	Lower	0* 5	5	1 7	6	0 6	6	18 (16.1%)
	Same	2 4	2	25 55	30	15 19	4	78 (69.6%)
	Higher	1 1	0	3 6	3	7 9	2	167 (14.3%)
		10 (8.9%)		68 (60.7%)		34 (30.4%)		112 (100.0%)

*Values in the upper left portion of the cells show the number of linkages in which the R&D/sales for the product of the alliance is greater or equal to 4 percent; centered number represents all alliances; values in the lower right portion of the cells show the number of linkages where the R&D/sales for the product of the alliance is less than 4 percent.

Table 3
Proportion of Joint Ventures versus Non-Equity Agreements

	Joint research and development		
	No	Yes	
Higher tech product*	.19	.62	.31
	(57)	(21)	(78)
Other industrial products	.48	.57	.49
	(85)	(14)	(99)
	.37	.60	.41
	(142)	(35)	(177)

*Technological level alliance product categorized on basis of average R&D/sales for U.S. firms in product's industry. "Higher" tech here refers to industries in which average R&D/sales $\geq$ 4 percent.

Values in parentheses represent the number of alliances recorded in each condition.

processes of higher technological intensity than generally produced in their primary line of activity.

The implications of this difference do not rest solely on the direction (higher or lower) of involvement, but on the actual technological level of the alliance product itself. Therefore, the above analysis was broken down by technological intensity of the alliance product. The upper left and lower right portion of each cell in Table 2 provide a breakdown by high and low tech alliances, respectively (using R&D/sales $=$ 4 percent for the technological intensity of the alliance product as a cutting value). Inspection of these data confirm the above discussion. The 2 to 1 ratio of Japanese to U.S. involvement in higher-than-core businesses is seen for both high and low tech product areas. However, some interesting differences as a function of technological level of product area are evident. Virtually all of the transactions of U.S. firms in product areas lower than that of their core business involve product areas associated with R&D/sales of less than 4 percent (see lower cell quadrants in Table 2).

In high tech alliances (those involving products in the electronics and higher tech industries) upward involvement is far more common than downward involvement for both U.S. and Japanese firms ($x^2_1 = 14.4$, p $<$ .001 for Japanese firms; $x^2 = 8.33$, p $<$ .001 for U.S. firms). However, while about 20 percent of these linkages involve U.S. firms engaging in product areas of higher technological intensity than that of their core business, over 40 percent of the linkages involve Japanese firms so engaged.

Tables 3 and 4 concern the form of the relationship established. The variables *technological intensity of the product* of the arrangement and whether the arrangement includes an announced

Table 4
Analysis of Variance: Technological Conditions Associated with Alliance Form

Effect	df	SS	MS	F Ratio
Technological intensity (T)	1	2.11	2.11	9.49**
Joint R&D (R)	1	2.12	2.12	9.51**
T × R	1	.77	.77	3.44
Total	176	42.89	.244	

**$P <$ .01.

intention to conduct joint research and development, were used in predicting whether the linkage will involve an *agreement* or *joint venture*.

In assessing these relationships, two-party relationships between industrial firms which did not involve an equity position in the partner were analyzed. As our data requirements for the following analyses were less severe than those utilized in Table 2, the number of arrangements available for subsequent analyses was increased. Though our measure of technological intensity of the product did not cover all of the product areas in which ventures were formed, it was relatively easy to dichotomously classify the arrangements as involving "higher" or "lower" tech products, using the same procedure (R&D/sales = 4 percent for industry of product as a cutting point) as described in the previous analysis. Therefore, alliances involving biotechnology, robotics, and nuclear related products ("high tech") as well as construction ("low tech") were able to be included to enhance the generalizability of the findings. The resulting sample size was 177.

In assessing the prediction of form, all joint ventures were scored as a "1," while other contractual agreements were scored as a "0." Therefore, the means under each condition of the predictors can be interpreted as the proportion of arrangements structured as joint ventures in that condition. As shown in Tables 3 and 4, both the technological intensity of the product and the decision to engage in joint R&D are related to the form of the arrangement. While 41 percent of the arrangements involved the formation of a joint venture, this was less common when the product of the alliance was associated with industries of technological intensity equal to, or greater than that of the electronics industry (31 percent, versus 49 percent for other industrial products). Joint R&D is positively associated with joint venture formation. When the firms announced an intention to conduct joint research and development, the joint venture form was most commonly used (60 percent). When there was no announced R&D intent, 37 percent of the arrangements utilized the joint venture form.

Table 4 also provides an indication of the effectiveness of these variables and their interaction in prediction of the form of the arrangement. Both technical intensity of the product area ($F = 9.49$, $p < .01$) and intention to conduct joint R&D ($F = 9.51$, $p < .01$) attain statistical significance in prediction of arrangement form. The two-way interaction of tech intensity and joint R&D does not achieve statistical significance at the .05 level ($F = 3.44$, $p < .07$). Inspection of Table 3 does show that contractual agreements are heavily favored when transactions involve high tech products in absence of joint R&D. Only 19 percent of such arrangements are structured as joint ventures.

These findings suggest some conflicting factors in the selection of transactional form. While research and development activity is generally positively associated with high tech areas (in this study a correlation of .16 ($p < .05$) was found between the dichotomous measure of technological intensity and intention to conduct joint R&D), high tech alliances led to a strong preference for market-mediated transactions, while joint R&D was associated with increased reliance on the joint venture option.

CONCLUSIONS

The listing of announced new cooperative relationships between U.S. and Japanese firms itself is quite revealing in that such a substantial number were in high tech areas. Arrangements in such areas as advanced materials, robotics, and computers not only involve technical development in these areas but also applications in more mature industries. An inspection of the within- and cross-industry linkages as well as the proportion of arrangements involving joint R&D also suggests that the development and commercialization of new technology is one hallmark of the new cooperative arrangements between U.S. and Japanese corporations.

Firms with similar commitment to R&D are more likely to link. It appears that this finding reflects an industry effect, as firms in developed nations that share an industry may have characteristically similar patterns of overall research and development expenditure. However, the between-industry analysis also suggests that firms of similar R&D commitment may perceive a greater likelihood of achieving synergy through the alliance and overcoming the transaction costs involved.

Comparing the positioning of U.S. firms to those of the Japanese raises some additional issues regarding the potential technological competitiveness of the U.S. While the vast bulk of the cooperations involve no change in product area positioning for the firms involved, a discernible pattern is still evident. Where the product of the alliance differed from that of the firm's core industry, the Japanese firm was much more likely to be moving to high tech areas through the alliance than was its U.S. counterpart. It appears that international linkages are being used as strategic mechanisms by Japanese firms to upgrade their technological prowess, not only within industries (Reich & Mankin 1986; Kotkin 1987), but through involvement in high tech industries.

Concerning the form of the arrangements, technological intensity of the product area for the new arrangement was important in predicting the form with high tech areas being associated with agreements as opposed to joint ventures. The intention to conduct joint R&D (though associated with high tech arrangements) led to an increased preference for joint ventures over agreements.

REFERENCES

Abernathy, W., Clark, K., & Kantrow, A. 1983. *Industrial renaissance: Producing a competitive future for America.* New York: Basic Books.

Astley, G., & Rajam, C. 1988. *The relevance of Porter's generic strategies for contemporary technological environments: A Schumpeterian view.* Working Paper, Pennsylvania State University.

Auster, E. 1986. *Industrial cooperation between Japan and the U.S.* Paper presented before the National Academy of Management, Chicago.

Beamish, P. W. 1985. The characteristics of joint ventures in developed and developing countries. *Columbia Journal of World Business,* 20(3): 13–19.

Bahrami, H., & Evans, S. 1987. Stratocracy in high-technology firms. *California Management Review.*

Business Week. 1985. R & D Scoreboard. July 8: 86–106.

Business Week. 1986. R & D Scoreboard. June 23: 139–156.

Business Week. 1987. R & D Scoreboard. June 22: 139–160.

Connolly, S. G. 1984. Joint ventures with third world multinationals: A new form of entry to national markets. *Columbia Journal of World Business,* 19(2): 18–22.

De Benedetti, C. 1987. Europe's new role in a global market. In A. Pierre (Ed.), *A high technology gap? Europe, America and Japan:* 67–87. New York: Council on Foreign Relations.

Doz, Y. 1986. *Strategic management in multinational companies.* New York: Pergamon Press.

Ettlie, J. E. 1986. Manufacturing technology policy and deployment of processing innovations. *Proceedings of the Second ORSA/TIMS Conference on Flexible Manufacturing Systems:* 1–15.

Franko, L. G. 1971. Joint venture divorce in the multinational company. *Columbia Journal of World Business,* 6(3): 13–22.

Franko, L. G. 1983. *The threat of Japanese multinationals: How the west can respond.* New York: John Wiley & Sons.

Ghoshal, S. 1987. Global strategy: An organizing framework. *Strategic Management Journal,* 5: 425–440.

Hamel, G., & Prahalad, C. 1985. Do you really have a global strategy? *Harvard Business Review,* 63(4): 139–148.

Harrigan, K. 1985. *Strategies for joint ventures.* Lexington, MA: D.C. Heath and Co.

Harrigan, K. 1987. Strategic alliances: Their new role in global competition. *Colombia Journal of World Business,* 22(2): 67–70.

Hennart, J. 1988. A transaction costs theory of equity joint ventures. *Strategic Management Journal*, 9: 361–374.

Japan Company Handbook: 2nd half 1984, 1985, 1986. Tokyo Keizai Shinposha Ltd. (The Oriental Economist).

Jauch, L., & Osborn, R. 1981. Toward an integrated theory of strategy. *Academy of Management Review*, 6(3): 491–498.

Jelnick, M., & Burnstein, M. 1982. The production administrative structure: A paradigm for strategic fit. *Academy of Management Review*, 7(2): 242–252.

Kotkin, J. 1987. Do the Japanese make good partners? *Inc.*, March: 27–39.

Main, J. 1988. The winning organization. *Fortune*, April 8: 50–60.

Osborn, R. N., Olson, J., & Hanada, M. 1985. *Analyzing U.S./Japanese joint research and development units.* Washington, D.C.: National Science Foundation.

Osborn, R. N., & Baughn, C. 1988. The role of technology in the formation and form of multinational cooperative arrangements. Paper presented before the Conference on Managing the High Technology Firm, Boulder.

Ouchi, W., & Bolton, M. 1988. The logic of joint research and development. *California Management Review*, 30(3): 9–33.

Penrose, E. T. 1959. *The theory of the growth of the firm.* London: Basil Blackwell.

Perlmutter, H., & Heenan, D. 1986. Cooperate to compete globally. *Harvard Business Review*, 64(2): 136–152.

Porter, M. 1986. Competition in global industries: A conceptual framework. In M. Porter (Ed.), *Competition in global industries*: 15–60. Boston: Harvard Business School Press.

Powell, W. 1987. Hybrid organizational arrangements: New form or transitional development? *California Management Review*, 30: 67–87.

Reich, R. B., & Mankin, R. D. 1986. Joint ventures with Japan give away our future. *Harvard Business Review*, 64(2): 78–86.

Roussel, P. 1984. Technological maturity proves a valid and important concept. *Research Management*, 27(1): 29–34.

Williamson, O. 1975. *Markets and hierarchies: Analysis and antitrust implications.* New York: The Free Press.

Zimmerman, M. 1985. *How to do business with the Japanese.* New York: Random House.

Part Five

Review and Questions

Review

The articles by Baughn and Osborn and by Contractor and Lorange both focus on factors affecting the type of cooperative arrangements between two or more firms. These arrangements differ from the traditional ones in that they involve firms of comparable size, the early stage of development, and an eye on the global market.

Baughn and Osborn see technology as playing the major role in formation of cooperative arrangements. Using data on announcements of new ventures between U.S. and Japanese firms over a three-year period, they examine the two firms entering each cooperative arrangement in terms of technological positions, product areas of linkages, and forms of relationship. They conclude that (1) many cooperative arrangements are in the high-tech areas, (2) joint ventures are the most common type of linkages, (3) the majority of linkages involve products within the core business area, (4) announcements of joint venture intention often lead to joint venture formation, and (5) nonequity arrangements are preferred in the high-tech areas.

Contractor and Lorange also see technology as an important determinant of the choice among various degrees of cooperation. They recognize many benefits of technology sharing, especially synergy and the reduction of risks. Technology is part of their comprehensive model for understanding the potential benefits versus the potential costs of a cooperative venture. The major benefits, in addition to combining technological skills, are market access, product diversification, and economies of scale. The major costs, besides the profits going to the cooperative partner, are additional overhead and the potential creation of a new competitor.

Both articles recognize that there is some evidence of technology transfer from U.S. to Japanese firms. Contractor and Lorange believe that the Japanese firms have used cooperative ventures to gain longer-term advantages. Baughn and Osborn's data show that outside of the primary business, the U.S.-Japanese linkages more often represent transfers that enhance the technology of Japanese firms.

Both studies point out that the trends in cooperative venture formation have been toward cooperation among large MNCs in competitive markets. They raise the issue of strategies of individual firms as the overriding factor in the formation of cooperative ventures. The framework offered by Contractor and Lorange is, in fact, intended to assist firms in selecting modes of cooperative ventures.

Questions

1. What strategies of international cooperative ventures have been most successful for MNCs?

2. How does a company measure the success of cooperative arrangements?

3. Do the Japanese firms have unique strategies, longer-term strategies, or better ways of using cooperative ventures for technological transfer and for other competitive advantages?

4. How do country differences, industry differences, and strategy differences affect the predisposition and outcomes of the various forms of cooperative ventures?

5. What is the common mode of cooperative arrangements in the "high- and low-tech" areas? Are the differences systematic?

6. Can the Contractor and Lorange framework be used to explain Baughn and Osborn's findings?

7. Is the R&D/sales average an appropriate measure of "technological intensitivity?" Should it be examined at a corporate or at a business level?

8. What are the public policy implications given the differences in the pattern of technological transfer between the United States and Japan?

9. What implications does the current trend of cooperative arrangements have for MNC managers?

10. What strategic explanation can one offer as to why some large corporations (for example, Bethlehem Steel) have no international cooperative arrangements?

Part Six
Managing the Political Environment

Chapter 14

Management of the Political Imperative in International Business

Peter Smith Ring, Stefanie Ann Lenway, and Michael Govekar
University of Minnesota

Abstract *In this paper we develop a framework for analyzing the political imperative. We argue that the effects of the political imperative on the firm will be a function of industry structure. Strategies that management employs in coping with the political imperative are a function of its impact on the firm and the firm's strategic predisposition. We also speculate on why strategic predisposition may lead firms to employ strategies that are not responsive to the demands of the political imperative.*

Models of management in international business have tended to be based on two perspectives of the interdependencies between a firm and its economic environments. Relatively less attention has been paid to theories that might explain interdependencies between the firm and its political environments.

Theories providing strategies for coping with firm-economic environment interdependencies tend to be grounded in industrial organization (I/O) economics (see e.g. Caves, 1982) or in theories of transaction cost economics (TCE) (see e.g. Rugman *et al.*, 1985; Teece, 1985). Explicit in I/O-based approaches (see e.g. Daniels *et al.*, 1985; Egelhoff, 1988; Porter, 1986) is the assumption that 'extra-organizational constraints are . . . seen as the determinants of a firm's success' (Jemison, 1981: 604). Thus the general paradigm is that industry structure determines firm conduct (strategy) which, in turn, determines performance. In transaction cost economics the driving force governing a firm's behavior is the principle of economic efficiency. Firms seek to minimize the combined effects of neo-classical production costs and transaction costs (Williamson, 1985: 61). For example, in response to market imperfections such as the failure of markets to price information, firms must create internal markets to be competitive across national boundaries (see e.g. Buckley and Casson, 1976; Hennart, 1982; Kogut, 1988). In both I/O- and TCE-based approaches, strategies are presumed to be a function of responses to economic environments.

In this paper we focus on the impact of political environments on the firm and its choices of strategy. We begin with a description of the kinds of government intervention that firms confront in the course of conducting international business. We go on to identify the types of risk asso-

Reproduced by permission of John Wiley and Sons Limited from *Strategic Management Journal*, Vol. II, 1990.

ciated with firm/state interdependencies (see e.g. Johansson, 1982) that result from government intervention, and argue that they will vary systematically according to industry structure. Next we investigate strategies designed to manage the firm/state interdependencies that result from industry structure, and address the impact that strategic predisposition can have on the choice of strategies that a firm employs in dealing with these interdependencies. We conclude with a brief discussion of the managerial and research implications of our analysis.

THE CONCEPTUAL FRAMEWORK

In Figure 1 the conceptual framework around which our argument is developed is set forth. Our point of departure is that managers of firms doing business in international markets confront two fundamental sets of threats and opportunities: economic and political. The economic set relates to the firm's need to determine what goods and services it can produce most competitively within and across national borders. Hamel and Prahalad (1983) describe these as 'the forces of integration'. In addition they identify a political set that stems from a corresponding need to cope with the economic policy objectives of nation-states, and describe these as 'the forces of responsiveness'. Chakravarthy and Perlmutter (1985) describe these two sets respectively as the economic and the political imperative.[1]

Building on the work of Porter (1986) and Root (1972), we argue that the firm-level effects of the political imperative will vary with industry structure. In contrast to the more deterministic arguments implicit in much of the literature on the strategic management of MNCs, we do not assume that the current structure of the firm is determined by industry structure. To the contrary, we argue that a firm's strategic predisposition (Miles, 1982), i.e. the pattern reflected in a firm's strategic choices, may be a greater determinant of a firm's structure and current strategies than economic or political imperatives. We further suggest that, within specific industries, some strategies may be more effective than others because they help to insulate the most vulnerable aspects of the firm from government intervention.

INDUSTRY STRUCTURE AND POLITICAL IMPERATIVES

The Political Imperative

In their explication of the political imperative, Prahalad and Doz (1987) tend to focus on host government intervention aimed at (1) the creation of new industries, (2) changes in competitive conditions within established industries and (3) the creation or protection of industries seen as vital to defense interests. In each of these cases the host government appears to be responding to changes in industry conditions caused by global changes in economic imperatives. Because their primary concern is with government intervention motivated by economic pressures, Prahalad and Doz's approach does not fully take account of government intervention in response to changes in political imperatives (e.g. for the imposition in the U.S. of import restraints in response to management and/or union demands for protection in the steel or auto industry). Interventions of this type typically have been described as creating political risk for firms.

---

[1] The economic and political imperatives also encompass, more parsimoniously, the four kinds of risk Ghoshal (1987) describes as being encountered by MNCs: macroeconomic risk, political (or policy) risk, competitive risk and resource risk. In addition, focusing on the imperatives permits managers to consider opportunities as well as risks in both political and economic imperatives.

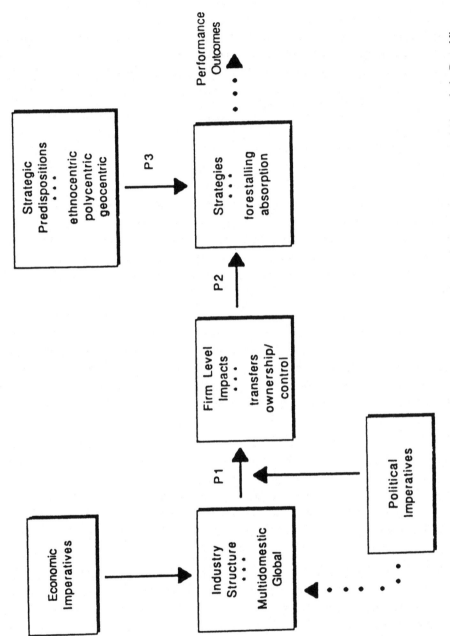

Figure 1 A framework for strategically managing political imperatives. Note: Solid lines reflect primary foci of this analysis. Dotted lines reflect secondary foci. P1, P2, P3 refer to propositions set forth in the paper.

A comprehensive review of the literature on the concept of political risk is beyond the scope of this paper (see e.g. Kobrin, 1979, 1982; Simon, 1984). Briefly, political risk is generally defined as home or host government intervention in international business activities. Its various forms are illustrated in Table 1.

The model outlined in Figure 1 is based on the premise that political risk (as one manifestation of the political imperative) is, and will remain, a strategic issue for firms engaged in international markets.[2] Relatively recent examples include: the 1978 American grain embargo protesting the Soviet invasion of Afghanistan, Canada's Foreign Investment Review Act (FIRA), the U.S. embargo of American and Western European equipment for construction of the trans-Siberian pipeline, the freezing of Libyan assets in the United States, or the imposition of limited sanctions against South Africa by Congress in 1986.

Industry Structure

In our analysis it is essential to distinguish between firms which are engaged in sectors of the economy which Porter (1986) describes as global from those which he describes as multi-domestic because they are subject to different political imperatives. In Figure 1 this distinction is reflected in the concept of industry structure. Our analysis is based on the assumption that industry structure is a consequence of economic imperatives, an assumption that underlines most of the dominant theories of MNC behavior in the strategic management literature (whether I/O-based—see e.g. Davidson and Haspeslagh, 1982) or transaction cost-based—see e.g. Hennart, 1988; Hill and Kim, 1988), although we will explore the way in which the political imperative can have an impact on industry structure.

Global industries present the managers of firms with the opportunity to benefit from differences in the comparative advantages of the countries in which they are located, and to derive a significant competitive advantage from worldwide volume.[3] In global industries, greater investment in R&D is likely to be essential to a firm's success. The firm's competitive advantage may be based on the low cost or high quality of the factors used in producing a product. The economies of scale which lead to these kinds of competitive advantage can be achieved if integration is possible between larger plants with longer production runs, or within channels of distribution designed to move high volumes. The costs of, and threats to, transfers (moving goods from country to country or plant to plant) should be low.

In contrast, in multi-domestic industries R&D spending is closely tied to particular markets, economies of scale are more modest, products differ significantly across national markets, or distribution, installation or other localized activity is emphasized. In addition, lead times may be short and transportation costs high. Distribution is frequently fragmented and hard to penetrate.

These differing characteristics of the two industry types are a consequence of the effects of economic, not political, imperatives. The utility of distinguishing between global and multi-domestic industries to our model is highlighted in Figure 1. Specifically, we suggest that the effect of political imperatives on the firm will differ according to the structure of the industry in which it competes.

---

[2]The other basic manifestation of the political imperative is political opportunity. In the discussion which follows we focus specifically on political risks. In our analysis we are primarily concerned with political risk which has negative effects on the firm, a result which is consistent with research on how managers view political risk. Hereafter, we simply refer to political risk as the political imperative.

[3]This discussion is based on an analysis of global industries by Hout *et al.*, 1982, pp. 99–100.

Table 1
Range of Host and Home Country Political Risks and Potential Impact on Firm

	Transfers	Ownership control
Host country		
Countertrade	×	
Import/export regulations	×	
Import restrictions	×	
Boycotts	×	
Currency restrictions	×	
Local content restrictions	×	
Export requirements	×	
War and revolution	×	×
Nationalization/expropriation		×
Protests, strikes, riots		×
Terrorist attacks		×
Indigenization		×
Environmental standards		×
Pressure for joint ventures		×
Disinvestment pressure		×
Local ownership requirements		×
Home country		
Countertrade	×	
Export requirements	×	
Taxation	×	
Import restrictions	×	
Loan restrictions	×	
Technology transfer controls	×	
Foreign Corrupt Practices Act enforcement	×	
Use of embargoes	×	
Price/wage controls		×
Production controls		×
Licensing requirements		×
Pressure for divestment		×
International		
War	×	×
Foreign policy disputes	×	×
Trade wars	×	
Blockades	×	
Embargoes	×	

We adopt Root's (1972) framework for analyzing the effects of the political imperative on firms in the two different types of industries. Root's framework suggests that the potential impact of the political imperative is to be found on the firm's ownership/control, transfers, and operations. Transfer risks refer to government interventions which may impede flows of products, capital, payments, people, or technology between a firm and its subsidiaries. Import quotas or local content requirements reflect two of the more frequently observed forms of transfer risk. Ownership and control risk stems from government policies designed to change firm ownership or influence managerial control. A classic example of ownership risk is the threat of expropriation. Demands by a government for significant minority interest in a joint venture reflect policies designed to constrain managerial control.

In contrast to Root's approach, we suggest that the effects of the political imperative on what Root describes as operations can be translated into effects either on transfers or ownership/control. For example, Root (1972: 357) defines 'monetary and fiscal policies, price controls, taxation, labor codes and regulations, [and] local content requirements', as operations risks. We argue that, in effect, these kinds of risk constitute transfer risks since their real impacts are felt on the movements of capital and human resources, or intermediate goods, among units of a firm. Root also describes 'general administrative behavior' of a government as a form of the political imperative that threatens operations. While he provides no concrete examples, we take his concept of 'general administrative behavior' to mean forms of social regulation such as environmental and product safety which, in our framework, affect managerial control since they limit management's discretion.

Specifically, we argue that risk arising out of the political imperative will have a greater impact on transfers for firms doing business in global industries than on ownership or managerial control. In contrast, for firms in multi-domestic industries these kinds of risk are more likely to affect the ownership and/or control of the firm.

We expect transfers to be relatively vulnerable in global industries because firms are likely to have decentralized critical production facilities in more than one country to gain the benefits of comparative advantage, thereby reducing the economic benefits to the host government of expropriation or other activities threatening ownership or control. This approach to configuration (Porter, 1986), however, leaves the firm vulnerable to threats to transfers such as the imposition of local content requirements, import or export controls, or currency restrictions.

In multi-domestic industries, threats to ownership and control are more probable because subsidiaries tend to be relatively autonomous and not dependent upon a parent or other subsidiaries for critical value chain activities (Porter, 1985). We expect that expropriation of a stand-alone subsidiary, or demands that a majority interest in it be ceded to the state or to a local firm, can provide sufficient economic benefit to a government to warrant such action. The autonomous, decentralized nature of firms in multi-domestic industries suggests that acquisition of ownership or control provides the state with a fully operational business. Even when the state does not have sufficient managerial capacity to sustain the operation, it is often able to 'buy' expatriate managers and thus insures itself of a 'going concern' (Bradley, 1977).[4] Thus, we offer the following propositions regarding relationships between industry structure and the firm level effects of the political imperative:

P1a: The primary effect of the political imperative will be on transfers for firms operating in global industries.

P1b: The primary effect of the political imperative will be on ownership/control for firms operating in multi-domestic industries.

In choosing how to manage the firm-level effects of the political imperative, managers can select from an array of strategies. We turn to a discussion of these strategies and their relationship to political imperatives.

---

[4]Note that this argument is not likely to hold in situations in which the firm over which the state acquires control is doing business in a 'weak' market. In such cases the newly acquired SOE is likely to be viewed as a supplier of last resort (Moran, 1974).

STRATEGIES AND POLITICAL IMPERATIVES

Ownership/control and transfer risks result from the strategic interdependence that exists between firms and nation-states. By strategic interdependence we mean a relationship in which the state and the MNC have to deal with each other to accomplish their objectives. Strategies, whether competitive or political, to manage this form of strategic interdependence can be classified using a typology developed by Pennings (1981).

Pennings (1981: 441) argues that, 'there are three categories of behavior that strategically interdependent organizations can display to coordinate their actions and to manage their interdependence: forestalling, forecasting, and absorption.' In our framework we do not treat forecasting (see e.g. Austin and Yoffie, 1984) as a separate category of strategic behavior since firms typically will forecast in the process of formulating either forestalling or absorption strategies.

Forestalling

Forestalling is 'coping behavior that prevents or controls the emergence of unpredictable behavior of other organizations. Coping by forestalling alters the structural arrangements of a strategic set' (Pennings, 1981: 441). For managers of MNCs a strategic set is the total mix of country/subsidiary interdependencies: the countries in which it has located operations and the relationships of those operations one to another. The structural arrangement in our case will be the result of decisions regarding the configuration and coordination of the firm's activities (Porter, 1986). Porter argues that configuration involves decisions on where the firm's activities are to be performed, including the decision as to the number of countries in which these activities will be performed. The coordination decision 'refers to how like or linked activities performed in different countries are coordinated with each other' (Porter, 1986: 23, 25). Because decisions on configuration and coordination determine the extent to which MNC subsidiaries are interdependent, they affect the way in which transfers within the firm take place. As a consequence of economic imperatives, however, firms operating in global industries have substantial flexibility in their configuration decisions. These options provide a basis for designing forestalling strategies to cope with the transfer risk inherent in global industries.

The objective of forestalling is to configure the firm's transfer processes such that they significantly increase the economic costs well beyond the political benefits derived by the nation-state from government intervention. By pursuing competitive forestalling strategies, firms in global industries obtain the cost advantages required for competitive advantage, while hedging against the effects of transfer risk. Carefully configured, competitive forestalling may minimize transfer risk arising from the actions of a single government, or from the concerted actions of a state-sponsored cartel or a customs union (see, Yarbrough and Yarbrough, 1987). For example, in the aftermath of the trans-Siberian pipeline embargo by the U.S. government, executives in some of the affected firms reported that they were giving serious consideration to locating production facilities outside the U.S.

Political forestalling strategies include public relations campaigns on trade issues such as those marshalled by Toshiba in the summer of 1987 (see e.g. *New York Times*, 1987; *Business Week*, 1987a, b, 1988) in response to a threatened embargo of the transfer of intermediate goods (semiconductor chips, components for microwave ovens and television sets) to its U.S. subsidiaries. The company took out full-page advertisements in many major American newspapers on 20 July 1987 arguing against the imposition of economic sanctions and detailing the potential harms such retaliation might have on the American economy. General Electric and Dresser Industries, among others, mounted similar political strategies in response to the imposition of an embargo on the transfer of technologies required to fulfill orders for compressors to be used in the trans-Siberian pipeline (see e.g. Lenway and Crawford, 1986).

The openness of the U.S. political system provides all firms with an opportunity to employ a broader range of political forestalling strategies than might be available to them elsewhere. Both U.S. and foreign firms can employ registered lobbyists, as well as create and fund foundations.[5] Constituency building and grass-roots lobbying (Baysinger, 1984) are examples of more recent forestalling strategies employed by politically active firms, both foreign—as Toshiba has demonstrated—and domestic. For U.S. firms there is the additional option of establishing corporate political action committees (PACS), whose campaign contributions (Maitland and Park, 1985) may help to forestall detrimental legislative or executive action. The implication of this line of reasoning for our analysis is that:

P2a: Forestalling strategies will be employed by firms in global industries to cope with political imperatives that threaten transfers.

Absorption

In multi-domestic industries, firms tend to locate a fuller and more concentrated array of value chain activities within a specific country. In these industries the strategic interdependence between the firm and the state is based on the firm's need for access to significant market share and a host country's propensity to use the attractiveness of that market share as leverage in dealing with the firm. This concentration of value chain activities provides potential benefits to governmental policies that affect ownership and control, as opposed to transfers.

To deal with these kinds of circumstances, Pennings (1981: 441) provides another generic strategy. He defines absorption as 'coping behavior that mitigates the negative consequences of other organizations [in our case, nation-states]'. As we define absorption, it is designed to minimize adverse effects of political imperatives by internalizing sources of political risk within the firm.

In the context of international business, absorption strategies include providing the host country with a measure of ownership through joint ventures or bringing nationals into management by including them on the board of directors or hiring them as managers. The political variant of these competitive absorbing strategies would involve legitimate activities such as absorbing host government political officials or state-owned enterprises within the firm (through the creation of a joint venture). In addition, absorption strategies could also include co-opting local government officials through pay-offs that are illegal under the Foreign Corrupt Practices Act.

If a firm's managers are concerned about threats to ownership or control after it makes a foreign direct investment, its preferred strategy will be to bring the threat into the organization at the time of the initial investment because internalizing the sources of political risk can lead to a public perception that the objectives of the firm and the state are congruent. These kinds of absorption strategies are also likely to provide an effective response to ownership/control risk because if the foreign nationals are not fully capable of running the multi-domestic firm as a going concern, they can become hostages. Once foreign nationals have been 'absorbed' by a multi-domestic firm, the state can acquire ownership and/or control over the firm, but only at the expense of the 'careers' of these individuals. Consequently, we offer the following proposition:

---

[5]The Japanese have become very aggressive in this area in recent years (see e.g. *Business Week*, 11 July 1988).

P2b: Absorption strategies will be employed by firms in multi-domestic industries to cope with political imperatives that threaten ownership/control.

These propositions are based on the assumption that industry structure and firm structure are isomorphic. We go on to relax this assumption for two reasons. First, the political imperative can lead to the threat (or to the imposition of) significant import or export barriers which may reduce the economic benefits of integration inherent in global industries. The result of this type of government intervention is that a global industry could take on many of the characteristics of a multi-domestic industry.

For example, the imposition of a stringent import quota may have the effect of fragmenting world markets, thereby reducing their scope and the economic attractiveness of world products, or creating conditions favorable to entry of new firms within the protected markets. Trade restrictions are further likely to reduce the intensity of price competition by artificially reducing supply. In response to the threatened imposition of trade restrictions, the management of the firm has to decide whether they are likely to be sufficiently permanent to warrant reconfiguring value chain activities. This can be seen in the need for managers of computer and consumer electronics firms in the U.S. and Japan to consider the possible effects of a 'fortress Europe' after 1992 on the continued viability of their current forestalling strategies.

A second reason that firms may not employ strategies that we would expect is the result of the strategic predisposition of a firm. In the following section of the paper we describe the impact that a firm's strategic predisposition has on the strategies it employs in dealing with the political imperative.

STRATEGIC PREDISPOSITION AND STRATEGY

Miles (1982: 238) defines strategic predisposition as 'the extent to which an organization exhibits a consistent pattern over time in the choices it makes about the formulation and implementation of its strategies'. Bartlett (1986: 372) observes that the antecedents of a firm's strategic predisposition include 'a company's existing asset configuration, its historical distribution of responsibilities, and the ingrained management norms [which] will greatly influence—and often constrain' the ability of a firm to respond to changes in industry structure (whatever the source). We argue that the combined effects of these institutionalization processes create a strategic predisposition that causes firms to do things today because 'they are taken for granted as "the way things are done"' (Scott, 1987: 505).

While we know of no research which has been conducted on the possible influence of strategic predisposition on the actions of firms in the course of coping with political imperatives, the Chakravarthy and Perlmutter (1985) typology provides a base for predicting the relationship between firm strategic predisposition and its choice of strategies. They describe four types of predisposition: ethnocentric, polycentric, regiocentric, and geocentric. Because characteristics of polycentric and geocentric firms tend to be reflected in regiocentric firms, excluding them simplifies the typology.

In an *ethnocentric* firm, strategic decisions for the firm as a whole tend to be dominated by the parent's needs and values. We expect that configuration and coordination trade-offs employed by firms with ethnocentric strategic predispositions would lead to high levels of interdependence between the parent and each subsidiary, thus enabling the parent to retain substantial control over its subsidiaries. For example, advanced technologies, R&D operations, and decisions concerning subsidiary financing are likely to be made at headquarters in top-down fashion. The need for headquarters control is also likely to preclude a firm with an ethnocentric predisposition from considering the creation of autonomous subsidiaries, even in multi-domestic industries.

The ethnocentric firm is likely to be more concerned with its economic viability than its political legitimacy, except in the home country. We expect that ethnocentric firms would use whatever leverage the home country can provide in dealing with their strategic interdependencies with host countries. As a consequence, ethnocentric firms are likely to assume that home government political support will help them to forestall transfer risks caused by political imperatives. Based on the above, we offer the following proposition:

> P3a: Regardless of industry structure, ethnocentric firms will rely primarily on forestalling strategies in coping with political imperatives.

In contrast, firms with a *polycentric* strategic predisposition tend to use autonomous wholly owned subsidiaries which seek political and economic advantages offered by host countries. Their concern is with their legitimacy in all the countries in which they do business. Thus, polycentric firms are likely to be predisposed to meet the political imperatives of all countries in which they operate head-on. As a result of this need for legitimacy, firms with a polycentric predisposition are likely to be sensitive to the values and the culture of the host country. They are also likely to have the capacity and to be receptive to working directly with host country nationals. Thus, we propose that:

> P3b: Regardless of industry structure, polycentric firms will rely primarily on absorption strategies in coping with political imperatives.

Geocentric firms tend to develop their own unique set of values. Their corporate culture is often distinct from that of the countries in which they do business. This enables them to benefit from country-specific advantages, while not discounting the need for political legitimacy in nation-states in which they have subsidiaries. Firms with a geocentric predisposition, because of their ability to balance the competing demands of economic viability and political legitimacy, are likely to experience fewer problems in coping with political imperatives, regardless of the structure of the industry in which they are competing. In global industries these firms are likely to be structured to take advantage of the economic benefits that result from creating strong interdependencies among subsidiaries. To protect these interdependencies, they are likely to engage in both competitive and political forestalling strategies.

In multi-domestic industries, geocentric firms may turn to competitive or political absorbing strategies (e.g. appointing foreign nationals to their board of directors or forming joint ventures with local companies) because their distinctive culture makes it possible to socialize foreign nationals into the norms and values of the geocentric firm. Consequently, we expect that:

> P3c: Geocentric firms will rely primarily on forestalling strategies in global industries and on absorption strategies in multi-domestic industries.

CONCLUSIONS

Strategic Predisposition and Competitiveness

In this section of the paper we conclude by considering some of the managerial and research implications of the relationships between strategic predisposition, strategies, and the structure of the industry in which the managers of the firm have chosen to compete. Our conclusions are derived from the observation that managers attempt (but do not always succeed) to restructure the firm in ways that they perceive will help them in coping with the economic and political imperatives inherent in international business. They do not succeed because in the process of restructuring they develop relationships with subsidiaries regarding product/market objectives, human resource practices, and performance goals (e.g. financial objectives) which Chakravarthy and Perlmutter (1985) describe as components of a firm's strategic predisposition. Over time, firms also institutionalize belief systems and values which are partially derived from home and host country cultural elements that further constrain their ability to respond to changes in the economic and political imperatives (see e.g. Scott, 1987). The failure of firms to adapt to the political demands of a specific industry structure is a consequence of the divergence between the strategy that is responsive to the political imperative within a specific industry structure and the strategy that firms adopt as a result of their strategic predisposition.

Ethnocentric firms, because they have tended to exercise high levels of control over their subsidiaries, may be relatively more competitive in global than in multi-domestic industries. Their competitive advantage in global industries typically stems from combining the parent's distinctive competence with the country-specific advantages of the host countries in which they have located subsidiaries. This pattern appears to have dominated in the textile, petroleum and mining industries (see e.g. Chandler, 1986). Yet, in global industries ethnocentric firms may not respond as effectively as geocentric firms to the political imperative, because they project home country economic and political values onto host country subsidiaries. This makes them less inclined to work directly with host country nationals and leaves them less sensitive to the nuances of host country political life and process. The intensity of the relationship between a parent and its subsidiaries in ethnocentric firms is also likely to preclude the creation of subsidiary-subsidiary interdependencies. In combination, these factors suggest that, in a global industry, ethnocentric firms may not employ the kinds of forestalling strategies necessary to insulate transfers from the political imperative as effectively as geocentric firms, since forestalling presumes a greater reliance on subsidiary-subsidiary interdependencies and an understanding of the host country political processes than the culture of the typical ethnocentric firm is likely to have fostered.

In multi-domestic industries, ethnocentric firms may find themselves at a serious competitive disadvantage because their reliance on forestalling strategies may leave them poorly prepared to deal with political threats to ownership/control. In addition, their need for control over their subsidiaries, as well as the dominance of the home country culture in dealing with their subsidiaries, may make them unwilling to use absorption strategies to insulate the firm from ownership/control risk.

For the polycentric firm, concern for political legitimacy in all the countries in which it operates may lead to undue reliance on absorption strategies in coping with the political imperative. In multi-domestic industries (e.g. branded and packaged goods industries) this is not likely to create problems, since the political imperative tends to threaten ownership/control. In global industries, however, the greater probability of threats to transfers requires a facility with the use of forestalling strategies. In addition, as Porter observes:

> In a global industry, managing international activities like a portfolio will undermine the possibility of achieving competitive advantage . . . . A firm may choose to compete with a country-centered strategy, focusing on specific market segments or countries where it can carve out a niche by responding to whatever local country differences are present. However, it does so at some considerable peril from competitors with global strategies (1986: 19).

Thus in global industries, polycentric firms may be disadvantaged in responding to both economic and political imperatives.

Our analysis leads us to conclude that a geocentric predisposition is likely to enhance the competitive position of a firm because of its ability to respond to the political imperative, regardless of industry structure. The unique culture of the geocentric firm that transcends national cultures enables the firm to develop a global perspective. Thus, in global industries (e.g. autos, consumer electronics) a geocentric strategic predisposition enables a firm to structure relationships with its subsidiaries to forestall threats to transfers while, at the same time, participating, when appropriate, in host country politics. On the other hand, in multi-domestic industries the unique cultures of firms with geocentric strategic predispositions allows them to absorb foreign nationals more readily than ethnocentrics (where the dominance of the home country culture may create tensions between headquarters and local management).

FUTURE RESEARCH

In the course of outlining our model we have offered a number of testable propositions which should be of interest to researchers in the fields of strategic management, political risk analysis, business-government relations and international management. For students of strategic management our analysis suggests that an effective response to the political imperative in international markets may require a mix of forestalling and absorption strategies. To date little attention has been paid to the need to formulate strategies designed to address the political imperative (e.g. home and host country import and export restrictions), especially as it increasingly affects the ability of firms to be competitive in international markets. There are signs, however, that this situation is beginning to change (see e.g. Doz, 1986; Kobrin, 1989).

The propositions we have offered require empirical testing. Unlike much of traditional political risk analysis and research in strategic management, the research program implied in this paper goes beyond an analysis of forecasting activities (e.g. Sethi and Luther, 1986). In addition to forecasting, it indicates the need for an analysis of the relationship between industry structure and firm-level effect of the political imperative, as well as the relationship between these firm-level effects and firm strategy. Investigation of the effects of strategic predisposition on strategy choices will require longitudinal studies, in addition to cross-sectional research.

Other issues not raised in this analysis, but germane to the topic, also require investigation. Further research of the effect of governmental bargaining power on strategic decisions (see e.g. Kobrin, 1986) would help us understand conditions that make the political imperative salient. An analysis of the relationship between the management of perceived commercial risk and political risk would provide insight into the extent to which management takes the political imperative into account in choosing between forestalling and absorption strategies. These and many more questions related to the analysis of business conducted in an international political and economic context remain open to those who are interested in increasing our overall understanding of the complex interplay between politics and markets.

ACKNOWLEDGMENTS

This research was supported, in part, by grants from the Graduate School, University of Minnesota and from a McKnight Foundation Research Grant from the Curtis L. Carlson School of Management. The authors wish to acknowledge the very helpful comments on previous drafts of this paper received from Carol Jacobson, Philip Bromiley, Balaji Chakravarthy, Larry Cummings, Richard Moxon and several anonymous referees.

REFERENCES

Austin, J. E. and D. Yoffie. 'Political forecasting as a management tool', *Journal of Forecasting*, 3, 1984, pp. 395–408.

Bartlett, C. A. 'Building and managing the transnational: The new organizational challenge'. In Porter, M. E. (ed.), *Competition in Global Industries*, Harvard Business School Press, Boston, MA, 1986, pp. 367–401.

Baysinger, B. D. 'Domain maintenance as an objective of business political activity: An expanded typology', *Academy of Management Review*, 9, 1984, pp. 248–258.

Bradley, D. G. 'Managing against expropriation', *Harvard Business Review*, July/August 1977, pp. 75–83.

Buckley, P. J. and M. Casson. *The Future of the Multinational Enterprise*, Macmillan, London, 1976.

Business Week, Japan's Clout in the U.S.: It's translating economic might into influence', 11 July 1988, pp. 64–75.

Business Week, 'The Toshiba scandal has exporters running for cover', 20 July 1987a, pp. 86–87.

Business Week, 'How Toshiba is beating American sanctions', 14 September 1987b, p. 58.

Caves, R. *Multinational Enterprise and Economic Analysis*, Cambridge University Press, Cambridge, 1982.

Chakravarthy, B. S. and H. B. Perlmutter, 'Strategic planning for a global business', *Columbia Journal of World Business*, 20, 1985, pp. 3–10.

Chandler, A. D. 'The evolution of modern global competition'. In Porter, M. E. (ed.), *Competition in Global Industries*, Harvard Business School Press, Boston, MA, 1986, pp. 405–448.

Daniels, J. D., R. A. Pitts and M. J. Tretter. 'Organizing for dual strategies of product diversity and international expansion', *Strategic Management Journal*, 6, 1985, pp. 223–237.

Davidson, W. H. and P. Haspeslagh. 'Shaping a global product organization', *Harvard Business Review*, 60, 1982, pp. 125–132.

Doz, Y. 'Government policies and global industries'. In Porter, M. E. (ed.), *Competition in Global Industries*, Harvard Business School Press, Boston, MA, 1986, pp. 225–226.

Egelhoff, W. G. 'Strategy and structure in multinational corporations: A revision of the Stopford and Wells model', *Strategic Management Journal*, 9, 1988, pp. 1–14.

Ghoshal, S. 'Global strategy: An organizing framework', *Strategic Management Journal*, 8, 1987, pp. 425–440.

Hamel, G. and C. K. Prahalad. 'Managing strategic responsibility in the MNC', *Strategic Management Journal*, 4, 1983, pp. 341–351.

Hennart, J. F. *A Theory of the Multinational Enterprise*, University of Michigan Press, Ann Arbor, MI, 1982.

Hennart, J. F. 'A transaction cost theory of equity joint ventures', *Strategic Management Journal*, 9, 1988, pp. 361–374.

Hill, C. W. and W. C. Kim. 'Searching for a dynamic theory of the multinational enterprise: A transaction cost model', *Strategic Management Journal*, 9 (special edition), 1988, pp. 93–104.

Hout, T., M. E. Porter and E. Rudden. 'How global companies win out', *Harvard Business Review*, September–October 1982, pp. 98–108.

Jemison, D. B. 'The importance of an integrative approach to strategic management research', *Academy of Management Review*, 6, 1981, pp. 601–608.

Johansson, J. K. 'A note on the managerial relevance of interdependence', *Journal of International Business Studies*, 6, 1982, pp. 143–145.

Kobrin, S. J. 'Enforcing export embargoes through multinational corporations: Why doesn't it work anymore?', *Business in the Contemporary World*, 1(2), 1989, pp. 31–42.

Kobrin, S. J. 'Testing the obsolescing bargain hypothesis in the manufacturing sector'. Paper delivered at the 1986 Annual Meeting of the American Political Science Association, Washington, DC, 28 August 1986.

Kobrin, S. J. *Managing Political Risk Assessment: Strategic Response to Environmental Change*, University of California Press, Berkeley, CA, 1982.

Kobrin, S. J. 'Political risk: A review and reconsideration', *Journal of International Business Studies*, 10, 1979, pp. 67–80.

Kogut, B. 'Joint ventures: Theoretical and empirical perspectives', *Strategic Management Journal*, 9, 1988, pp. 319–332.

Lenway, S. A. and B. Crawford. 'When business becomes politics: The involvement of western firms in east-west trade'. In Preston, L. (ed.), *Research in Corporate Social Performance and Policy*, JAI Press, Greenwich, CT, 1986.

Maitland, I. and D. S. Park. 'A model of corporate PAC strategy'. In Robinson, R. and Pearce, J. (eds), *Academy of Management Proceedings*, University of South Carolina, Columbia, SC, 1985.

Miles, R. *Coffin Nails and Corporate Strategy*, Prentice-Hall, Englewood Cliffs, NJ, 1982.

Moran, T. H. *Multinational Corporations and the Politics of Dependence: Copper in Chile*, Princeton University Press, Princeton, NJ, 1974.

New York Times, 2 July 1987, IV, p. 1:6.

Pennings, J. M. 'Strategically interdependent organizations'. In Nystrom, P. C. and Starbuck, W. H. (eds), *Handbook of Organizational Design*, Oxford University Press, New York, 1981, pp. 433–455.

Porter, M. E. 'Competition in global industries: A conceptual framework'. In Porter, M. E. (ed.), *Competition in Global Industries*, Free Press, New York, 1986, pp. 15–60.

Porter, M. E. *Competitive Advantage*, Free Press, New York, 1985.

Porter, M. E. *Competitive Strategies*, Free Press, New York, 1980.

Prahalad, C. K. and Y. L. Doz, *The Multinational Mission*, Free Press, New York, 1987.

Root, F. R. 'Analyzing political risks in international business'. In Kapoor, A. and Brub, P. (eds), *Multinational Enterprise in Transition: Selected Readings and Essays*, Darwin Press, Detroit, MI, 1972, pp. 354–365.

Rugman, A. M., D. J. LeCraw and L. D. Booth. *International Business: Firm and Environment*, McGraw-Hill, New York, 1985.

Scott, W. R. 'The adolescence of institutional theory', *Administrative Science Quarterly*, 32, 1987, pp. 493–511.

Sethi, P. and K. Luther. 'Political risk analysis and direct foreign investment: Some problems of definition and measurement', *California Management Review*, 28, 1986, pp. 57–68.

Simon, J. D. 'A theoretical perspective on political risk', *Journal of International Business Studies*, 15, 1984, pp. 123–143.

Teece, D. J. 'Multinational enterprise, internal governance, and industrial organization', *American Economic Review*, 75, 1985, pp. 233–238.

Williamson, O. E. *The Economic Institutions of Capitalism*, Free Press, New York, 1985.

Yarbrough, B. V. and R. M. Yarbrough. 'Institutions for the governance of opportunism in international trade', *Journal of Law, Economics and Organization*, 3, 1987, pp. 129–139.

Part Six

Review and Questions

Review

The paper by Ring, Lenway, and Govekar constructs a framework for analyzing the political imperative in international management. It focuses on what impact the political environment has on the firm's choice of strategy.

The point of departure in the conceptual framework is the proposition that managers of firms involved in international markets confront two fundamental sets of threats and opportunities. The *economic* set is variously designated as "forces of integration" or "economic imperative." The *political* set is variously designated as "forces of responsiveness" or "political imperative." The authors postulate that the firm-level effects of the political imperative vary with industry structure (which itself is determined by the economic imperative), but the current structure of the firm is *not* fully or even primarily determined by industry structure. Instead, the firm's *strategic predisposition*, as shown by the pattern reflected in the firm's strategic choices, may exert a greater influence on the firm's structure and current strategies.

The political imperative is discussed in terms of political *risks* relating to home and host government intervention in international business activities, although the authors recognize that the political imperative may also create opportunities for firms. The effects of the political imperative (risk) breaks down into *transfer* effects and *ownership/control* risks. Two hypotheses distinguish the effects of the political imperative for firms in global industries and in multidomestic industries.

The paper next addresses the management of risks resulting from the strategic interdependence between firms and nation-states in terms of *forestalling* and *absorption* strategies. Two hypotheses specify which of these strategies will be employed by managers in global industries and in multidomestic industries. The remainder of the paper discusses the influences of ethnocentric, polycentric, or geocentric strategic predispositions on forestalling and absorption strategies and concludes with three hypotheses.

This paper bears on several of the preceding papers in this book. In particular, it strengthens the treatment of the political imperative by Chakravarthy and Perlmutter, and it complements the economic emphasis of the Ghoshal and Porter models.

Questions

1. What is the meaning of "political imperative?"
2. What are the transfer effects of political risk? Of ownership/control risks?

3. Why do the authors hypothesize that the primary effect of the political imperative will be on transfers for firms operating in global industries?
4. In managing political risks, what is *forestalling* behavior by the firm?
5. What is strategic predisposition?
6. How does the strategic predisposition of a firm influence its use of forestalling or absorption strategies?

Postscript

The Current State of Research on International Strategic Management

Growing interest in the field of international strategic management in recent years raises questions on the emerging directions of research. To gain some insight on current trends, we studied the domains and methods of the journals and articles collected for this book.

We focused on fifteen leading research journals over the five-year period 1985–1989. To the fourteen journals considered as appropriate outlets for scholarly research in the business policy field (McMillan 1989), we added the *Journal of International Business Studies*. We applied the selection criteria that, (1) the articles deal explicitly with the strategic management of U.S. as well as non-U.S. multinational corporations (MNCs), and (2) the articles report attempts to validate strategic management models in a foreign context or address strategic management issues in non-U.S. MNCs. We collected 101 such articles.[1] The Appendix lists the journals consulted and the number of articles selected. We first categorized the articles according to the topic, the approach, and the level of analysis. Next, we examined the theories used in the articles and their findings.

Table 1 presents the distribution of articles by topic. During the period examined, general research interest centered on the three areas of strategy, strategy implementation, and relations among environment, strategy, structure, and performance. Researchers paid particular attention to two variables: the environment, including environmental analysis (18%), and organizational structure, including cooperative ventures (18%).[2]

Table 2 provides information about types of research. One-half of the articles are empirically oriented, of which two-thirds use a deductive approach and one-third an inductive approach. One-third of the articles are conceptual, dealing with issues such as a typology of global strategy, forms of alliances, and a framework for strategy formulation. Nine percent of the articles are descriptive, focusing mainly on strategic management practice of U.S. as well as foreign companies. The remaining articles (8%) are comparative studies.

The majority of studies examine U.S. MNCs. However, 20% employ a non-U.S. sample set. Attempts to validate strategic management models in a foreign context are made in 14% of the studies. The models of Miles and Snow, Porter, and Rumelt receive the most attention.

---

[1]We used these same criteria for the first cut in our search process for the articles in this book. Schendel and Hofer (1979, p. 11) define strategic management as a process that deals with the entrepreneurial work of organizational renewal and growth and, more particularly, with developing and utilizing the strategies that guide organizational goals and goal formulation, environmental analysis, strategy formulation, strategy evaluation, strategy implementation, strategic control, and the role of management.

[2]Four out of ten articles studying networks/joint ventures/alliances focus on structural issues.

Table 1

Distribution of Journal Articles by Main Topics on International Strategic Management

Topic	SMJ	ASQ	AMJ	MGS	HBR	AMR	SMR	CMR	JMS	ORD	JBS	LRP	JMG	INF	JIB	Number of articles
Strategy (typology and concept)	5	—	—	—	2	—	—	2	—	—	1	2	—	—	3	15
Networks/joint ventures/alliances	1	—	—	—	4	—	1	3	—	—	—	—	—	—	1	10
Subtotal																25
Organizational goals	—	—	—	—	1	—	—	—	—	—	1	—	—	—	—	2
Goal formation	—	—	—	—	—	—	—	—	—	—	—	—	—	—	—	—
Environmental analysis	2	—	—	—	—	—	—	—	—	—	1	—	—	—	1	4
Strategy formulation	3	—	—	—	—	—	1	—	—	—	—	—	—	—	—	4
Strategy design	—	—	—	—	—	—	1	—	—	—	—	—	—	—	—	1
Subtotal																5
Strategy evaluation																
Strategic group	1	—	—	—	—	—	—	—	—	—	—	—	—	—	—	1
Self-renewal process	—	—	—	—	—	—	—	1	—	—	—	—	—	—	—	1
Subtotal																2
Strategy implementation	—	—	—	—	—	—	—	—	1	—	—	—	—	—	—	1
Strategic planning	—	—	—	—	—	—	—	—	—	—	2	1	—	—	—	3
Management	—	—	—	—	—	1	1	1	—	—	—	—	—	—	1	4
Organizational control	1	—	—	—	—	1	—	—	—	—	—	—	—	—	1	3
Organizational structure	1	—	—	—	—	—	1	1	—	—	—	—	—	—	1	4
HQs-Subsidiary relations	1	—	—	—	1	—	1	1	—	—	—	—	—	—	2	6
Subtotal																21
Strategy control	—	—	—	—	—	—	—	—	—	—	1	—	—	—	—	1
Role of management	2	—	—	—	—	—	1	—	—	—	—	—	—	—	1	4

Table 1
Distribution of Journal Articles by Main Topics on International Strategic Management (*Continued*)

Topic	SMJ	ASQ	AMJ	MGS	HBR	AMR	SMR	CMR	JMS	ORD	JBS	LRP	JMG	INF	JIB	Number of articles
Environment																
Strategy	1	—	—	—	—	—	1	1	—	—	2	1	—	—	—	6
Structure	1	2	—	—	—	—	1	—	—	—	—	—	—	—	—	4
Planning	1	—	—	—	—	—	—	—	—	—	—	—	—	—	—	1
Competitiveness	1	—	—	—	—	—	—	—	—	—	—	—	—	—	—	1
Strategy and structure	—	—	1	—	—	—	—	—	—	—	—	—	—	—	—	1
Strategy and performance	—	—	—	—	—	—	—	—	—	—	—	—	—	—	1	1
Subtotal																14
Strategy																
Structure	1	—	—	—	—	—	1	—	—	—	—	—	—	—	—	2
Performance	4	—	1	—	—	—	—	—	—	—	1	—	—	—	—	6
Structure-performance	2	—	—	—	—	—	—	—	—	—	—	—	—	—	—	2
Subtotal																10
R&D strategy	2	—	—	2	—	—	—	1	—	—	—	—	—	—	—	5
Manufacturing strategy	1	—	—	—	—	—	1	—	—	—	2	—	—	—	—	4
Sourcing strategy	—	—	—	—	—	—	—	—	—	—	—	—	—	—	1	1
Human-Resource management	—	—	—	—	—	1	—	—	—	—	—	—	—	—	—	1
Information Technology	—	—	—	—	—	—	1	1	—	—	—	—	—	—	—	2
Total	31	2	2	2	8	2	12	11	2	—	11	5	—	—	13	101

The abbreviated journal titles are defined in the Appendix.

Table 2
Distribution of Journal Articles by Type of Research on International Strategic Management

Type of research	SMJ	ASQ	AMJ	MGS	HBR	AMR	SMR	CMR	JMS	JBS	LRP	JIB	Number of articles	Percentage
Conceptual	7	—	—	—	7	2	3	2	—	7	3	3	34	33.7
Empirical														
Deductive	17	2	2	2	—	—	1	—	2	2	—	4	32	31.7
Inductive	3	—	—	—	1	—	5	5	—	1	2	1	18	17.8
Comparative	2	—	—	—	—	—	—	1	—	1	—	4	8	7.9
Descriptive	2	—	—	—	—	—	3	3	—	—	—	1	9	8.9
Total	31	2	2	2	8	2	12	11	2	11	5	13	101	100.0
Verification in foreign context*	4	2	1	—	—	—	—	—	—	2	1	—	4	14
Research in non-U.S. based MNCs[†]	2	—	—	2	2	1	3	4	—	3	—	3	20	

The abbreviated journal titles are defined in the Appendix.
*Studies are conducted solely to verify strategic management models using non-U.S. MNCs as samples.
[†]Studies are conducted to learn about strategic management practices in non-U.S. MNCs.

Table 3 presents the distribution of articles by level of analysis. The majority (70.1%) address strategic management issues at an individual company level. Only 10% address an industry level, and even fewer (4.5% each) address the business, subsidiary, and individual (manager) levels. Articles dealing with conceptual research are not included. Research interest on cooperative ventures brings about a new level of analysis involving two or more firms.

Table 4 shows the distribution of MNCs by nation of origin used as samples in the empirical, comparative, and descriptive studies. Researchers have a strong interest in strategic management in the Asian context and in Asian countries, notably Japan. British companies are the ones most studied among the European MNCs. Articles dealing with conceptual research are not included.

With respect to theoretical grounding, we found that virtually none of the articles derives its theory from a single discipline. The two most cited disciplines are organizational theory and business policy/strategic management, followed by economics/industrial organization. In a small number of studies, researchers also draw theories from organizational behavior, industrial psychology, international affairs, and anthropology.

Our examination of research findings was the most challenging task. To gain some sense of the current level of knowledge, we classified each article by topic and summarized the research findings. Where possible, we grouped the findings. We also made notes of conflicting or competing results and of unanswered questions. The following list summarizes the results of our examination.[3]

---

[3]This summary should not in any way be treated as a generalization of findings, but merely a reflection of our own deductions from reading the articles.

Table 3
Distribution of Journal Articles on International Strategic Management
by Level of Analysis

Level of analysis	Number of articles	Percentage
Industry	7	10.4
Company	47	70.1
Cooperative venture	4	6.0
Business	3	4.5
Subsidiary	3	4.5
Individual (manager)	3	4.5
Total	67	100.0

Articles dealing with conceptual research are not included.

On Strategy

1. Critical elements of global competitiveness consist of quality, cost, R&D, information technology, and cross subsidization in MNCs. The use of cooperative ventures is increasingly important for MNCs.
2. Factors that may influence a company's choice of strategy are concentration of industry, competitive position, strategic objectives, country's comparative advantages, rate of change of technology, host-country government, and task ambiguity.
3. Researchers offer several typologies of global strategy and of cooperative ventures, each with a different classification scheme. Some apply to certain types of industry, for example, high-tech versus low-tech industries.

Table 4
Distribution of MNCs by Nation of Origin Used as Samples in the Journal Articles

Country	SMJ	ASQ	AMJ	MGS	HBR	AMR	SMR	CMR	JMS	JBS	LRP	JIB	Total
Europe	14	—	—	1	1	—	1	1	3	—	2	6	29
United Kingdom	6	—	—	1	—	—	1	—	2	—	2	2	14
Others	8	—	—	—	1	—	—	1	1	—	—	4	15
Asia*	4	2	1	1	5	1	2	6	1	4	1	3	31
Japan	2	1	—	—	5	1	2	5	1	2	—	1	20
Others	2	1	1	1	—	—	—	1	—	2	1	2	11
North America	14	2	—	—	—	—	2	2	1	5	1	10	37
Canada	1	—	—	—	—	—	—	—	—	1	—	1	3
United States	13	2	—	—	—	—	2	2	1	4	1	9	34
South America	1	—	—	—	—	—	—	—	—	—	—	—	1
Not identified	—	—	—	—	—	—	—	—	—	2	1	—	3

The abbreviated journal titles are defined in the Appendix.
Articles dealing with conceptual research are not included.
*Includes Australia and New Zealand.

On Diversification Strategy

The optimal level of company diversification is determined by the balance between economies of scope and scale. There is some evidence that a strategy of international diversification pursued from a narrow core skill outperformed that with high product diversity.

On R&D and Manufacturing

1. A company's innovation is a function of its principal activity and size. Intercompany dynamics within an industry can contribute to a company innovation.
2. The superior performance of the Japanese manufacturing system is due to its ability to balance flexibility and efficiency, the use of a lean production system, and the use of a small number of supply sources.

On Organizational Structure

1. International divisions are still used in nonconglomerates, whereas conglomerates use the global product structure.
2. One study proposed a new organizational structure called "transnational structure," which would enable an MNC to achieve global competitiveness through efficiency and flexibility of international operations and through organizational learning.
3. The issue of whether an organizational structure is "culture free" or "cultural bound" is still unresolved.

Based on our examination of research findings, we conclude that there is no common knowledge base in international strategic management study. However, it is evident from the several conceptual and empirical approaches to research that theory and model building have made a good start. Since international strategic management is, indeed, an emerging field, several issues need to be more adequately addressed by researchers. First, the articles in this book pay too little attention to industry issues. Are mergers and acquisitions, technology, and cooperative ventures blurring industry boundaries? In the past, researchers often used industry as a "control" variable. If that variable becomes less relevant, what other variables can be substituted? Should we use the strategic group concept? If so, should we then focus on international strategic groups?

Second, the MNC's environment, though frequently mentioned, needs more attention. At present, researchers simply classify international business environment in such broad terms as free versus regulated, or they focus on such characteristics as hostile/cooperative or ambiguous/nonambiguous. But what specifically are the environmental contigencies underlying international strategic management concepts and theories? If the MNC environment is to be treated as differentiated and fluid as Rosenzweig and Singh propose, how can we measure it empirically? How should environmental variables, both opportunities and risks, be used in designing international business strategy?

Third, researchers have proposed many typologies, in particular, for global strategy and cooperative ventures. The question thus arises as to whether there should be one common and generally accepted typology, or whether we need to understand the company, industry, market, and other attributes that are appropriate to each typology.

Fourth, there remains a forum, confined to four or five journals, for researchers in international strategic management that is different from the forum used by researchers in traditional strategic management. How can we encourage more dialogue between international and general management scholars? Each group can learn much from the other, and thus serve to enrich management disciplines in ways that would benefit both.

BIBLIOGRAPHY

Dyment, J. J. "Strategies, Market Controls for Global Corporations." *Journal of Business Strategy* 7 (no 4, 1987).

Frohman, A. L. "Putting Technology into Strategic Planning." *California Management Review* 27 (no. 2, 1985).

Kuhn, T. *The Structure of Scientific Revolutions*. 2nd ed. Chicago: University of Chicago Press, 1970.

Leontiades, J. "Market Share and Corporate Strategy in International Industry." *Journal of Business Strategy*, 5 (no. 1, 1984).

McMillan, I. C. "Delineating a Forum for Business Policy Scholars." *Strategic Management Journal* July–August (1989).

Ritzer, G. *Sociology: A Multiple Paradigm Science*. Rev. ed. Boston: Allyn and Bacon, Inc., 1980.

Schendel, D. E., and Hofer, C.W. *Strategic Management: A New View of Business Policy and Planning*. Boston: Little, Brown & Company, 1979.

Appendix: Journals Consulted and Number of Articles Selected

Journal	Abbreviation	Number of articles
Strategic Management Journal	SMJ	31
Administrative Science Quarterly	ASQ	2
Academy of Management Journal	AMJ	2
Management Science	MGS	2
Harvard Business Review	HBR	8
Academy of Management Review	AMR	2
Sloan Management Review	SMR	12
California Management Review	CMR	11
Journal of Management Studies	JMS	2
Organizational Dynamic	ORD	—
Journal of Business Strategy	JBS	11
Long Range Planning	LRP	5
Journal of Management	JMG	—
Interfaces	INF	—
Journal of International Business Studies	JIB	13
Total		101

Index

About the Editors

Franklin R. Root is Professor of International Business and Management at the Wharton School. A graduate of Trinity College, he has an MBA from the Wharton School and a PhD from the University of Pennsylvania.

Dr. Root has lectured in several countries in the fields of international business and economics. He has served on the faculties of the University of Maryland, the Copenhagen School of Economics and Business Administration, and the Naval War College. During the summer of 1970, he was Regional Advisor on Export Promotion for the Economic Commission for Latin America in Santiago, Chile. He is also a past President of the Academy of International Business and a Dean of the Fellows of the Academy of International Business.

Dr. Root's books include *International Trade and Investment*, 6th edition (South-Western, 1990), and *Entry Strategies for International Markets* (Lexington, 1987).

Kanoknart Visudtibhan is Assistant Professor in the International Business Department of George Washington University. She graduated with honors from the University of Western Australia and received her MBA from the Australia Graduate School of Management. She earned her PhD at the Wharton School, University of Pennsylvania.

Dr. Visudtibhan is a native of Thailand, where she has conducted several management development programs on international business and human resource management. She has also lectured at Chulalongkorn University in Bangkok.

Dr. Visudtibhan has presented papers in the field of international business at conferences in several countries. She recently coauthored an article that appeared in the *Journal of European Operation Research*.